Solutions
in Schools

Edited by
Yasmin Ajmal and Ioan Rees

BT Press

First published March 2001
Published by BT Press
17 Avenue Mansions, Finchley Road, London NW3 7AX

© the individual authors 2001

Layout by Alex Gollner

ISBN 1 871697 75 1

CONTENTS

ACKNOWLEDGEMENTS

Watching Steve de Shazer presenting a conference several years ago, we wondered what it must be like to have been a part of a team that has developed a way of working that has had such a profound effect on the world and lives of so many people. No writing about solution-focused therapy and thinking would be complete without acknowledging the pioneering work and continued innovation of Steve and his team at the Brief Therapy Centre in Milwaukee.

Our thanks also to Evan George, Chris Iveson and Harvey Ratner, at the Brief Therapy Practice in London, whose interest in providing a context for these ideas in Great Britain gave us all the opportunity to learn. Their continued interest in Education and the desire to promote projects and ideas has been invaluable. True to form, their comments and the time they have given to this book have been characteristically 'spot on'. Mariama's 'behind the scenes' technological advice and support has also been greatly appreciated.

As for the authors themselves, we are sure none of them will have anticipated the amount of work involved in taking up the invitation to expand into a book what started out as a workshop presentation at a conference. The fact that they have succeeded is a testament to their commitment and belief – and also to the optimism of the people they work with and the work they are doing.

Finally, our gratitude to Tehmeena (Yasmin's sister) whose knowledge of grammar, ideas about structure and clarity of thought has greatly contributed to the readability of this book.

On a more personal, note Ioan would like to thank his family for their unwavering support in all his solution-focused adventures and John Murphy for inspiring him to stay focused on respect for the child above all else.

Yasmin would like to thank her family and all the people she has met in the course of her work whose ideas, questions, patience and courage has kept her interest alive.

We wish to thank Michael Durrant for his support during the writing of this book and for making an invaluable contribution. His work is an inspiration for all who work in Solution-Focused Brief Therapy around the world.

FOREWORD

BY MICHAEL DURRANT

Some years ago, I met with a group of educational psychologists in the United States. Despite the stated focus of our seminar as being on Solution-Focused Brief Therapy, the real talk of the meeting – the discussions that went on at lunchtime and during the breaks – were all about diagnosis. In particular, there was much discussion and debate about the finer points of differentiating whether a child showed signs of 'ADD' or of 'PDD'. I was intrigued by the extent and vigour of this discussion, particularly since the very fact that these psychologists were attending a seminar on Solution-Focused Brief Therapy suggested that they may not so readily embrace traditional diagnostic concepts. After some time, I asked about the significance of the debate and was told that distinguishing between ADD and PDD was particularly important since, in this district, additional support and funding was available for students with one disorder but not for those with the other!

This experience reminded me of one of the powerful aspects of the school context for welfare and therapy professionals. In schools, our client population is defined very much by particular problems and deficits. Problems are writ large, since problems are the things that set certain students apart from the otherwise undifferentiated mass of the school population. Problems may bring notoriety, problems may bring increased status among peers, problems may bring special attention from a support teacher or problems may bring individual sessions with a psychologist. Most teachers can readily tell you who the 'problem kids' are.

Referral for special assistance is often couched in terms that suggest a disorder, condition or illness. That is, students who, for whatever reason, stand out from the rest are given some kind of psychological label. However, in the minds of many teachers, these students are not 'disordered' or 'disturbed'; they are disorderly and disturbing. The boundary between 'therapy' and 'discipline' is not always clear and the counsellor or psychologist struggles not to be seen just as yet another part of 'the system' that is seeking to deliver peace and conformity.

Cade (1995) suggests that school systems, understandably, easily become caught in 'more of the same' escalating cycles when dealing with difficult or challenging students. Recognising that it is the way in which problems, and the students presenting them, are perceived that determines how they will be tackled, he suggests that the school easily falls prey to a self-fulfilling pattern, leading to the point at which 'teachers cease to see the pupil and see only his or her "reputation" (or diagnosis or label).' It becomes a screen that stands between them and the pupil such that teachers tend to notice and react mainly to those behaviours and attitudes that confirm that 'reputation' (Cade, 1995).

We all know that once we are 'looking' for a particular problem or pathology we tend to find it. Rosenthal (Rosenthal & Jacobsen, 1968) showed that teachers' preconceived ideas about students' IQs actually affected the students' performances. When teachers thought of students as being bright, the students tended to perform in ways that supported this. Thus, this view suggests that the behaviour and academic performance of students is connected with the beliefs of teachers and other adults with whom they interact.

Harry Korman, a Swedish psychiatrist, commented about the effect of what we think on what we see. In the midst of a debate about the usefulness of labels such as 'borderline personality disorder', he suggested that 'borderline' actually means someone who is on the border of being completely well and/or a really nice person. He went on to comment that when he began to look out for examples of that kind of 'borderline' behaviour, that is exactly what he began to notice (Korman, 1998).

Against that background, four things strike me about this present book. The book is a collection of examples of professional practice that is radical, is elegant, is dynamic and reflects the influence of a particular group of people.

First, the chapters in this book represent professional practice that is radical. I'm sure that the chapter authors, writing about their own work with students, families and schools, did not consider themselves to be radicals. However, set against the prevailing climate that is problem-determined, these examples of therapeutic work within the education sphere are radical indeed. Take, for example, a seemingly innocuous aspect of the work described by Gillian Strachan. Faced with a student who was chronically refusing to attend school, she introduced a programme that included school work being sent home to the student, since keeping up with the work was important to her. Gillian comments that, previously, she might not have considered this an appropriate or helpful step. One can understand the view that sending work home was contributing to the problem. The girl wants to continue with her work but sending work home is simply reinforcing her school refusal! Instead, her desire to do her work should be used as leverage to cajole her back to school.

Standard professional practice offers a multitude of reasons why sending work home to a student who refuses to attend is colluding with the problem. However, the psychologist in this case was concerned to discover what the student wanted and then to find a way to co-operate with that and harness that in the construction of a solution. Such a stance is truly radical; radical co-operation, perhaps or, as Steve de Shazer, one of the founders of the solution-focused approach described the stance, 'radical acceptance' (de Shazer, 1999).

Second, the practice reflected in this book is elegant. The practitioners whose work makes up this volume are pragmatic. In my initial example about diagnosis, the psychologists were concerned first with what would achieve appropriate funding and support for their students. Similarly, the examples in this book are concerned with how to achieve the best possible outcome for all concerned. Many of the examples are elegant but their elegance is not necessarily in the 'purity' of the therapeutic approach. Rather, the elegance of these stories is in the way that the practical and often competing demands of the different parts of the education system are worked with and respected, always with the pragmatic goal of helping things change.

Third, the approach described in this book is dynamic. This is not polished presentations of work that is over. These are not stories in which the authors can sit back, put their feet up and reflect that 'it is finished'. Rather, this book reflects 'work in progress'. These people and their work are learning and growing and changing and evolving. That's another thing that makes these accounts so real.

Fourth, the work described in this book reflects the significant and pervasive influence of a particular group of people. Many times throughout the book, writers refer to having been introduced to Solution-Focused Brief Therapy through training conducted by the Brief Therapy Practice in London. Chris Iveson, Harvey Ratner and Evan George (with Diana Iveson and Jane Lethem) caught the Solution-Focused Brief Therapy bug and established a centre of excellence for training and practice in London. As their training activities began to extend more and more widely throughout Britain, one of the areas on which they focused was that of schools and educational issues. They offered a practical and helpful framework for people working within the educational arena that moved completely away from a focus on problems and assessment to a focus on solution and co-operation. Educational psychologists, teachers, social workers and others found this useful. One of the most intelligent things that 'briefthree' (as Chris, Harvey and Evan were sometimes known) ever did was to invite Yasmin Ajmal (one of the authors of this volume) to join the practice. The addition of an educational psychologist who knew what it was like to use Solution-Focused Brief Therapy within the day-to-day reality of the school setting was a significant step forward. Thus, this volume is testimony not only to the visionary work of the various authors but also to the pivotal contribution of the Brief Therapy Practice to the expansion of Solution-Focused Brief Therapy in real life settings in Britain.

In one of many striking and poignant moments in the stories presented in this book, a young client talks about her experience of therapy and says, 'I liked being listened to in that way,' The stories in this book demonstrate a variety of techniques and a variety of applications of Solution-Focused Brief Therapy within the school setting. Most importantly, they demonstrate what can happen when we are able to put aside our diagnostic frameworks, our normative views of behaviour and our expert opinions about what should work. They show what can happen when we begin to listen differently to the people with whom we work.

Michael Durrant
Director, Brief Therapy Institute of Sydney, Sydney Australia

Author of Creative Strategies for School Problems: Solutions for Psychologists and teachers (W.W. Norton, 1995).

CHAPTER ONE

INTRODUCING
SOLUTION-FOCUSED THINKING

BY YASMIN AJMAL

'I like this life better than my other one.' (Thomas, aged 14).

Solution-Focused Brief Therapy (SFBT) is a means of helping people find ways to create the life that they want. Over the past twenty years the work of Steve de Shazer and his team at the Brief Family Centre in Milwaukee have offered this innovative approach in the field of therapy. Their interest in looking at what works and what motivates people has led to a creative and respectful practice to help people move forward in difficult situations. The interest in solutions rather than problems, the future rather than the past and people's resources rather than deficits, provides a structure which is encouraging, effective and economical of time and resources.

Over the past ten years these ideas have been taken up by professionals in education and developed in a creative and inspiring way. Ideas first encompassed in a therapeutic setting have been developed into a way of thinking that can fit well into any situation. From working with individuals and groups to whole systems and anti-bullying campaigns, SFBT offers a means of developing constructive and co-operative dialogues with young people and all those who work with them in the school setting.

Solutions in Schools is a book for those who use or wish to use SFBT thinking and skills within schools. Those who have contributed are all employed in the field of education and have been interested in relating solution-focused thinking to their work. The chapters in this book are 'richly' different, yet also alike. What we have is an exciting range of accounts representing their think-ing-in-progress. None of the authors would claim to have the definitive answers; what they all share is a desire to find a way through, in even the most discouraging of situations. Within a context of tightening resources and time constraints they describe a pragmatic, time-sensitive and cost-effective approach to the discovery of solutions and new possibilities during difficult times. Most importantly they demonstrate how this popular approach is able to offer the hope of change with its respectful, future-oriented and goal-focused emphasis.

Overview of underpinning philosophy

Looking at problems or looking for solutions: what forms the basis for solution- focused thinking?

I remember speaking to a harassed head teacher who had spent a whole morning trying to get to the bottom of an incident between two boys: why had they fought, what had led up to the incident, who had said what and so on. He was frustrated and tired – not just because he hadn't got anywhere but also because he hadn't been able to do all the other things demanding his time. I asked him how he would know that things were improving between the two boys and we then discussed how he could use this to move things forward with them. When I talked to him again he told me that focusing on what would be happening once the problem was resolved, rather than on the problem itself, had created clear pointers for changing behaviour and had moved things on much more quickly. More importantly he felt much more refreshed after dis-cussions with students about incidents – saving his own energy to deal with other things.

Solution-focused thinking is a way of looking at the world, at situations and at people that is associated with change and with hope. Our behaviour is affected by what we believe and our beliefs are affected by our experiences. Thus the basis for change can be located in a difference in how people come to view their situation ('new viewing') or through it do something differently ('new doing').

Thus the questions aim to orientate people towards a future where the presenting difficulties are resolved. For example:

> 'How will you know things have improved in this situation?'
> 'What are the minimum signs of progress you will need to see
> in order to tell things are moving on?'

The past is explored as a source of possible successes which can be built on. Thus small behaviours and ideas can be highlighted and developed to become the basis for significant change. For example:

> 'What have you done since our last meeting which has been good for you?'
> 'When was the last time that you could have lost your temper and didn't?'
> 'In the past when you have felt things slipping out of your control, what have you done that has helped?'

There is no view of pathology. A certain behaviour or difficulty is viewed as something the person we are working with needs to change and not as a symptom of anything else. This frees up the thinking of the worker to be alert to the possibilities and potential for change. As soon as we start categorising someone what we listen out for and our view of what we hear can be quickly reduced to the options contained within the label.

The process of solution-focused thinking is guided by the following pragmatic assumptions.

1. Students, parents and teachers have capacities to resolve difficulties.
2. Big problems do not need big solutions (Murphy 2000).
3. We need to catch hold of what is already working.
4. It's important to know where you are heading.
5. Carry on doing what works. If it isn't working, do something different.
6. A problem is simply something a person wishes to do without.

The task of the worker

The task of the worker is to highlight in conversation what appear to be solution thoughts and behaviours and thus guide the conversation towards a way of thinking and doing that may make a difference. The stance is one of curiosity to ensure that any ideas which emerge are firmly rooted in the thinking and experience of the person or people we are working with. By focusing on small details the attempt is to build up layers of complexity of description in small stages. At the core of any work is the co-operation and relationship between those involved. Thus importance is placed on the feedback we receive (non-verbally, e.g. smiles and shrugs as well as what is said) to help us assess whether the track we are on is a useful one. If a particular question is not answered the worker assumes the responsibility for asking it differently or asking it again. The assumption is that they will be able to answer the question when we ask it in the right way and when it is about something that has meaning to them.

The next section of this chapter seeks to explore these ideas in practice. The first part examines ways of orientating thinking and conversations towards resources and co-operation under the following headings:
- Creating a context of competence.
- What we listen out for and how we listen.
- Activating existing knowledge and skills.
- Seeking out co-operation.
- Retaining a non-judgemental stance.
- Building collaboration – finding out what someone wants as the basis for a discussion.

The second part looks at some of the useful techniques for building solutions. It includes:
- A future when the problem is resolved. Looking at questions which open up and develop a description of what a future would look like if there was no longer a problem.
- Sometimes the preferred future is already happening a little. Finding out about the exception times when things may already be a little better in relation to the difficulty.
- How far have we come and how will we know we are moving on? Using rating scales to look at where people are now and what the next steps would look like.
- Rounding it all off. Some ideas about what to include at the end of a discussion.

Orientating thinking and conversations towards resources and co-operation

Creating a context of competence

I can remember sitting on a bus during my first year of teaching after a day at school and sobbing. The last 10 minutes of the day – 'tidying up' had been a disaster. I sat and replayed it over and over in my mind. By the time I got home I had a list of defects which would have covered most of the south of England and had convinced myself that teaching was beyond me. I ignored the rest of the day which had gone well and instead reduced my confidence to an all time low.

It is important to relate to the people with whom we are working as being resourceful and capable. It is all too easy, amidst overwhelming difficulties, for us to lose sight of our own and others' capabilities and resources. However, at

the heart of change is a person's knowledge and belief of their own self efficacy. Therefore questions seek to highlight people's abilities to solve their own
problems. For example:

> 'Tell me about a change you have made' (the message here is
> 'you are a person who makes changes').
> 'What did stopping yourself yesterday from hitting out when
> you were angry tell you about yourself?'
> 'What sorts of things do you need to be able to do to be a sea
> cadet?' – 'and which of these can you already do?'

This interest in a person can be established right at the beginning of a discussion. A few minutes getting to know a little about somebody – what they enjoy,
hobbies, areas of their lives that are going well – can begin the search for
strengths and the development of a perspective where people are seen (by
themselves and the workers) as skilled problem- solvers and active contributors to their lives in positive ways. Sometimes it can be useful to use the perspective of others to build up this description, for example asking a parent,
'What is it that James does which you like?' or a student, 'What might your
teachers say about you that you have not mentioned?' One student who was in
trouble with most teachers liked his history teacher. What he liked about the
teacher was his fairness, humour and the fact that he was interested in the students' views rather than just telling them what they should think. When this
was developed to think about what the teacher might say about him as a
student a whole list of strengths emerged including the fact that he showed an
interest, that he was able to state his views clearly, that he was helpful, and that
he worked well with other students.

These ideas can be used equally well with groups or with a class. For
example, during work with a group of boys in a secondary school brought
together because of concerns about their behaviour, the following questions
were used as a starting point: 'What do you like?' and 'Tell us about a difficult
situation which you think you handled well, which you handled in a way that
made you feel good about yourselves'. Similarly, a Spanish teacher related a
time when she had wanted to talk to a class about their behaviour during her
lessons. She began by being interested in things they enjoyed doing and their
favourite lessons in school. The initial reaction from the students was thinly
disguised surprise. However she persisted and later described the conversation as the best she had ever had with the class. She was astonished by the
group's openness and co-operation. The teacher also commented that she
found herself viewing the students more positively.

Listening out for strengths and helping someone to build a helpful
description of themselves can be a powerful starting point for change. It starts

the search from a different place and can rekindle belief that change can occur. Even in very difficult circumstances we can help people get in touch with their strengths by asking them how they are coping, how are they managing to get by, how come they haven't given up even when they have wanted to and when they cannot see anything ever being different. For example asking a student with multiple exclusions how s/he managed to hang in and not be permanently excluded gets right to the heart of the matter whilst at the same time focusing on the strengths and resources of the students.

What we listen for and how we listen

The solution-focused approach emphasises the development of a dialogue in which the worker builds on what has been said. The skill is to listen out for anything that might be helpful and to persist, gently, in the belief that the person does bring something positive to their situation.
I was asked to talk with an experienced teacher who had been asked to cover a class for a term. She had previously taught the class for few periods and had found it very difficult.

YA: You say you have been teaching for a long time – what sorts of things have you been doing?
Teacher: Well, I have been working in schools for nearly 20 years.
YA: Gosh, that's a lot of sticking power.
Teacher: I'm basically a class teacher but I've also been a maths post-holder, a language post-holder and worked with children with special needs. Oh yes, and in my last school I covered a deputy post for about 6 months.
YA: So it would seem you have an extensive overview of what goes on in a school. What do you enjoy about teaching?
Teacher: Hmm – sometimes just leaving at the end of the day.
YA: I'm sure. What else?
Teacher: Well I love seeing children settled and learning. Knowing actually that I can teach and I like seeing kids get to know how to do something.
YA: What do you think the children who you have taught would say they liked about what you do?
Teacher: I think some might say they like my enthusiasm and humour and um … making things exciting. I like to keep a good pace going. That's what bothers me about this class – we keep having to stop and so the creative pace is lost.
YA: Uh-huh. What else might children say they like about you as a teacher?
Teacher: Well I'm very fair and even when I have a go at them I make a

point of talking to them about it and will say when I was wrong.

YA: So it seems that you make it very clear to the children through your own behaviour what is right and what is important to you.

Teacher: Yes – well I guess so.

YA: What about this class – what would they say they value about you in the short space of time they have known you?

Teacher: Probably not much.

YA: If you had to guess?

Teacher: Well some might say we do interesting work.

YA: Anything else?

Teacher: That I listen to them.

YA: Uh-huh.

Teacher: And that I try not to punish them all; rather just the people who deserve it.

YA: And what would you say that the class do that you like?

Teacher: God that's a hard one! … They have some good ideas about things – but there's not enough space for them to get it out.

YA: So they've managed to hang to their creativity even though it hasn't been given a lot of space?

Teacher: I suppose so – I hadn't thought of it like that. There are some children in there who want to learn.

YA: What have you noticed that tells you this?

Teacher: Well they listen and sometimes they have brought in things to show me about what we have been talking about – and that's nice because you think well at least someone was interested.

When the teacher and I first started talking, the worries and difficulties were uppermost in her mind. During the discussion the intention was to acknowledge these and also to find out about other aspects of the situation which might be helpful. There were several times when the teacher's initial response showed that she found the question difficult. Often when people are asked to think about something in a different way they do not immediately know what they want to say. This does not mean they do not have anything to say. At these times the intention was to give her a bit more time by repeating the question or using a prompt such as 'if you had to guess?' The information about the class and her own teaching strengths were also true of her experiences and offered more scope for thinking about the current dilemma.

Activating existing knowledge and skills

Setting up a dialogue which values what a person can do, can be the first step towards helping to activate existing knowledge and creating a context for people to do what they already know how to do.

I was asked to talk with Andrew, a year 11 pupil, who had been diagnosed as having dyspraxia. He was described as someone who couldn't organise himself and with his GCSE exams coming up this was a source of concern for his parents and teachers. When he walked into the room my eyes alighted on the Gunners badge on his football shirt and I asked him about this. He was a keen Arsenal supporter and liked to go to the home games. However, because they are such a popular team, he told me you had to send off for tickets in advance. I asked him how he did this. He told me that he had a yearly planner on his wall and when the fixtures came in at the beginning of the season he would note down when all the home fixtures were to be played. He then went through and put a note two weeks before that to remind him to send off for tickets. After establishing that I was in fact talking with the right pupil(!), I asked him more about how he managed to make this system work. It was a very useful introduction to a more general discussion about organisation which now began from a position of competence and knowledge.

Seeking out co-operation

Finding out about someone, offering the opportunity to show a different side of themselves can also be an important first step in the development of a co-operative relationship. I heard an example from a head of year who was in her office when a student noisily entered. He had been sent out of class to be 'dealt with'. The head of year began by asking him if he could help her organise her desk as the paperwork had got out of hand and was danger of taking over the whole office. The pupil obliged and after a few minutes she thanked him for his help and then asked how she in turn could help him. This question within the framework of mutual helpfulness gave a very different starting point from the one which had existed five minutes previously.

Retaining a non-judgemental stance

In schools there are occasions when you have to deal directly with the problem in line with school policy. Alongside this is the opportunity to work with the student to develop solutions for the future. A powerful way to develop co-operation is to acknowledge people's feelings and views of a situation in a way that is not judgmental. This is not always easy to do – we might indeed have very strong views from our own perspective about what is right and wrong, acceptable or unacceptable. Nevertheless, if we want someone to engage in a constructive discussion where they feel encouraged to speak openly, it is helpful to be neutral about what is being said. If people feel you are judging them they might either clam up or spend time defending their position. When, following a discussion, we ask people what they have found helpful, they often comment with surprise at how open they have been – commonly attributing this to the feeling that they have not in any way been judged.

People are sometimes worried that they could be seen as condoning bad behaviour or situations. Being non-judgemental is not the same as condoning. One way to be clear about this is through the language used, not by presuming an understanding of what has been said, but rather by consistently checking it out.

For example:

> 'So have I got it straight … you don't feel that there is anything wrong from your point of view. That other people are on your back and you are fed up with this'.
>
> 'Let's see if I've got this right … it seems what you are saying is that you feel pretty hopeless at the moment and can't see it ever being different'.
>
> Also by emphasising the source of the viewpoint: 'So from your point of view the teachers are just picking on you', 'So what is important to you is to stick up for yourself', 'So what you think is that he deserved what he got'.

Building co-operation: finding out what someone wants as the basis for a discussion

> 'If you don't know where you are going chances are you will end up somewhere else' (Steve de Shazer).

Finding a clear goal helps to define areas to work on and ensures people are clear when they get there. Research (Murphy 2000) has shown that work is more effective when it addresses what the people we are working with see as important. Thus the focus for the work is best achieved through collaboration between all those involved. Consider the following example. I was asked to work with Lucy, a year 9 pupil, because she was being asked to leave a number of lessons on a regular basis. She was loud and confrontational with teachers and refused to apologise. The school wanted Lucy to stop arguing with teachers and to be polite and respectful, to settle to her work in class and to talk to teachers if there was a problem.

When I met Lucy she was full of indignation at how she was being treated and felt strongly that she needed to stick up for herself when people were being unfair. I wasn't sure this was the best time to introduce the school's goals! Instead I asked her what ideas she had about what she wanted to do when she left school. She was very clear. She wanted to be a beautician and had already identified the qualifications she needed to attend the college of her choice. I was curious about what she was doing at the moment that was helpful to her in achieving this, and what else would need to happen to ensure she was able to continue on her chosen path. Amongst other things she talked about staying in class. Acknowledging that this was not always easy, various strategies were discussed – including how she could stick up for herself in a way that was good for her. The head of year grabbed me the following week and asked what I had done to Lucy. He described the change as so phenomenal that it could not be ignored by anyone. What I had done was to listen to Lucy's views, identify what was important to her, and work within her own frame of reference.

The following questions may be useful to start the search for the direction in which someone is interested in going:

> 'What are your best hopes for this discussion?'
> 'What would make this discussion worthwhile?'
> 'Imagine you are walking away from this discussion and are thinking, 'I'm glad I came'. What is it we would be talking about that would have made you think this?'
> 'What would need to change as a result of us talking that will tell you this has been worthwhile?'

The stance is one of curiosity, and the assumption that people attend/participate in a discussion for a reason. This reason may be that they want to avoid something such as permanent exclusion, court, or being grounded, and as such this may be their motivation for engaging in a discussion. The following extract illustrates this:

Rachael came into the room with her mother and sat with her body turned away. Her head was bent downwards and her face was hidden by her hair.

Worker: What would make this discussion worthwhile from your point of view?

Rachael: I don't speak to anyone.

Worker: Is that something you would like to change?

Rachael: No, I can sort my own problems out.

Worker: So how come you're here?

Rachael: My mother made me.

Worker: So how come you decided you would do what your mother asked you to this time?

Rachael: I just want people to get off my back.

Worker: And if coming here helped with that would that make it worthwhile?

Rachael: Yes.

When working with students we continually search to locate the co-operative part of someone's behaviour as the starting point. The assumption is that people usually have a reason for doing things. In the above example the fact that Rachael had attended the meeting suggested there was something she wanted or didn't want.

Summary

In this first section the following assumptions and idea have been explored:

– People are more than just a problem.
– People have the skills, resources and qualities they will need to resolve their difficulties.
– These strengths are an important basis for change and as workers we need to help people remember, discover and find out about them as soon as possible.
– Everybody has their own unique way of co-operating – we need to find this out.
– The basis for any piece of work is to find out what people want. What is their motivation for attending a meeting?
– Our role as workers is to adopt a stance of curiosity about beliefs, views and behaviour, and to create a way of talking that is more likely to lead to change.

Building solutions – useful techniques

A future when the problem is resolved

Future orientated questions are a creative way to look for goals for change. The worker is interested in helping the person they are working with clarify the future they hope to have if the problem is resolved. Rather than becoming bogged down in the details of what **is** 'wrong' the focus is instead on what will be 'right'. The picture promotes a positive expectancy of change and rekindles hope that things can be different. Talking with a mother who felt depressed and hopeless, I asked her if she would find it helpful to think about how she would like things to be. She replied 'Oh yes, it would be lovely to think about my life being good. I think I need that right now to get me through this'.

There are a number of questions that can be used to provide a useful context in which people can think about how they would like things to be. One of the questions most commonly referred to in this book is the 'Miracle Question'(de Shazer, 1988):

'Suppose that tonight while you were asleep, there was a miracle and this problem was solved. The miracle occurs while you are sleeping so you do not immediately know that it has happened. When you wake up, what is the first thing you will notice that will let you know that there has been a miracle?'

Other frameworks include:

'If tomorrow turned out to be a good day for you, how will you know your day was going well?'

'How will you know you have done yourself justice despite the difficulties?'

'How will you know we don't need to meet any more?'

When people are asked to think in a future framework it frees their thinking from the limitations of what is not right: the doubts, the difficulties, the reasons not even to try. The clearer the description of a 'do-able' future, the easier it is to work out ways of getting there. The more details there are, the more possibilities for change are opened up, the more clues there are about what will be helpful.

For example, one girl who felt isolated and worried about what she said, what she looked like and how others viewed her, talked about joining in with the other pupils in her class more and not always being on the sidelines. Examples of this included walking to school with two friends in the morning and joining in their chatter about what they would do after school rather than only thinking about her studies. By accepting some of the offers she received to go out, she also felt she would have something to add when they examined what had happened the night before under the microscope.

To help build a rich description (Michael White) workers ask about the fine details of what people do, thus locating the future description firmly in the context of their lives at home, e.g. 'When you wake up tomorrow, what time will that be, what is the first thing that will tell you that the miracle has happened, that things are different?' Or at school: 'What is your first lesson, what will be different when you enter the classroom that will tell you that things are different?'

Widening the description to incorporate other people's perceptions can also be useful. For example, 'What will your mum notice about you first thing in the morning that will let her know that things were different?' Or 'Who will be the first to notice in school? What will they notice?' Or 'What will tell your friends that the miracle has happened?'

By drawing in significant people to develop the description, further details emerge. It also places the person in a context of interaction. Thus the question, 'And how will you know they have noticed things were different?' encourages the person to further consider their actions from other perspectives.

For example when I asked Gillian (a year 9 student) how her teacher would know that the miracle had happened, she responded that if she had all her equipment with her, her form tutor would probably comment on the effort she was making. I checked whether this was something Gillian would like. She thought she would, and as a result she would probably feel less picked on first thing in the morning. This might make her feel better about settling to her work.

Sometimes people will tell us that they will feel differently: 'I will feel happy'. To draw out more concrete details the worker will be curious about the differences in behaviour that would accompany this. For example, 'If you are feeling happier, what sorts of things will you find yourself doing?' or 'What will be different about the way you do things?'

The more a person can describe in detail what they would be doing if the problem was gone the more real the possibility becomes. So if the first part of a description focuses on something that will not be happening, e.g. 'I will not be starting on her as soon as I enter the room' we would find out about what would be happening instead, so that the description is something observable and tangible. For example, 'If you are not starting on her, what will you be doing instead?'

Catch hold of what is already working (Exceptions)

No situation is 100% the same as another. There are times when it is better and there are times when it is worse. People often dismiss the better times as flukes or aberrations and yet it is precisely what was happening at those times that may hold the key to significant change.

As the future becomes more vivid so the past can be drawn in. The bits of the past we are interested in are those experiences which highlight capacities which are already there. Consider the following extract: Linda (a parent) arrived at a discussion in a distressed state. She felt she was failing her daughter as a parent by not providing the care she should. Linda wanted to show more concern when Donna was upset about something and not just dismiss her as being a 'drama queen.' I asked Linda if there were any times recently when she felt that she had reacted to Donna in a way that she liked. She replied 'This morning'. Linda already knew how to do what she wanted to do. When Linda thought about what had happened that morning she picked out three things she felt pleased with. First, she had shown sympathy about a sore elbow by kissing it ('Even though I wasn't sure it really hurt, Donna thought it did!'). Second, she had given her own views about a sling Donna had wanted to wear ('I think it is important to be open with Donna. It is important in our relationship'). Third, she had asked Donna what she wanted to do ('Normally I would just tell her'). Donna had gone away happily and Linda felt she had supported her well. Linda commented afterwards that the discussion had made her think differently and she wrote down her stages for future reference.

Finding an exception can occur in different ways. Sometimes people reflect and comment spontaneously on what they are saying. 'I would feel so much better if he could come in and settle for the first few minutes on the mat. Mind you, he did this on Tuesday – I was really surprised.' We need to listen for and hear these clues which are often buried.

Sometimes the worker can introduce the context for thinking through a general enquiry, such as 'Which small bits of the miracle are already happening?'

Or it can be helpful to pick up a specific detail. For example a student who wants to improve his work might be asked, 'When recently have you felt more able to do the work you are set?'

The skill of the worker is to help someone think about what has already happened in a way that might be helpful in the future. Thinking about 'who, what, where, when, how' can encourage an examination of details which have been overlooked and yet are useful.

Sometimes people describe what has happened as being in the control of someone or something else. In these situations it can be useful to explore at least some small sign of something they did themselves to contribute to the change happening. What we are looking for is an action that can be repeated in the future. For example, 'My first day went OK but people are always nice on your first day' could be developed with 'That's what they did to help you settle in, and what did you do to help?' Or how they responded to the change. For example, 'He came in quietly – well he can if he has a mind to do it' could be explored with 'And when he was coming in quietly what did you then do?'

Where people report no positive changes, the worker can enquire how they have managed to cope and stop things getting from getting worse. Again the aim will be to draw out as much specific detail as possible and to remind people of their strengths and resources in the face of such difficulties.

How far have we already come and how will we know we are moving on?

One of the most accessible and flexible tools are rating scales which are essentially conversational frameworks. A 0-to-10 scale provides the structure to develop a dialogue about how far someone has come, what would be good enough, what the next step would look like, how others would rate their progress, etc. A typical way of using the scale framework is as follows:

'Let's say that 10 is the best things could be and 0 is the complete opposite of this. Where between 0 and 10 would you say you are today?'

'What is it that puts you at a 3 and not a 0?'

'Where on the scale would be good enough? And how will you know you have reached this point?'

How will you know you have reached 1 point up on the scale? Who else will notice and what will they notice?'

In the above questions the intention is to reinforce bits of the miracle or exceptions that the person is already doing, and to identify the next steps. The smaller and more concrete these steps are, the more likely it is that the pupil, teacher or parent you are working with will experience success. And the motivation to take these next steps is related to how closely the 'ten' on the scale represents the goal of the person you are working with.

Any number of scales can be used to map progress in different aspects of situations: learning, behaviour, classroom management, coping with change. It is also common to talk with people about their confidence in maintaining or making the changes they have outlined. This again can be framed within a scale:

'On a scale of 0 to 10, where 10 represents your total confidence that you will reach your good enough point/next step on the scale and 0 represents that you think there is not a hope, where between 0 and 10 would you say your confidence is at the moment? How come? What would increase your confidence to the next point on the scale?'

Scales seem to offer a structure that makes sense to pupils and enables them to express their ideas in a concrete and tangible form. In the same way the flexibility of movement up and down a scale can help to move away from the 'fixed' nature of difficulties and encourage a greater sense of control. I can remember sitting in the office of the Special Needs Co-ordinator (Senco) when we were interrupted by Darren and Tony. Tony stood moving from foot to foot while Darren introduced what they had been doing. A week previously Darren had used a scale with the Senco to think about his behaviour. On returning to class he had decided that Tony's behaviour needed a bit of 'sorting out' and so had drawn out a scale for him to use. At this point Tony stepped forward: 'Yeah, see, my behaviour is on a 6 today but I reckon I'm going to aim for an 8 tomorrow'.

Rounding it all off

We end where we start. At the beginning of the chapter we looked at the importance of highlighting the strengths and resources of the people we are working with. At the end of a discussion we would take time to emphasise their skills, qualities and determination, and anything else useful or helpful to them.

Any feedback need not take long but what is said and how it is said can increase the usefulness. Importance is given to the skills, qualities and determination which have been evident in the discussion. Any steps people have already taken will be emphasised and they are often asked to look out for further signs of change and progress:

> 'Watch out for times when you are teased and hold back.'
> 'Notice what you are doing that moves you up the scale.'
> 'Notice times he is more settled in class.'
> 'Pay attention to the times she answers you back and you keep your temper.'

Summary of words that are useful

The language we use can have a powerful effect on the context being discussed.

'How' rather than 'why' focuses on helpful behaviours.

'When' rather than 'if' sets up an expectation of change.

'Will' rather than 'would' creates a tangible rather than a hypothetical future.

'What will be happening (instead)' rather than 'what won't be happening' replaces a negative with something positive and tangible.

Second and subsequent discussions

The interest is in what has been better between the last discussion and today. The questions seek to highlight the smallest signs of progress and look at how the person could begin to do more of it. Useful questions could include:

> 'How did you do that?'
> 'What did it take to get that to happen'
> 'What did you do differently – that you liked?'
> 'What would it take for that to happen again?'

The description is built up with small concrete details. Asking about what others would have noticed can add rich and useful details and also, if they were pleased with the progress, could be a source of motivation to continue:

> 'Was your mother pleased with the letter from your form teacher?'

'Yes.'
'Did you like the fact that she was pleased?'
'Yes. There wasn't so much stress'
'What was there instead that you liked?'
'We ended up having a really good talk about lots of things. We haven't
   done that in a long time'

Revisiting a scale can also be a useful way to highlight improvements and
to locate next steps. However, it is important to be sensitive to the effort it will
have taken someone to make the changes they have. It may therefore be
important to explore someone's confidence in maintaining the changes they
have made.

'What will it take to keep at a 4 for the next week?'
'How confident are you that you will be able to maintain the
changes you have made?'

There are times when there have been no changes or indeed things have
grown worse. The worker will need to ensure that they take things slowly,
acknowledging the frustration and disappointment and also the fact that
despite the difficulties, they have turned up. In some cases this will have taken
a lot of courage and determination.
There are several areas of enquiry which might be useful.

1. Breaking down the period into smaller chunks. For example, asking
   someone to rate each day on a scale, or looking at the different subjects
   in school. What we would be looking out for are the times when things
   were maybe a fraction better, as a starting point to explore what was different at those times.
2. Asking people how they have been coping, getting by or stopping things
   from getting worse can focus on the strengths people have drawn on to
   get them through the difficult situations.
3. Starting to focus on signs to look out for that would tell them things were
   starting to improve again, gently rekindling hope that things can be different, however unlikely it might seem at present.

Applications to Education

Schools have offered a unique opportunity to take the principles of solution-
focused thinking and apply them creatively in a variety of ways. The educational environment provides flexibility to work with individuals, groups, whole
classes, parents and other professionals. It also poses the challenge of time
and the need for efficiency, both of which are instrumental factors in guiding

the work described in this book. Individual chapters speak to these and other such issues, and in doing so provide useful hints in learning about the application of Solution-Focused Brief Therapy within this unique and challenging environment.

Time

Part of the tradition of thinking underlying Solution-Focused Brief Therapy is to treat each conversation as if it could be the last. Thus the emphasis is to ensure that there is something useful in each conversation and that the solution-focused ideas also serve us as workers, liberating us rather than forcing us to work in a different way. For example, in schools, any work needs to be cognizant of the fact that school staff have to fit a great many activities into an already crowded day. The challenge may be seen as to make best use of any time that is set aside to deal with a given issue. In Chapter Two the author explores the potential in meetings. He questions the amount of time commonly set aside to look at what has already happened and suggests a change in emphasis which values looking forward. Chapter Three also looks at what can be achieved through a series of short meetings to encourage change. These accounts also relate well to how Steve de Shazer talks about 'going slow in order to go faster' as they illustrate how going at the pace of those we work with can lead to a quicker resolution.

Groups

People do not change by drawing on their deficits, they use their resources. However skilled a member of staff is, in the end it is the students drawing on their own skills that makes a difference, and it is the purpose of any solution-focused interview is to highlight these. Moreover, there has been a lot of interest over a number of years about what students themselves can bring to each other through sharing learning, behaviour and emotional issues with each other. Chapter Four explores the value of students learning from and supporting each other in group settings. Taking as its starting point the influence of peers in affecting behaviour, their work provides a context in which young people can learn from each other's experiences and in doing so reveal possibilities that are salient. Chapter Five gives an inspirational account of how students' resources can be harnessed in peer counselling and peer support as part of an anti-bullying initiative. In Chapter Six the work described has, at its core, valuing the strengths, skills and problem-solving capacities of students. Drawing together groups of students and doing just this can lead to remarkable changes in behaviour and in situations where bullying is a serious cause for concern. The results described speak for themselves.

The home/school interface

In our experience, to leave young people with the major onus and responsibility for change is often too much to shoulder in difficult times. However, when a young person, their family and the school can work jointly together the likelihood of change is much enhanced, particularly if those involved are able and willing to notice the changes people are making. Increasingly, the involvement of 'parents as partners' is testimony to the welcomed shift in education toward including the home in solution finding. This is reflected in the Code of Practice which states 'If they (parents) feel confident that schools and professionals actively involve them, take account of their wishes, feelings and unique perspectives on their children's development, then the work of those schools and professionals can be more effective' – Special Educational Needs code of Practice (2000 p.11). At times this can challenge professionals and requires sensitive handling. Chapter Seven explores the effect of finding and building on common goals, identifying what works and making the ordinary extraordinary. The attention to the very small signs of progress gives a powerful example of the importance of rekindling people's belief that change can occur. Chapters Eight, Nine and Ten all provide an intensely practical focus and a fund of ideas to open up a dialogue between home and school that values the positive and celebrates the contribution of all involved. Attention is paid to the language and techniques that can lead to possibilities, inviting co-operation where challenging behaviour is concerned.

Supporting the wider systems of change

Finding solutions is usually a shared experience. Supporting the whole school system as a way of supporting individuals and groups of students during the journey of change is an important application of solution-focused thinking. The model provides a clear structure which enhances the move away being an 'expert/advisor' model to one of collaboration. Chapter Eleven looks at how solution-focused questions can enhance the process of consultation and assist schools in doing what they already know how to do. Chapter Twelve is essential reading for all those who are interested in working outwards from individual cases towards intervention at a systems level. In chapter 13 the fruits of a well-established Solution-Focused Brief Therapy support system are described. With great experience and vision, solution-focused ideas are drawn together into a blueprint for establishing an educational counselling service.

Effectiveness and students views

Solution-focused workers are always interested in feedback from the people they work with to determine what has been useful and what to do more of.

This enables the worker to get the best possible 'fit' with whoever they are working with, and the better the fit the more useful the work is likely to be. This is taken up in Chapter Fifteen where the following questions are looked at: does Solution-Focused Brief Therapy work with students and what do they say about it? It provides interesting evidence about what students find useful about the approach and some ideas about how we can use this information in our work. Applying one of the ideas described by children as being useful is taken up in chapter Fourteen, in which an exploration takes place regarding ways of supporting parents, staff and students in between the 'formal' discussions through the writing of letters. The workers use the letters as a way of highlighting what has been useful in a meeting and any ideas people may have had. The feedback about this feedback would suggest the writing of letters has enormous possibilities.

CHAPTER TWO

HOW TO BUILD SOLUTIONS AT MEETINGS

BY MICHAEL HARKER

Introduction

As helping professionals, we work in a problem-generated, problem-generating environment. Talking to other professionals about problems is an integral part of our daily work practice. Other professionals assume that we are interested in hearing about the details of a problem, because this will lead to further understanding and perhaps the identification of a cause, and the formulation of a solution. This type of discussion continues naturally within the context of multi-agency meetings convened to discuss children's and young people's needs.

In many such meetings there is a natural tendency to want to know more information and to understand how a problem has evolved, and what factors may be underlying the difficulties. Very often, however, this information does not lead directly to the formulation of solutions.

This paper describes attempts to integrate solution-focused questioning within the context of interdisciplinary and multi-agency meetings held to discuss the particular needs of children and young people.

Developing solution-focused practice

Over the last six years or so, I have been working with colleagues in Renfrewshire and Inverclyde Psychological Services to introduce and develop solution-focused principles and practice in the daily work of local authority educational psychologists. Our service has a statutory remit within the Department of Education Services, and offers consultancy, casework, training and project work to schools within the Inverclyde Council area. Within our casework role, our clients tend to be children, young people and parents, who agree to a referral being made to us on their behalf by schools. We also accept direct referrals from parents. Our consultancy role involves a regular pattern of visits to pre-5 centres, primary, secondary and SEN schools. This consultancy may also lead to requests for training or longer-term project work.

Initially, we began to use the approach with young people and their families where behavioural difficulties had been identified. As we became more familiar with this development in casework, a number of other natural applications of solution-focused approaches emerged within the context of the day-to-day work of the educational psychologist (EP). The challenge became how to apply these methods within a problem-driven environment. A number of other practitioners were also beginning to explore ways to use solution-focused approaches within educational settings (Durrant 1993; Rhodes 1993; Rhodes & Ajmal 1995).

We now have a broad solution-focused practice within which we continue to work to maintain and develop solution-focused approaches in the work of educational psychologists. (Redpath and Harker, 1999).

The problem with problem solving

The belief that solutions will only arise from a full and detailed discussion of problems seems to be deeply embedded within our society's view of how to solve problems. The 'problem solving paradigm' has become the dominant model for the helping professions. De Jong & Berg (1998) give an excellent account of the historical reasons for this development. They suggest that problem solving in the helping professions has been strongly influenced by the 'medical model' of diagnosis and treatment. McMahon (1990) outlines the stages of the problem-solving model as follows:

1. Description of problem(s) and Data Collection
2. Problem Assessment
3. Intervention Planning
4. Intervention
5. Evaluation & Follow-up.

This generic structure of problem solving, first determining the nature of the problem and then intervening, influences much of the interaction and discussion at inter-agency meetings. Thus, in many meetings, professionals and families spend time sharing information and describing and detailing the nature and cause of problems. The aim is to arrive at an agreed problem definition, and by so doing, to agree a plan of action.

Figure 1 outlines some of the activities which might take place within a 'problem solving meeting'. Within this discussion framework, a 'problem focus' can remain for the majority of the meeting, leaving the concluding 5 or 10 minutes for intervention and evaluation planning.

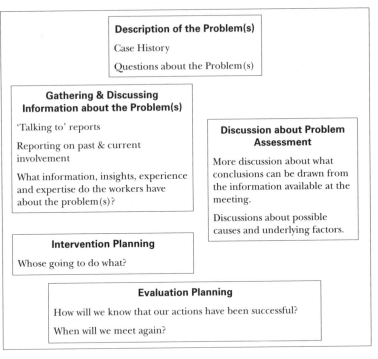

Description of the Problem(s)

Case History

Questions about the Problem(s)

Gathering & Discussing Information about the Problem(s)

'Talking to' reports

Reporting on past & current involvement

What information, insights, experience and expertise do the workers have about the problem(s)?

Discussion about Problem Assessment

More discussion about what conclusions can be drawn from the information available at the meeting.

Discussions about possible causes and underlying factors.

Intervention Planning

Whose going to do what?

Evaluation Planning

How will we know that our actions have been successful?

When will we meet again?

Figure 1. Some typical activities at a 'problem solving meeting'.

This underlying problem-solving model tends to be adopted by statutory agencies, such as the Courts, Social Services and, in Scotland, the Children's Hearing system. These sources regularly make referrals for 'assessment'. For example, Children's Hearing requests regularly contain phrases such as, 'there is a need to get to the bottom of Frank's difficulties', or, 'the assessment should help to determine why Sharon is not going to school.'

Unfortunately, as is often realised, very rarely is a cause of a problem identified and generally agreed; nor does the identification of the cause generally lead to a practical solution to the presenting problem. However, this does not stop people wanting to know 'why?' and arrive at an understanding of the situation. The result is that people tend to get sucked into ever-decreasing circles of problem descriptions and hypotheses about the causes of problems.

Solution patterns can be unique to individuals and are often not predicted by professionals' theories or hypotheses about underlying causative factors.

One pupil referred for school refusal had successfully attended school on the day of her appointment with me. She explained this success as being due to her family's activities the previous evening. They had ordered a take-away meal and had sat together enjoying the Lily Savage Show on television. This had reduced her anxiety and taken her mind off going to school the next day. The 'Lily Savage Solution' is not one to be found in any textbooks about school refusal.

Within a problem-solving context it is not surprising that meetings frequently act to confirm professionals' problem-focused view of the clients and their situations. Workers can feel de-skilled and can begin to feel powerless in the face of often appalling social deprivation, abuse and poverty. Families can end up being vindicated in their belief that they are powerless to change.

The net result is that seldom does a meeting of this kind result in positive change. Outcomes are very often discussed in advance of the full meeting and the meeting serves simply to ratify decisions which have already been formulated. Thus, a powerful context for change is lost and often the problem is confirmed in its place as the central factor in the situation.

Building solutions in meetings

Using a solution-focused approach; a meeting can become a powerful vehicle for change. Solution-focused questioning can be used to transform the discussion so that meetings become integral to solution-focused interventions rather than additional or parallel to any ongoing work. Figure 2 contrasts the different structures of a 'problem-solving' and a 'solution-building' meeting. In the latter, discussion about problems quickly moves on to discussion about solutions.

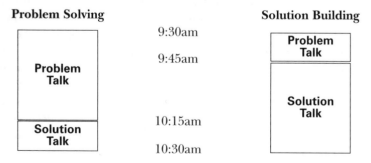

Figure 2. The structure of meetings.

Figure 3 outlines some of the activities which might take place within a 'solution-building' meeting. The focus here is on empowerment rather than problem description and analysis. The meeting can be viewed as a co-operative exploration to help uncover the client's hidden strengths and resources.

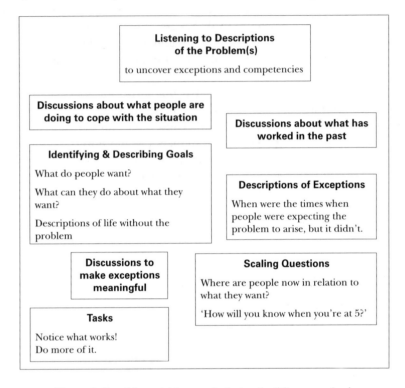

Figure 3. Possible activities at a 'solution building meeting'.

Your role within the meeting will largely determine whether or not, and to what extent, you can facilitate the introduction of solution-focused questioning. If you are chairing the meeting you will have the best opportunity to set a solution-focused agenda. Even within your own input to the meeting you should be able to introduce an element of solution-focused questioning. The tradition in many meetings is for each participant to report on their involvement in a rather passive way. Try to adopt a more interactive style, using your 'slot' at the meeting to ask a number of solution-focused questions which might relate to issues raised in your individual contact with the clients. It can be helpful to decide which questions to ask in advance of the meeting. Introducing a solution-focused approach at a meeting can be stressful, in that you are going 'against the grain' and not conforming to the traditional meeting protocol.

Creating a positive context for change

The chairperson has maximum opportunity to create a solution-focused context at a meeting. The role should be to offer a sense of hope for the participants, creating positive context for change in much the same way as in a therapeutic context.

Thus, following the customary welcome and introduction, the chairperson might begin with:

> 'So, we are all here today to find a way forward for Jim (or "to find a solution to the problem"). Everyone has read the background reports so we should all have a clear idea about how things got to where they are today. Perhaps we could start with finding out what has changed since the reports were written.'

It may or may not also be helpful to follow your opening remarks by seeking agreement as to the purpose of the meeting. For example:

> 'Can we agree that we are all here because we want Jim to be settled and learning in school?'

At this point the chairperson could go straight in to a scaling exercise (see below), or he/she could ask the parents, the social worker or the school the question:

> 'What progress has there been since the reports were written?'

Or:

> 'What has been working since we last met?'

This should initiate a search for 'pre-meeting' change and exceptions to the problem pattern. This type of opening also takes away the need for people to 'speak' to their reports.

After some discussion about this, a scaling exercise could be introduced by asking:

> 'I'm still a bit confused about how things have been going. Let's say we have a scale from 1 to 10, where 1 is the worst things could possibly be and 10 is no further need for these sorts of meetings (or, 'the best things could be expected to be'). Where is Susan today?'

Invite each person in turn to give Susan a number on the scale. Allow people the flexibility to scale for different aspects separately (e.g. home and school). A flip chart or note pad could be used if required. Then ask everyone to give their reasons for their replies and ask them to focus on:

'What has got Susan to ...?' or 'What's keeping her at ...?'

These questions will inevitably result in the generation of a great number of strengths and coping strategies.

Then consider asking:

'What number would you settle for?'

And:

'What would things have to get to for the school to feel that Susan no longer needed to be discussed at meetings like this one?'

And:

'What would things have to get to for the Panel/Court to discharge Susan?'

Follow up these questions with questions which help people describe in detail what will be different when things are at their selected number, e.g.

'How will you know when Susan is at...? What will be different?'

These questions will help people clarify their expectations of the client(s) and help set realistic and observable goals. The differences between people's scalings can often be an interesting source of exceptions and differences.

The next stage might be to invite more detailed discussion about some of the times when the pupil was 1 point up the scale. Consider, e.g.

'When does he get to 4?'

And:

'What was happening the last time he was at 6?'

And:

'What's different when he's at 3?'

In these questions it is assumed that there are some times when things are not quite so bad, or a bit better. In most meetings these exceptions to the problem pattern are usually overlooked or disregarded in the search for the 'cause' of the difficulties, or in the detailed specification of the problem. In asking these questions, the chairperson immediately gives credibility to those times when the problem is not dominating the situation. This will shift people's focus and help re-frame these occasions as meaningful and helpful in the development of a solution.

Very often as workers, we tend to attribute positive change to factors outside our direct control, e.g., 'he was just in a good mood that day', or 'his friends were absent on that occasion.' It is important to encourage workers to consider what they themselves have done to contribute to the positive changes. Thus, in this discussion, it is useful to ask further questions which seek to implicate the teachers, social workers or parents in these exceptions, e.g.

'So, what were you doing the last time things were at 8?'

Or:

'How did you manage to get him to do that?'

Or:

'Did you plan your strategy well in advance or did the change just come to you all of a sudden?'

In this way successful strategies can be identified and reinforced.

If no exceptions are elicited, ask questions that get people to describe a future when the problem is not quite so bad, e.g.

'Let's say things get to 6 (1 point up the scale), what will be different?'

'What will Billy be doing that tells you that things are now at 6?'

'What will you be doing differently when things are 9?'

'How will you know when things move to 3, what will be different?'

'Let's say that when we all meet again things have moved up to 6. What will have been happening that has got things to this point?'

These types of questions help to set short-term goals and expectations for the clients. They also help people recognise and acknowledge movement toward solutions. Solution-focused meetings can be concluded by summarising progress to date and any exceptions noted. Responses to the various scaling questions can be summarised and long and short-term goals listed.

If the conclusion of the meeting is that the situation has deteriorated, it is important to honestly acknowledge the seriousness of the situation, and perhaps ask some questions which seek to discover the ways in which people are coping with the ongoing difficulties, e.g.

'What are people doing to maintain the situation at the moment?'

'What's stopping things getting even worse?'

If appropriate, some form of task could be set for each person present, e.g.

'Notice the times when things move 1 point up the scale.'

Or:

'Notice what it is you are doing that is different when things get to 7.'

Or:

'Do more of what you were doing the last times things were at 2.'

Secondary school solutions

Subject teacher 'case conferences' have been a regular feature of many secondary schools for some years. At these meetings you often find that most of the time is taken up with each teacher telling the meeting how 'Billy' is behaving in class. The result is a detailed description of 'Billy's' disruptive behaviour in a variety of contexts. The danger is that the meeting simply serves to reinforce the pupil's disruptive reputation and enhance the teacher's feelings of helplessness. It is often the case in such meetings that one or two teachers observe that 'Billy' is actually 'no problem' with them. However, these exceptions are rarely used in a positive way to construct solutions and management strategies. At the end of such meetings there is usually insufficient time to move toward the development of solutions to the presenting problems.

A 'solution-focused strategy meeting' is essentially a solution-focused version of the subject teacher 'case conference.' The focus is on the development of solutions rather than the description of problems. The purpose of this type of meeting is to bring together secondary school subject teachers in order to identify and develop improved strategies for dealing with a particular disruptive pupil. The aim is to support positive changes where they occur and to help teachers manage pupils with challenging behaviour. The focus is away from a detailed exposé of a pupil's 'horrendous' behaviour towards a joint construction of strategies, which will work in the classroom context.

A simple scaling exercise is used where each teacher is asked to place the pupil on a scale in terms of where they think he/she is in their class (see Figures 5 and 6). This scale then becomes the focus for discussion and interaction at the meeting. It enables a clear identification of where the pupil is in terms of acceptable behaviour, facilitates goal-setting and determines the limits of acceptable behaviour. It is also a powerful way to illustrate to teachers that the pupil behaves differently in different classes and with different teachers.

The following section describes one such meeting, which took place in a large secondary school in Greenock. The meeting was convened to discuss the re-integration of a pupil ('Ryan') into secondary school. Ryan was a second-year pupil with a long history of disruptive behaviour. He had been attending a part-time off-site behaviour unit with the aim of maintaining his attendance at secondary school. The plan was to work to improve his behaviour and class-work and improve the chances of him coping better at school. The meeting was held following a recent setback that had resulted in Ryan serving a short-term exclusion from school. Despite his difficulties, Ryan could be a likeable young person and there was some goodwill remaining amongst staff members.

Planning

Advance planning and liaison were essential. A member of the senior management team was asked to co-ordinate arrangements for the meeting. Such a meeting is an extremely difficult thing for most schools to organise. It is usually impossible to arrange cover for 10 to 12 subject teachers to attend the same meeting. There clearly has to be a strong desire for it to take place and it has to be given sufficient status by the head teacher and the rest of the senior management team. At the school in question, the morning interval was extended for 15 minutes in order for the meeting to take place. Even after this, however, only 25 minutes was available for the meeting.

Ryan's parents were not present at the meeting but were informed that it was taking place by the school and were given feedback after the meeting.

The aim of the meeting was to develop detailed descriptions of what teachers were already doing that was working for Ryan and the school. Thus, the plan was to discuss the problems and the descriptions of Ryan's disruptive behaviour within a context that looked at what was working.

In this type of meeting, the assumption is that a focus on successful strategies and on what is happening when the pupil is not behaving in a disruptive manner will lead to the development of more effective behaviour-management strategies. The aim is to recognise, acknowledge and build upon the skills and resources which the teachers are already bringing to the situation.

It is important to acknowledge that at some point in the process the teachers may feel a need to talk about the problem. In Ryan's meeting, this was achieved by circulating a pro-forma some weeks prior to the meeting which gave teachers the opportunity to put their concerns down in writing and also began to enable them to notice possible exceptions to the problem. (see Figure 4). This information was collected on the day of the meeting and acknowledged by the chairperson. However, it was not discussed in detail at the meeting.

Teacher Information Sheet

Name.. Class...........................

Has the pupil been referred to me in the past? YES / NO

Please give a brief description of the behaviour that gives cause for concern at the moment

....

....

....

Now take a moment to think of some of the times when you have noticed the pupil doing a bit better in class. These observations will be helpful as we try to develop some solutions to the current difficulties.

Please be specific. For example, 'John does better in class when he is on time for class and when he is not sitting with his friends'.

1...

....

2. ....

....

3. ....

....

4. ....

....

Teacher's Signature .... Date...........................

Thank you very much for your help

Figure 4. Teacher Information Sheet.

Structure of the meeting

Almost all of Ryan's subject teachers attended the meeting, together with the head teacher, senior management, guidance staff and staff from the off-site unit. It was explained that the meeting has been arranged to help improve the pupil's behaviour at school. The initial focus was to be Ryan's behaviour, rather than the teachers' management skills. The teachers should not be made to feel threatened or undermined by the meeting. The explicit focus was on the pupil, his behaviour and what had happened (and needed to happen) to improve it. The implicit effect was that the teachers would be helped to an awareness of what they did in class which made a difference and helped to manage Ryan and his behaviour. The scaling exercise would focus on Ryan's behaviour and not the teachers' management skills. However, discussion around the scaling responses would aim to highlight what the teachers were doing which was helpful.

It was explained that due to the seriousness of the situation, the head teacher had agreed to take the unusual step of bringing everyone together to discuss Ryan. It was further explained that due to time restraints it would not be possible to go into much detail about the nature of the problem. The teachers were thanked for the return of the information sheets, which had helped to provide a clear picture of the problems presented by the pupil.

SThe scaling sheet (Figure 5) was distributed and the first question was asked (see Figure 6):

> 'Based on your contact with Ryan, where is he at the moment on this scale?'

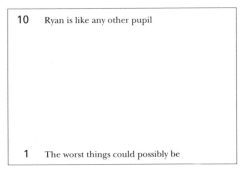

10   Ryan is like any other pupil

1   The worst things could possibly be

Figure 5. Scaling Sheet

Q1 Where is Ryan at the moment on the scale?

Q2 What has been happening that has got things to....?

Q3 What would you settle for?

Q4 What would have to happen for Ryan to have moved one point up the scale? (How will you know? What will be different?)

Figure 6. Questions for Scaling Exercise

It was explained to teachers that they should complete this task individually, either by marking the sheet with a number or simply using the scale to arrive at a number in their heads. Each person was then invited to respond in turn, stating the number they had given Ryan. The responses were marked on a communal scale on flipchart paper or blackboard. Teachers were allowed as much qualification as they wished and different ratings for different contexts were accepted, e.g. 'Well, I get him for registration and he's OK then, say at about 7, but in my maths class he's only at about 3.'

Figure 7 illustrates the range of responses given at the meeting to question 1.

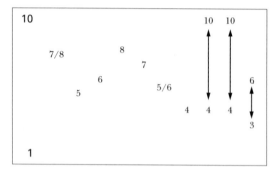

Figure 7. Range of responses to question 1: 'Where is Ryan at the moment?'

It was immediately obvious that Ryan was being given different ratings by different teachers, and was being rated differently by the same teacher in different contexts. This allowed the beginnings of a discussion, which focused on exceptions to the problems, e.g. times when things weren't quite so bad.

The second question was then asked (see figure 6):

'What has been happening that has got things to ...?'

This question enabled a discussion of some of the positive strategies, which were already in place in the school to support Ryan. In response to this question, the teachers tended to talk about examples of Ryan's better behaviour, situations when he could behave well, or gave summaries of what he was good at. For example:

'When Ryan is caught he accepts it.'
'He is totally controlled, therefore he behaves.'
'Better than some, he doesn't argue back.'
'I like him.'
'He has ability.'

Ryan's meeting ran out of time before questions 3 and 4 were asked. The meeting was concluded by summarising people's responses to the two scaling questions. Feedback was given in terms of what was happening in the school to stop the situation getting worse. The staff were complimented in relation to the positive management strategies which had been elicited.

It was suggested that the teachers should continue to do what they feel was working for the pupil. They were asked to notice what was happening on the occasions when Ryan moved 1 point up the scale.

If there had been sufficient time left, the next question would have been asked:

'What would you settle for on this scale?'

This question enables the teachers to set a realistic target for improvements. The number teachers choose will depend upon what you have set up 10 to be. For example, if 10 is 'Ryan is like any other pupil', then most teachers may want him to achieve 10. If 10 is 'Ryan is a perfect pupil', then most teachers may settle for around 7 or 8.

Question 4 could then be asked:

'What would have to happen for Ryan to have moved 1 point up the scale?'

Or

'How will you know when Ryan has moved 1 point up the scale?'

This question opens up a discussion of the small steps required for the pupil to move towards the goals set by each teacher. In this discussion it is essential to elicit clear, unambiguous, observable descriptions about what will be happening when the pupil is 1 point up the scale. The scope of the discussion can be expanded by asking what the teacher will be doing that is different: 'How will the rest of the class know that Ryan has moved up the scale?' etc.

Further descriptions of exceptions can be elicited by asking the teachers to describe occasions in the past when things got to ... (e.g. 1 point up the scale) for just a short while. Asking the teachers to explain how they managed to do this can help them to accept some responsibility for this change.

The meeting could then be concluded with some feedback, summarising what is already happening that is maintaining the pupil at the existing level. This should include a summary of what the teachers are doing that is making a difference (i.e. 'What has been happening that has got him to 4?'), should subsequently move on to summarise the goals set for the pupil by the teachers (i.e. 'What would you settle for?'), and finally feed back the strategies required to move the pupil 1 point up the scale (e.g. 'What would have to happen for Billy to have moved 1 point up the scale?').

If you choose to work with a colleague or a support teacher, he/she could be responsible for taking notes during the meeting and providing verbal feedback. If it seems appropriate it may be useful to offer to provide written feedback in the form of a 'Management Strategy Sheet.'

It is possible that this sort of meeting has maximum effect if it is used alongside other interventions, e.g. support teaching or individual work with the pupil and/or the family. The teachers are then perhaps more inclined to view the process as a way to provide you with information that will help you in your individual contact with the pupil. As a result, they may be more open to discuss their experiences with the pupil.

As with all solution-focused approaches, flexibility is the key.

Comments/Reflections

Remaining solution-focused requires self-belief, commitment and ingenuity. Initial changes in our approach to casework triggered a desire to explore the broader applications of solution-focused principles. This chapter has outlined how meetings can become powerful forums for change.

The sample questions quoted here have all been used by myself and colleagues in meetings successfully to help people move towards solutions in their lives. Our continuing task is to maintain the energy, enthusiasm and humour which is required to continue to develop these approaches.

The use of solution-focused approaches in our wider practice has altered the way in which we see ourselves applying psychology within educational settings. We have been trying to develop new and more creative relationships with clients and other professionals. In many instances this has created a joint context within which practical solutions can be identified, nurtured and developed. We are moving away from 'psychologist as expert scientist', towards 'psychologist as co-creator and facilitator.' Our role in this context is to join with our clients, be they teachers, parents, young people or other professionals, in a solution-focused way. Our work is to encourage and facilitate the identification of goals and the creation of meaningful solutions.

The challenge for professional helpers is to remain optimistic and 'solution-focused' within a problem-driven environment. If we assume that our clients (children, parents, teachers and other professionals) have within them the strengths and resources required to bring about positive change in their lives, our role is to help them realise this and develop their own unique solutions.

CHAPTER THREE

FROM THE IMPOSSIBLE TO THE SOLUTION

BY GILLIAN STRACHAN

This chapter illustrates the application of the solution-focused approach in practice with two cases, which were previously seen by others as 'impossible'. It gave the worker the confidence to approach these cases when other professionals felt they had been unable to resolve the difficulties and were 'stuck'.

Introduction

The School and Family Support Service (SFSS) is a small team of social workers (one senior, three professionally qualified and two trainees) employed by Angus Council Education Department. Our client groups are young people and children, their families and school staff. All members of the team have been trained in Solution Focused Brief Therapy by members of the Brief Therapy Practice.

Solution Focused Brief Therapy is the framework within which team members operate. We use the method in the following areas of service delivery: school attendance; behavioural difficulties; anti bullying; exclusion from school; home-school partnerships; child protection; counselling. The main function of the Service is to establish links between schools and families and young people through a professional and solution focused approach.

Our Service has no statutory basis. However, we are involved with cases which are referred to the Reporter to the Children's Panel. Young people are referred to the Service by school staff with parents' permission. Thereafter, contact agreement, approach and matters to be resolved are agreed between the young people, families and school. Contact agreement is reached through discussion with the Young Person, the family and school staff. This is negotiated by the worker who ensures all those involved are in agreement. We believe working in collaboration increases our client groups' motivation to engage, as opposed to statutory orders.

Rationale for solution-focused brief therapy

Two members of the School and Family Support Service and one member of the Educational Psychology Service were trained in Edinburgh by Harvey Ratner from the Brief Therapy Practice. Following that training we found the solution-focused approach extremely effective in our casework. It also enabled us to support school staff with cases and challenging situations previously seen as being 'stuck'. It helped us remain focused and work across the Department within a clear framework. As a social worker, I find that the emphasis of the approach on respect and genuineness fits with my professional values. The framework initially appears deceptively simple but I found it had enormous scope for greater 'connection' with clients. Greater depth of empathic understanding is achieved by the detailed questioning and language. It provides me with a more powerful tool for therapeutic change. The identification of clear goals and the use of 'scaling' to measure and monitor progress are most helpful. The fun aspects of the method were most enjoyable to clients and myself. In terms of applying the method within the department, initial feedback from schools and colleagues was positive and encouraging.

We encouraged other members of the Department to take up training and were actively supported by a member of the Directorate team. Then, as interest and confidence in applying the method grew, we bought training into Angus. Yasmin Ajmal from the Brief Therapy Practice has trained staff over four, two-day sessions. Initially, training was offered to staff required to employ problem-solving skills in supporting young people, i.e. guidance and support for learning staff (latterly we have included class teachers), community education workers, advisers and members of the Educational Development Service. Most recently we have trained head teachers and those in management positions in schools. As numbers of solution-focused trained staff grew in schools, so did some frustrations; this led to the training of management staff to enable them to lead others in a solution-focused manner. We are now focusing on implementing the method in more detail in each school, by providing support and follow-up, in-service training. As more staff are trained they apply the method in their own context. It is expanding constantly, with new applications in different branches including in the most 'stuck' of situations with the least motivated clients.

Solution-focused practice

I agreed to give a presentation to the conference in September 1999 for two main reasons: first, since undertaking my professional training thirteen years ago, I have found Solution-Focused Brief Therapy to be the most effective method I have used in my work with schools and families. Second, to show my appreciation to members of the Brief Therapy Practice.

The first case, outlined below, was one of the earliest where I applied the approach following one, two-day 'School-Related Problems' course given by Harvey Ratner from the Brief Therapy Practice.

'Nikki'

Nikki was referred following an absence from school of a year. Others described her as school phobic, with anxiety disorder. The case was referred to our Service as an interim measure whilst the family were waiting to be seen by Child and Family Psychiatry.

Establishing clear goals

I met with Nikki and her mum in the family home. I also supported school staff along with the Educational Psychologist. During the first session Nikki was able to set goals and had a clear preferred future. Steve De Shazer (1985) states, 'one of the most common reasons for failure is a poorly defined goal.' It was important at this stage for Nikki to have clear goals. She wanted to have a 'normal' life. So using solution-focused questioning, in order to clarify her meaning of 'normal', I established what she would be doing in a 'normal' life. She said she would be 'seeing friends, going out and going to school,' in that order. 'Going to school' was her third goal. It was necessary to build Nikki's confidence and gently acclimatise her to school by beginning with goals one and two.

Small steps towards change

In Solution-Focused Brief Therapy, I like the way the questions lead to detail and depth of description, and how talking about change is enough to make it happen. George, Iveson and Ratner (1990 and 1999) describe the solution-focused question leading to description 'that is rich in small, concrete, behavioural detail.' With each of Nikki's goals we achieved extensive, detailed description. For Nikki, the first sign things would be beginning to improve was her getting out of bed. With very small steps, using scaling to monitor progress and highlight what she had done, she set goals for each session. I used a scale of 1 to 10, but with experience, I realise that I should have used a larger scale to allow for greater movement.

Going out of house scale

1	2	3	4	5	6	7	8	9	10
Staying in bed									Going out of house

Session 1
I don't stay in bed all day, I get up, Gran comes round

Session 2
Moving to 3
I got up earlier, did my hair.

Session 3
Moving to 3½
Stayed up, stayed dressed

Session 4
Moved up to 4
Phoned my friend, mum encouraged me, I have to do this. I'm feeling better, said to my friend I'd go out. I'll be at 5 when I go out and I'll meet people and feel better.

Session 5
Moved back to 3½
Didn't go out with my friend. We stayed in, I enjoyed it. To move up to 4, I'll be going out with friend.

Session 6
Moved to 5½
Phoned friend. Planned to go to Oasis fashion show. I'm nervous but want to do it.

Session 7
Moved to 8
Went with friend for a walk around twice. I felt funny but I was okay. To get to 10 I'll go to the fashion show.

Session 8
Moved to 8½
I went to fashion show but was really scared. I stayed outside for ages. When I

went in I met people from school. I managed because I was determined and my friend helped me. Some of the school staff were models.

Her goals included:

- staying out of bed
- doing her hair
- dressing
- going out of the house
- going out of the house and down the road
- having a friend around

Moving with Nikki at her pace

Nikki took very small steps towards her normal life. Rhodes and Ajmal (1995) bring to our attention that some people may be clear about their goal but such a huge step can be overwhelming! This was the case for Nikki. At these times taking small steps (a quarter and a half on the scale) appeared to make her progress more achievable.

Whilst Nikki was absent from school, work was sent home for her. Continuing with work was important to her (prior to using the solution-focused approach, I would have thought this was keeping her at home). Her Mum was involved in making helpful suggestions which included doing some of the work in her local library. Nikki also took her little sister to the primary school and gradually she was getting nearer to her own school building and her third goal.

Staying brief

In the initial three weeks, I met Nikki over eight, fifteen-minute contacts; previously, I would have planned an hour's visit weekly. My contacts were brief and I came out of the house thinking, 'Is that it?' Things moved very quickly but sometimes up and down the scale. Nikki's next goal was to get into the school building and, after a few attempts, she managed this. Again, Nikki set goals, going back to small steps when 'the going got tough.' When Nikki was helping me prepare this, she remembered usually managing to do more than she thought she would. She thought the look of surprise on my face, when she told me what she had managed, was funny! This was a genuine response on my part, not only to what Nikki had achieved but how this method was working. After five weeks Nikki managed to go into school.

Enabling school staff in the use of the approach

The focus of my work then moved to supporting school staff in more detail with the same approach. Nikki set the goals with her guidance teacher, who monitored her progress again using scales, and highlighted the great strengths Nikki had. They did this by Nikki selecting the subjects she would go into first and using a confidence scale to monitor how confident she felt in each. They looked in detail at what Nikki had done, or how friends had helped her to move up the scale, by looking at what others saw Nikki doing.

What was important to Nikki

Later, in preparation of these materials, Nikki said it made a big difference to her, knowing her guidance teacher 'really cared.' Again, the authenticity of the approach, or the teacher, had shone through and was important. Once inside school, Nikki began to make rapid progress. She moved from inside the door to staying for five minutes, meeting friends in the social area, going with friends to one class, then two, then three. After three classes things moved very quickly. Nikki was referred to the School and Family Support Service in September and resumed all her classes by December. She beat the case conference goals which were to have her in all classes by March the next year. The views of significant others, especially her peer group, were important to Nikki. So much so that she found great difficulty overcoming fear of her peers enquiring about the problem which led her to stop attending school. She agreed an excuse with her guidance teacher, who told the class she had been ill for a long time. This was the only time the problem was referred to by Nikki. Rhodes and Ajmal (1995) suggest 'extended discussion of the past can actually be unhelpful as it can lead to feelings of hopelessness.' There had been a number of other professionals involved with Nikki before myself who had all looked in detail at the problem with Nikki and her family. For me, doing something different was vital.

Coping with setbacks

Following the Christmas holiday period there were a few setbacks: normal attendance problems; testing out of her parents; illness extended by a few days.

School staff and a few telephone conversations between the mother and myself dealt with these setbacks. One of the siblings began to have an attendance problem and mirrored some of Nikki's previous behaviour, again, this was quickly resolved. The educational psychologist for the primary school who also uses solution-focused approaches, liaised with myself about what had worked previously and drew on existing strengths within the family.

Nikki has been at school for two years since, without any further difficulties and is sitting seven Standard Grade exams.

Respecting Nikki's wishes

When the final preparations for the conference were complete, I contacted Nikki and her Mum to check they were happy with my presentation. I asked if there was anything else they would like me to say on their behalf. I received two letters (see below) which they asked me to read out. I struggled with this initially – firstly because Scottish culture does not allow for 'boastfulness' and secondly, because I was surprised by the impact the work had had on them. However, to respect their wishes I read out the letters. In the letters, Gillian is only a name, it could be you or any other worker.

> My first year of high school started off OK, then one of my class mates began to bother me, not physically but I'd say her attitude was nasty and bitchy. The more I let her bother me, the more I found excuses to stay off school and the more anxious I became. I got to the stage where I was having panic attacks and didn't feel like I could go to school at all. Often I thought I would never go back and that this was my life.
>
> Gillian advised me to take things step by step. We talked a lot and took things at my own pace, which made it easier for me to cope. With the help of my guidance teacher, we arranged for friends to meet with me in the library at school, and gradually I made it back into my first practical classes. When I walked into my class alone, it felt as if everyone was looking at me and I was the topic of the day. If I was with a friend it eased the pressure and I was able to distract myself from attention. I felt most nervous when fellow classmates queried me about why I had been off for so long. My guidance teacher once again spoke to my classmates and explained that I was ill. They said no more after that. Gillian helped me through one of the biggest problems of my life. Myself and my whole family are very grateful for everything she did to help.
>
> As things progressed I saw less of Gillian, but whenever I do see her, even now, I thank her for all of her help and I am always happy to mention 'what's going well.' I couldn't have changed without her help.
>
> From Nikki

And from her mother:

> We are only too pleased to allow Gillian to use Nikki's situation in her speech to you tonight and feel it's the least we can do to say

thank you.

After much stress and 'end of tether' scenes, Gillian stepped in with help, not only for Nikki but also myself. The advice and guidance she gave was invaluable; we couldn't have done it alone and the whole family was affected by this major problem.

To see Nikki today it is hard to believe she is the same girl. The help she received has undoubtedly changed her life.

Yours sincerely

Phyllis

The impact of the approach

I thought I had achieved the goal of helping Nikki back to school. Sometimes, we are unaware of the impact we can have on people's lives and when they tell us, it is difficult to accept. As part of the education system, we are privileged to be in such a position, but should perhaps be aware that this impact can be both positive and negative. At a recent seminar given by Ben Furman, he stressed the importance of celebrating success or progress within the young person's environment, in order to encourage the school or community's acceptance of the achieved goal. Furman and Aloha (1992) show the benefits in clients giving credit for their progress to family, friends and professional helpers.

Celebrating success

Although Furman and Aloha talk about 'coaching' clients to celebrate success as part of the piece of work, Nikki and her Mum did this naturally by thanking friends, taking flowers to the school and thanking other professional helpers. Such expressions of gratitude were a sign of acceptance of their achieved goals and possibly meant less likelihood of relapse.

Susan

Have you ever had a case referred where lots of other professionals have been involved and the problems have been around for a number of years?

Susan was referred due to continuous unresolved group bullying. This was her third secondary school. Her parents chose this school because they believed she wouldn't be bullied there.

Susan was the victim in a group of four girls who were once friends. She didn't want anything done about the bullying as she believed it could not be resolved. School staff had tried before and she felt things became worse. Her mother had phoned the school when she realised it was happening again.

Susan began shutting herself in her room, crying, and in bad moods denying there was anything wrong.

How many of us have felt under pressure by a referral? I certainly did with this one; I could be the next to fail this girl.

School staff felt it was something in Susan's behaviour which provoked the bullying. She had strong opinions and other girls didn't like her confident manner. She also told stories which the other girls didn't believe.

Engaging with the pupil and building trust

Susan didn't want anything done about the bullying, and if this remained the case, we were 'stuck'. The guidance teacher and I met with Susan, went over the proposed piece of work and considered what we would do and how we would do it:

– Trying to install some confidence in Susan by sharing what had worked before in similar pieces of work, where long-term bullying had been resolved using the Shared Concern method.
– Being honest and telling her there were no guarantees, but reassuring her the work would go at her pace and stop at her request.
– Giving her back control of her life.

That is one of the things I like about this method: the pupil is in control and sets the agenda. George, Iveson and Ratner (1990 and 1999) describe 'communicating the worker's belief in the client's ability to change things, that change is under their control, not ours.' Clearly, Susan felt let down by the previous help being repeatedly unsuccessful. It was important she felt she had choices, was clear about the proposed work and had control throughout in order to feel safe.

This approach is one of enabling and supporting rather than being seen as the expert coming into school. My role was to support Susan, school staff and in particular the guidance teacher. Susan, the guidance teacher and I agreed that the guidance teacher would work with the group of girls and I would work with Susan.

Working in partnership with school staff

Recognising the guidance teacher's strengths and skills, we agreed to work in partnership and were clear about one another's roles. All this was with Susan's agreement. The guidance teacher used the 'Shared Concern Method', which is a solution-focused method of resolving group bullying which was devised by Anatol Pikas, a Swedish psychologist. This involved meeting with individual members of the bullying group in order to establish their suggestions of what they would do to improve the situation, then encouraging them to try out these suggestions and let the teacher know at the next meeting what had changed as a result of their help. This piece of work with the group was successful and the group began to move towards a more positive relationship with Susan. My work with Susan led on from there.

Pre-session change

Between my introductory meeting with Susan and my first session, she had begun to feel more confident. This was due to the group beginning to make positive moves towards her. I assessed this using a confidence scale.

1	2	3	4	5	6	7	8	9	10
Having no confidence									Feeling more confidence

At the time of our first meeting, Susan rated herself at 2. She was not at one because she was determined not to give in to the other girls and she spoke to her Gran, who helped. She moved from a 2 to a 4 because she wanted 'things to get better' and some of the girls were speaking to her. But she still didn't trust them.

The tool bag

Having some previous anti-bullying experience prior to my solution Focused training, which included counselling, I used a counselling approach as well as a Solution-focused approach during the first session. This involved active listening and empathising. The use of both approaches led to greater depth of understanding. Susan describes how she felt listened to on the video transcript which follows.

Goal setting

One of the criticisms made by some of the solution-focused approach is its lack of depth in terms of feelings and emotions. I haven't found this, and my experience is demonstrated clearly in this case. Susan set the goal for change. These were the things she wanted help with: her confidence, emotions and opinions.

Preferred future and role play

By asking Susan what she would be doing when she was more confident, I established she wanted to return the group's positive moves – but she was afraid they would 'trick' her and upset her again. She said she would be returning a smile and having 'normal conversations with them.' I asked her what difference that would make when she was having 'normal conversations.'

She said the others would accept her.

In order to establish greater depth and clarity to Susan's wish to return a smile, have 'normal' conversations and to assert her confidence, I invited Susan to improvise a role play. She found this very amusing and we both laughed a lot, particularly when I tried to have a normal conversation as a 15 year-old girl. Susan ended up playing both roles. This appeared to be her adjusting the unbelievable stories and practising the 'normal conversation.' We also practised Susan returning the smile, paying particular attention to body language.

Second session moving fast

There was a physical difference when I saw Susan in the second session. She appeared happier and her hair was different. She felt her relationship with the other girls was much better but most of all she felt more confident. Again we used the confidence scale to look in more depth at what she had done. She had moved from a 4 to a 6 and gave detailed description in metaphors to describe her courage. She will tell you about this in the video transcript. Rhodes and Ajmal (1995) refer to clients' use of metaphors in describing their situation and how the therapist 'also co-operates by sometimes using the exact language of the client.'

The third and final session

By the third session Susan felt she had reached her goals. Three of the four girls were friends. On the confidence scale she was at an 8 which was good enough for her. This is what she did to move from 6 to 8 on the scale : she had spoken to her parents about the upset, had no further days off school and felt she was accepted by the group. She had gone back to the Army Cadets, to which she had belonged prior to the bullying in school. Clare, one of the group, had apologised.

Outcome

Susan had six months of happiness before she left school the following May. The other girls in the group learned about their relationships with one another through the Shared Concern Process.

Video

Susan agreed to the interview being video recorded where no rehearsal took place. The video focused on the process, as I thought it would be interesting to hear a pupil's perspective of the approach. I use solution-focused questions but it is mainly Susan's detailed description of the process and the work we did together.

Transcript

This is an unedited transcript of the video conversation with Susan. I open the session by reminding Susan that we met in September 1998 and finished working together about December.

G: So how are things now, since we last met?
> (I met up with Susan for the purposes of making the video for the conference and hadn't seen her since I finished working with her four months previously.)

S: Things are going fine. I've got my Sergeants back.
> (Prior to the difficulties she had in school, she had been a Sergeant in the Cadets.)

S: I've left school now. I left on the thirty-first of May and I started my new job on the fifth of July.

S: So, you've been away from school just a week or so and you've managed to get a job already?

S: Yes, second interview in my life and I've got a job already.

G: Well done Susan, and thank you very much for agreeing to come along today to help me with this video for the conference. The conference I am going to is about the work that I do, and people will be interested in hearing from you about what you thought was helpful in the work we did together.
Can you tell me Susan, what it was you liked about the way we worked together?

S: I think it was just because we worked one-to-one and I was able to talk just to you and say what I was feeling, and talked to you about what I was keeping back from my parents because I couldn't really speak to my parents, because they were always busy.

G: So you liked just having one person to speak to. What did you like particularly, if anything, in the way that we worked together?

S: I think it was something to do with the way you asked the questions.

G: Can you tell me a bit more about the questions? You said you liked the questions.

S: Erm, I don't know. A lot of people didn't ask questions like that and you just sat there and listened to what I said, whereas many people don't.
> (Steve De Shazer [1994] in his chapter, 'Freud Was Wrong: Words Have Lost None Of Their Magic' suggests, 'Perhaps we have been asking the wrong questions, or asking our questions the wrong way.' Although the questions can sometimes be difficult, clients seem to like them.)

G: So, it was the listening that you liked as well?

S: Yes, I liked being listened to in that way.
> (It appeared that the solution-focused questions made Susan feel that she was being listened to, whereas my previous counselling approach did not have the effect of

solution-focused questions).

G: Lots of other people tried to help you before in the past.

S: Yes, but they didn't really listen to what I said. They had selective hearing really and heard what they wanted to. I'd never really had to push myself to think about the answers before.

G: Yes, you did all the hard work and I asked the unusual questions. Thinking back to how things became better for you, can you think what you did that began to make things better?

S: Mm, yes, well, speaking to you and then I decided I would speak to my parents. I spoke to them and I spoke to my gran and I really just took a different look on life. I stopped living in the past and started to move forward and it's been fantastic since then.

G: That's great! How did you manage that?

S: I don't know really. It was to do with the girls in the school.

G: What was it you did that helped make these changes for you?

S: I made contact with them and smiled just like we had practised, and tried to be pleasant to them.

G: How did you manage that?

S: And, if they didn't return it I would keep trying. And then, eventually, I kept trying and they did start to return the smiles. And then they said hello in the passing and then I said it back. And then, we got into hello, how are you doing. And then I would speak back. And then it kept going and going. It took a lot of time and effort from me, and probably them as well and then we ended up becoming friends again, and I never thought we would.

G: You began to do that at a time when things were still quite painful for you. How did you actually manage to smile at them at this time, it takes great courage?

S: It did take a lot of courage and I think it was all bottled up, and I just had to let it out. It was like a balloon and you blow and blow into the balloon, and tie it into a knot and your courage is inside. And then, if you let the balloon go it whooshes all around the room and your courage is coming out of you, and you just burst with courage and go with the flow really.

G: So your courage helped you through everything really?

S: And all that helped me in school.

G: Remember the scaling questions I used?

S: Yeah, I remember them, the confidence scale especially. I started off at a four and then I think it was about three times I saw you later, I was up at an eight because everything had changed and things were much better really, moving into the future.

G: So, what did you think about the way we used the scale? Can you remember how it was helpful?

S: Well, it was because I thought I'm on a four and the reason I'm not on a three is because I am happier sitting at four but, I'm not at a five because I would be more confident if I was at a five. And then, gradually, I could see myself moving up and then, four, five, six, seven, eight, and eventually in school I stopped at an eight. But now, everything's going really great and I've ended up with a job and I think right now I'm sitting about an eleven. Even though it just goes one to ten, I think I'm still an eleven.

G: That's great Susan, you've done so well. I recall you remembered the exact numbers of the scale [we laugh a lot together]. You remembered the numbers and I always had to write them down for the next time we met. I never had to prompt you, you always wanted to go back to the scaling and that was why I thought I would ask you what you thought about it because the people at the conference may be using it in their work.

S: Yes, it really helps you and I liked it because it helped you and I to understand where I was at. If I was at a four, it helped me explain and understand why I was at four, and then when I moved up to eight it helped me explain how I'd got to an eight. It helped me to see all the good stuff that was happening that helped me get to an eight. It helped me to see what I needed to do to move up a number.

G: So that was a useful way for us to look at things?

S: Yes, definitely.

G: The things you overcame when we worked together and the things you learned about yourself, your own strengths, Susan, and your courage, and the balloon that you talked about, and the confidence scaling, and how much your confidence grew. You've managed to secure a job in two interviews. What does that tell you about your confidence?

S: It came out as I used the balloon for my courage. I think my confidence was locked behind a door someplace and I didn't have the key to unlock the door, somebody else did. And as soon as I got to the point where I needed it, somebody handed me the key and out it came.

G: I must say, it's great you've done so well and managed to get a job on top of all this, especially after just two interviews.

S: I know. So many people have to go through so many interviews here and still they don't get jobs. I think I'm just a really lucky girl. I can't believe my luck, everything has just kept turning good now.

G: And are people around you pleased at your success?

S: Yes. When I got the job my friends were phoning to see how I'd got on. When I told them I'd got the job they were saying great, great, I'm so pleased for you. And these were the friends before who had said you'll never get a job because I didn't have the qualifications or anything but, there you go I didn't need them.

G: So what's the difference now, Susan, since I first met you?

S: I've changed a lot. I've grown up I think and I take a different look on life now. What happened in the past is in the past and if God made a time thing and I could go back and change it, I don't think I would change it because it's given me a different look on life now and you can't change your past, and you can't be scared of your past, and even although there's so much terrible stuff that's happened to you, you can't live in the past for the rest of your life. I've closed that nasty book.

G: Good.

S: Thank you very much.

G: And thank you Susan, for all your help, and good luck in the future.

Neil Logue, Head of Educational Services, Angus Council. made the following statement: 'Over the past four years, staff from Angus Council have benefited from the training provided through international speakers and by Yasmin Ajmal, whose training and support in implementing the method in Angus has been invaluable. There is a growing interest in and commitment to solution-focused approaches within the Education Service in Angus and I am confident this will be of benefit to young people in our schools.'

Stuck cases – some reflections

Feeling in control is important to most adolescents and certainly was to Nikki and Susan. Moving at their pace and being with them in the work seemed to enhance their feeling of being in control. The most striking reflection for me, which Susan talks about, is being 'listened to.' This approach helps people feel heard and seems to make a connection for them between what they say and what they find helpful. The solution-focused approach continues to give me the confidence to approach challenging cases and situations. It gave me a sense of hope and this transferred to Susan and Nikki, who previously believed their stuck situations 'would be their life.'

CHAPTER FOUR

BRIEF THERAPY APPROACHES
WITH GROUPS AND FAMILIES
IN AN EDUCATION SUPPORT SERVICE

BY MADAN MALL AND BERNADETTE STRINGER

A reflection on developments in working with groups and families where children's entitlement to education is being affected by emotional and behavioural difficulties.

For the purposes of this chapter we will be discussing our experiences of using Solution-Focused Brief therapy in group work situations, with children, and their families.

Introduction

Setting

Birmingham is home to the largest Education Service and Social Services Department in the country. The Child Advisory Social Work Service (CASWS) is located within the Children's Division of the Local Authority Social Services department and functions across the organisational boundary between that Department and the Education Service. CASWS, as part of the Birmingham Child and Adolescent Mental Health Service, provides a therapeutic service to troubled children and their families, including looked-after children and their families/carers.

The service delivered is informed by a variety of theoretical frameworks including psychodynamic, psychoanalytic, systemic, cognitive and behavioural. The Service has a well-established team. All team members are qualified and experienced social workers who have additional qualifications in counselling, psychotherapy, teaching or psychology.

History

Some team members have used Solution-Focused Brief Therapy since 1993. We have found that the model is consistently useful and empowering of clients, and offers the worker the possibility of managing stuckness both in long- and short-term situations. We have worked as individuals, and as co-workers with groups, in family situations, and with adults and children individually. We have also offered consultations to other professionals and systems. The authors became interested in a solution-focused approach at a time when:

– we were regularly requested to work with children who displayed high levels of aggressive behaviour, including bullying at school and at home;
– research by Madan Mall (1993) involving interviews with white and black children who had been excluded, indicated that excluded children were gaining kudos from aggressive and violent behaviour. These children were not seen by a psychiatrist or diagnosed as ADD/ADHD;
– there was an increasing awareness amongst LEAs nationally that African-Caribbean boys were being excluded from schools. (Education Guardian, 1:21:92).

We were concerned to intervene with disruptive pupils individually and in the classroom, particularly as Mall's research, based on interviews with black and white boys and girls, suggested that some excluded children aligned themselves to peer groups where their troublesome behaviour was reinforced.

Children indicated that name-calling and racist remarks were common in their experience in schools and that there was a problem in teacher and pupil relationships. This in turn could lead to outbursts of angry or aggressive behaviour for which the child was disciplined or excluded.

The research suggested that the children were not aiming to disrupt school, nor were they anti-school. The results also showed that they were either aiming to hold their position with their peer group or that it was their reaction to situations which led them into difficulties. The sample of children interviewed did not necessarily actively set out to seek arguments with their teachers, but situations in which arguments took place caused children to speak their minds.

Why groupwork?

The authors decided the most effective way to manage the high number of referrals would be to work with groups of children. Using groups to help young people look at their social roles and to learn through challenge and counter challenge was a popular method at the time (David Broadbent 1991, 'Make or Break,' Social Work Today 1: 8: 91, Beck & Emery 1985).

We were experienced in running groups and aware of how the power of peer group influence could be used to stimulate and motivate troubled young people in a group setting.

> Peer groups can provide the presence or absence of supportive relationships, role models, rewarding consequences, instruction, information, opportunity, challenge and confrontation. (Nelson-Jones 1991).

Children who presented angry behaviour were referred to us with labels such as 'aggressive', 'resistant' and 'defiant'. Surprisingly, we found that children formed friendships very quickly and exchanged phone numbers for support between meetings.

The formulation of attachments in groups is not uncommon. All people have various degrees of connectedness to others who can support them (Acock and Hurlbert, 1990). The children who were referred to us were disconnected from the majority of the school population but connected to a minority group of peers who gained status by reinforcing their own anti-social behaviour.

Solution-focused groupwork

As we increasingly used the collaborative methods of solution-focused work, we observed that connecting children by their experience, strengths and problem solving skills, encouraged by their peers as well as adults, enabled them to accept change without threat to their status.

As the demand for places in the groups increased, we continued to run them twice a year. Not every group was the same and the duration and frequency of meetings changed with every new group of children. We were also influenced by other work pressures and demands, and the wishes of group members.

What developed as a method for managing the groups was an ongoing focus on possibility and change, an emphasis on the young person's knowledge about their concern, and an understanding of why other people were concerned about them.

We continued to run the groups using a solution-focused approach because we found that children responded readily. They told us in feedback that they liked:

– the questions and the ratings, which gave a visual indicator of progress or deterioration;
– the style of the facilitators and the way discussions about their difficulties were approached;
– the activities in pairs and groups, individual attention and interesting homework (see appendix);
– that we looked for their successes and encouraged their peers in the group to do so.

This way of working was successful – so we used more of it! The referrals continued to come from other professionals when it was known that we were offering anger-management groups with some success.

Co-working

We find it is vital when working with groups to co-work. It is an advantage that we are a south-east Asian man and White/Irish woman working together. We strive continually as part of our work to be aware of issues relating to race and gender and other forms of oppression.

One of our own aims was to raise with the members of the group an awareness of oppressive language and attitudes. It was encouraging to hear the children become more aware in perceiving oppressive comments towards themselves and others, and becoming more confident in challenging these in an appropriate way (i.e. one which could not then be framed as anger or bullying). The children learned to be assertive by seeing it modelled by people coming from different perspectives. The children were comfortable with discussing issues in this way, because the co-workers were comfortable sharing them. We used examples from our own lives and the knowledge and experiences of group members.

We continued to develop the model in regular sessions with families, again using a co-work approach. The effectiveness soon became apparent in feedback from service users. We noticed differences in sessions because we were actively looking for them, e.g. in non-verbal cues such as how relaxed people were, how they smiled more, seemed less burdened and were lighter in tone.

We found it helpful to use the co-worker when working with families to notice change and difference and to record it. This is a move away from using co-work as a means of mutual support for the workers when managing stressful issues.

Pre-session interview

We always preceded the setting up of a group by interviewing the children. This was easily arranged when we were facilitating a group in a school, because we could see the children within a morning. When children had been referred from a variety of places we found it easier to visit them at home.

The pre-session interview was very useful to us and to the group members. We were able to meet the children and their carers, explain the aims of the group and hear the children's and their parents'/carers' views about attending – particularly important if someone else referred the child.

By placing an emphasis on future-orientated questions and seeking the child's views about his/her concerns, the tone was set for the rest of the work. The information was recorded and we were able to refer back to the child's comments through the life of the group.

We also explained to the child and the significant adults how we would work and encouraged those who saw the child between the group meetings to support him/her and reinforce the group by noticing and commenting on changes. This was especially important when the children were not at the same school and the groups met at the Centre.

Beginning a session

It was important to arrive before the children and to have the room ready. We were then free to greet them as they entered the room. We would ask the parents or carers what they had noticed during the week and to comment on any differences in behaviour and presentation. If no examples came from them we would offer some comments from our observations of the group.

Problem-free talk

By the time everyone arrived the children would have inevitably begun to compare stories. Although we had no 'control' over whether 'problem free talk' took place or not, we could have some influence on the tone of the discussions by asking questions such as 'How has it been?', through welcoming the children back, and by looking forward to their news.

If homework had been set the previous week, we reviewed and discussed it. The homework was always arranged to bring out examples of coping and managing. Sharing experiences within the group encouraged learning from each other and the choice to use other children's wisdom. This made them feel important and needed, and increased their feeling of belonging to the group and each other (Nelson-Jones 1991).

If a child had had a 'bad' week, we asked about their coping strategies and also generated support from the other children's collective experience. As facilitators our role was to enable each child to tell his/her story rather than for us to comment directly on each child's experience. We would also listen carefully to the examples and redirected discussions towards strengths and skills. We listened carefully to the language used, e.g. 'I decided to ...' and picked up on any exceptions.

Co-constructing goals, agendas and preferred futures

Our goal in setting up Anger Management groups was to:

- help children keep control more often;
- manage a high number of referrals.

We hoped to enable children who had shown themselves to be impulsive and assertive in character to have a choice about how they reacted to provocation.

There was also an agenda set by the referrers, for example that the aggressive and confrontational behaviour would diminish, and that the children would become more manageable in the classroom. In this way the referrer is stating his/her own preferred future for the children. They will have made an assessment, and will have an idea of what they hope will be achieved by referring for counselling/support. Our preferred future for the children also included the possibility that they could access educational opportunity, which in the long term would enhance their life chances. New experiences, which provide a 'turning point' for an individual, assist in reducing negative and increasing positive chain reactions in human interactions and increase the possibility of change being reinforced. This is supported by Rutter (1999) who states that:

> 'Experiences tend to impinge on individual children in quite different ways; the reduction of negative, and increase of positive, chain reactions influences the extent to which the effects of adversity persist over time; new experiences which open up opportunities can provide beneficial "turning - point" effects.'

This is not necessarily what children want.

It is important to find out what children do want. When listening to children's experiences we became increasingly aware that some behave in defensive and aggressive ways to survive in the environment, family or neighbourhood in which they live.

We hope that after the pre-session interview, each child joining the group would have had the opportunity to think about his/her own reasons for coming – and was not attending just because he/she had been told to or was under threat of exclusion.

We also gave some thought to the responsibility of the facilitators to create an ethos whereby children feel they belong and are important in the group. Thus the facilitators enable the members, each with their own agenda, to create a group identity whilst preserving their own. The child has an allegiance and a sense of belonging because he/she has been instrumental in creating it. The child is prepared to take part in the collective responsibility for the group and its success. This does not detract from the child's individual agenda, because he/she has autonomy within the group.

We aimed to do this in practical ways:

– by giving the group a name, chosen by the children;
– including fun activities;
– setting ground rules with the children based on care and respect for each other;
– encouraging the children to respect the confidentiality boundaries of the group, but also to talk about their achievements to significant adults and friends outside the group;
– using the ideas within the Solution-Focused Brief Therapy model to validate each member.

Our experience when working in schools, with established peers who knew each other, was that the group became 'the place to be.'

Constructing goals with family groups

When working with a family group, a discussion of preferred futures can open up different possibilities for each member.

However, one has to be aware of the consequences of a particular solution preferred by a family member. For example, a seventeen-year-old Asian man was convinced that the solution to resolving friction with his father was to leave the family home. For the young man, it was an adventurous period in his life. For his family, it would be a devastating course of action. His parents felt they had failed, and their extended family and distant family would only think of the negative reasons for the young man's departure.

Once all these issues were discussed, the family planned a strategy whereby the young man would enrol at college/university, and live in alternative accommodation. This alleviated the notion of 'disgrace' – i.e. the young man leaving the home in conflict – and replaced it with pride that the young man was a scholar and was integrating with society independently. Had this situation involved a young woman, the discussion with the family may have led to a very different set of co-constructed goals, within the culture and belief system of the family.

Here then is a dilemma. Whilst, in theory, working towards individual preferred futures is empowering of the individual, it can be difficult to marry the preferred futures of individuals when working in groups or family groups.

In a family group the worker helps the family to collaborate, each member with the other, to set goals which will benefit the family. Within this, the individual may have a choice of goals, whilst maintaining his/her part in the collective responsibility for the family wellbeing. The choices that an individual makes in constructing goals and agendas are therefore determined by surrounding influences.

Exceptions

In seeking exceptions it is important not to negate or minimise the child's or family's story by focusing solely on the times that the problem does not happen or happens less. Timing, pacing and matching is of the essence. We have heard attempts to elicit exceptions which can become oppressive and, if not timed and paced with the client, can lead the client believing that he/she is not being heard or taken seriously. We have learned that if exceptions are not forthcoming, one should listen some more, to what the client is bringing to the discussion.

When listening to a child's story, particularly when it has gone terribly wrong or is exaggerated, loud or unconnected, it is easy to miss exceptions. The value of co-working is that a worker can listen specifically for exceptions and possibilities.

Children have told us that adults sometimes 'talk' to them in an attempt to get them to see the trouble they have caused after a crisis incident involving aggression and lack of control. In this way of working we might be interested to explore the question 'How did you stop yourself?' before reflecting on what happened. If it can be asked, it can be developed to look at times when the child has managed to stop things before, or other times when he/she has managed to avoid trouble.

Matching the language and using metaphor

Previously in group work, we found that using questions based in 'problem talk' brought forward the depth of a problem, as memories of negative experiences and helplessness covered by anger broke the surface. We actively sought more detail to assist us in solving or diagnosing the 'cause' of the aggressive behaviour, or as a means of leading the group to gaining some 'insight'. What these discussions did not encourage was a view that the anger expressed by the children could be an attempt to resolve or cope with the tensions around them, i.e. a way of managing their distress. Rather, it seemed to reinforce and highlight their inability to control themselves.

We also found that children were often skilled in offering us learned scripts to manage their angry behaviour, e.g. count to ten, punch a cushion, and walk away. They had been well schooled and rehearsed in these 'be good' responses.

What we were interested in was discovering how the use of different language can affect how we think about events, ideas, thoughts and perceptions(Sapir (1929), Wharf (1956), Vygotsky (1962, 1978). Thus, when working with children who get angry, we have found a powerful way of engaging them is to pick up and track the metaphor that is offered to us to explain or tell their story. One can choose to pick up and track the language of anger, or pick up and track the language of calm. We have learned that hints or glimmers of change are often hidden in the language used by the child or family and one has to attend to this with great care to hear possibilities and bring them to their attention.

We found in the group that the children began to use the language of possibility and change with each other. We realised that we were effectively modelling the model to group members and became aware of the potential usefulness of this in enabling families to communicate with each other about their needs.

Sometimes people ask what to do when the information given is not believed to be accurate. We have experienced this in anger-management groups. Within a strengths-and-skills focus it does not really matter if the story is exaggerated, or even untrue, because the worker is seeking out the strengths, skills and knowledge that the child has in relation to their story. The worker is in effect helping the child with an internal rehearsal for future possibilities.

Our emphasis is on listening with a different ear … or from a different perspective. The aim is to notice difference and coping within the story the child is telling and to focus on these and reflect them back. Reflecting back is a core counselling skill (Carl Rogers 1951, Dryden and Feltham 1992). What we reflect back is competence and skills and knowledge gained from coping thus far. We aim always to seek competence even if it seems that things have gone terribly wrong.

Case illustrations

Single-session groupwork

We were asked to see the residents of a unit for looked-after young people, after the death of a peer. The young people were angry and upset about the experience but chose to focus their frustration on the number of rules that governed their lives in care. This had regularly led to confrontation between the staff and the young people.

The young people used their time with us to work out their own individual plan of action which would open the possibilities to change their situation, both in their accommodation and in relation to their power over their own lives. In finding ways to manage their dissatisfaction with their living situation, we also heard them deal with much of the distress and sense of powerlessness that they brought to this situation from their own life experiences, and which had been brought to the forefront by this most recent loss.

We continued to work with metaphor because the subject matter was too painful for the group at that time. The referrers wanted us to see the young people in order to offer them individual therapy to work through the unresolved issues of separation and loss the referrers perceived were at the root of an angry grief reaction.

> However, we sensed the importance of attending to the agenda that the young people brought rather than push them into dealing with their grief. By working out action plans, they were managing an angry grief reaction in a concrete way. (Wendy Latham, 'Letting Go', Social Work Today, May 1991).

At the end of the first session we asked what each member of the group would take from the meeting. The group members told us that they were surprised and relieved at the way the session had gone. They had felt intimidated to come to the meeting and although individual appointments had been offered they decided to come as a group for mutual support. They had feared that a counselling session might be too difficult for them, but felt motivated to support each other as a group.

Single-session family work

This extract is taken from a single session to illustrate the way in which the tools of solution-focused therapy are used in a conversation with a young person and his mother. Names have been changed to preserve confidentiality.

The referral was from the Senior Clinical Medical Officer attached to the school:

> 'I should be grateful if you could see Malcolm and his mother regarding the possibility of working with them to bring about a change in Malcolm's anti-social behaviour patterns.'

The problems were described as:

– he has a short temper;
– he retaliates when taunted by peers, both verbally and physically;
– he is involved with youngsters on the estate who encourage his behaviour and this is causing conflict with the neighbours;

- he is disruptive and aggressive towards teachers;
- he has undergone repeated exclusions;
- his supports in school have failed. He is attending an exclusion unit.

The session

The session was co worked, with one worker making notes and the other interviewing.

The social worker began the session with:

Social worker to Mother: 'What differences have you noticed since you saw the school doctor?' (Pre-session change)

Mother: 'Malcolm has been permanently excluded, he's been arrested twice, because he's been hanging around with the wrong crowd.' (Problem talk)

Social worker to Malcolm: ' What else is different since you saw the doctor?'

Malcolm told us that since he had been attending the exclusion unit, he had become 'less stressed and not in trouble all the time.' (Exception)

Social worker to Mother: 'Have you noticed he's been … less stressed and that he's not in trouble all the time.' (Notice use of client's language)

Mother: 'I've been pleased with Malcolm's behaviour lately.'

Social Worker: 'What are you most pleased about?' (Enquiry, tracking differences)

Mother: 'I can trust him now.'

Social Worker: 'You can trust him? How come?' (Concretising the behavioural change)

Mother: 'He stays in the house during school hours and he doesn't react so much to other kids' teasing.'

Social worker: (nodding) ' Uh-huh! So all of this has happened since Malcolm has been excluded?' (Summarise with emphasis on 'all of this has happened')

Mother: 'The education welfare has found another school for him. It'll be a new start.'

Social worker: 'So exclusion can be a fresh beginning?' (Reframe)

Social worker to Malcolm: ' What do you need to do to improve things further, to carry on the fresh start?' (Goal setting)

With prompting, (what else, seeking small concrete changes), Malcolm told us that:

I need to ignore other children;
I need to keep my self-control;
I will gain positive reports from school;
I will help around the house;

I will help my dad.

Malcolm and his mother agreed that Malcolm should show his dad that he is making an effort, by doing what he is told.

Social worker to Malcolm: ' Who can help you to feel better about your efforts?'

Malcolm: 'Mum.'

Social worker: 'How does she do that?' (Concrete behaviours sought)

Malcolm: 'Don't know!'

Social worker to Mother: 'How would Malcolm's father know you were pleased with him? What do you see Malcolm doing which shows his dad that this is going to be OK?' (Circular question)

Mother: 'More Patience – his father just sees the bad side of Malcolm.'

Notice that Mother has reinterpreted the question so the social worker builds on Mother's idea of what needs to happen but also deflects the possibility of stuckness by asking:

Mother: 'What helps you to hold the good bits about Malcolm?' (Seeking Mother's strengths i.e. that which is useful to this situation)

Mother: 'He has a caring nature, for instance a cat got run over by a car. Steven stamped on the cat, Malcolm became upset and tearful of the incident.'

Social worker: 'So this shows how sensitive Malcolm can be?' (Reflecting and reinforcing mothers view about Malcolm)

Mother: 'Yes, Malcolm is worried about carrying his aggressive reputation with him to the new school.' (Mother's acknowledgement of Malcolm's concern about his label, and recognising new beginnings)

Social worker to Malcolm: 'What reputation would you like to take with you to the new school.'

Malcolm: 'Being honest, not stealing.' (Preferred future)

Social worker to Mother: 'What would you choose?' (Mother's preferred future)

Mother: 'He needs to become more active.' (Future Goals)

Social worker: ' What else?'

Mother: 'Go to bed early.'

Social worker: 'Uh-hmm. What else?'

Malcolm: 'Get up early to go to school,'

Social worker: 'And?'

Malcolm: 'Go swimming.'

Mother: 'Do his homework.'

Social worker: 'Anything else?'

Mother: 'Keep out of his father's way when he is angry.'

Malcolm and his mother have given us direct information about what is going on at school and also indirect information about family dynamics at home. We do not know yet if this is going to be more than one session, but we are aware that there may be other issues which are underpinning Malcolm's behaviour.

As social workers practicing family therapy we have a dilemma. We would normally track the family dynamics surrounding the referred behaviour and probably seek to punctuate the dynamics in the system at the level of the parents, based on the hypothesis we had constructed. During the session we took a break to discuss how to proceed.

We decided to continue to assist Malcolm and his mother to construct their own goals and in doing so helping them to maintain control and management of the problem that they brought to the session. On a large flip chart we had written down exceptions, goals, scaling etc. Sometimes families ask to take them away. On other occasions we type them and send it to them. We have found that people appreciate having a personalised account of the session to reflect upon and remind them about the decisions that they have made. We believe that this validates and reinforces the family's knowledge and skills.

Six weeks later the family telephoned to say that they no longer required further appointments, as the situation had improved. We liaised with staff at Malcolm's school who told us that Malcolm was attending his new school and, whilst still challenging, he had received no further exclusions.

To date, two years later, there has been no re-referral.

Conclusion

Over time we have developed ways of working which may complement the original model in its purest form. We feel that this is inevitable because we bring a variety of experiences and a wide knowledge base of other therapeutic models to our practice. We are comfortable in assuming the role of facilitator, guest teacher or mentor on the journey to solutions – whatever our clients find useful.

The benefit of co-work from our different gender and cultural perspectives is repeatedly reinforced as we are always learning from each other, our team and our service users about the delivery of an effective service.

We are presently exploring the use of language in therapy, particularly attending to the emphasis one can give to strengths and skills through the use of specific language. As a culturally mixed team we are aware of the power of language in changing people's perceptions about themselves and others and how this relates to the concept of attitudinal and behavioural change.

We are continually developing the model. The process of working within a competence frame is continually evolving; we do not get it right every time.

However, we have found our most useful assets in developing this model are our counselling skills with an emphasis on rapport building, timing, matching and pacing with individuals, families and groups. This is perhaps the most significant principle for us. Solution-focused work is easy to learn but must be used with skill.

CHAPTER FIVE

EMPOWERING STUDENTS TO EMPOWER OTHERS

BY THE ABC PEER SUPPORT SCHEME
AT ACLAND BURGHLEY SCHOOL
VAVI HILLEL AND ELIZA SMITH,
CO-ORDINATORS

Introduction

'We don't have a bullying problem in our school.' This is a common fallacy that perpetuates the suffering of many school students. In reality, bullying goes on in every school and occurs at every level of society.

Acland Burghley is not unusual, in that we have similar issues of bullying to other inner-London comprehensive schools. Our students are no more enthusiastic, committed or willing to take on responsibility than those in other schools. What makes our school unique is the way in which these qualities have been harnessed and put to use in the form of a peer-support scheme that has become an integral part of the school community.

The ABC scheme was piloted in 1993 in conjunction with Sheffield University research (Sharp & Smith, 1993). Initially developed to combat bullying through individual counselling, the scheme has evolved and created opportunities for student and teacher involvement through a range of activities.

In this chapter we have included real experiences written by students, about students empowering other students. The case studies are a testament to the skills and confidence with which the peer counsellors have been equipped as a result of effective training in solution-focused thinking. The peer counsellors have requested permission from those with whom they have worked to include their stories in the case studies. All of the names of the individuals concerned have been changed to ensure confidentiality. In this first short extract, the benefits of peer counselling are powerfully illustrated.

'Matthew': case study by Polly Robbins (aged 12)

Matthew approached me in the playground saying he was upset. I asked if he wanted to talk to me and he nodded. We found a room and, as we knew each other fairly well, we could bypass the 'getting to know you' and could start straight away. Matthew had seen me on other occasions about different subjects, all of which had been solved in one session. Matthew started off by saying that his so called 'best friend', Toby, had been very nasty to him. In Games, his last lesson, Toby hadn't been talking to him. Also, when Matthew had asked Toby if he wanted to be his partner, Toby had been rude. Throughout the last few days Matthew felt that Toby had been 'taking away' another close friend of Matthew's, Daniel. Matthew felt that if these two friends abandoned him he wouldn't have anyone to turn to as he did not have a very strong circle of friends.

I asked a number of questions, but to get the picture clear for both of us I thought a scale would be best. I offered him a 0 and then suggested that he made up his own 0 and 10. He said 0 is 'terrible', that is, Toby is being really horrible, taking all his friends away and he has no friends as a result. He said that 10 is having Toby as a really good friend and having a lot of other friends. When asked to put himself on this scale, Matthew put himself on a 6, a fairly good mark, I thought. He said he wasn't a 5 or lower, 'because I've still got you lot', meaning his wider circle of friends. He said he still had friends at least, even if they weren't that close or in his class. He would be a 7 if he had someone in his class.

We then moved onto solutions. He'd tried a lot of ideas:

– being really nice to Toby: this worked for around half a day, but Matthew felt that it was fake and unreal;

– being horrible to Toby: although Matthew felt this portrayed his feelings well, he also felt it was slightly mean and that it didn't work too well. This worked for around two hours;

– Matthew's last idea was ignoring Toby: this was still working and he had started it the day before. It was the best solution so far.

As ignoring Toby had worked well, Matthew decided to carry on with this idea. He didn't want to be too spiteful so he decided that if Toby was asking a reasonable question or something, he would answer nicely.

About two weeks later, I asked Matthew casually in the playground how things were going and he said that he had stuck with targets and that now Toby and he were just as good friends as ever. He didn't actually say so, but I guessed that he had gone up the scale to an '8' or '9'. I thought this, as he seemed a lot happier in general. He smiled and stood up straight and when I talked to him, whereas before he had looked unhappy, avoided looking at me and slouched when he walked.

I learned a lot from this case. Matthew made it easier for me as he came in and started talking straight away; he didn't need much prompting. I think that Matthew also got a lot out of the session, as developing his own ideas seemed to boost his self-esteem almost straight away. He left the session looking happier than when he had approached me in the playground and with something he could do. I'm very pleased that we had held the session and that both of us got something out of it.

Training for peer counsellors

As teachers trained in solution-focused therapy, we felt that this approach could capture the imagination of young people and could be applied in practical terms to our scheme.

Our idea was enthusiastically received by the Brief Therapy Practice, who welcomed the unique opportunity of working with teenagers. We decided to undertake eight, two-hour training sessions after school, over several weeks. After much consultation, a programme was adapted from the training designed for adults, suitably differentiated to cater for younger trainees.

Our aim was to create a training programme that was both fun and accessible to student counsellors. The intention was to explore the principles of solution-focused therapy in a practical way, linking the concepts to activities and ideas to which the pupils could immediately relate. The freshness and enthusiasm of the students made this a tremendously rewarding experience for all those involved in training.

A variety of activities was devised, including the use of prompt sheets, role-play, games, brainstorming, video case-studies and video extracts. The activities were of short length to ensure concentration and stimulation, and we actively participated in the sessions.

One of the most popular and challenging exercises involved a video extract from the cartoon programme 'The Simpsons', in which the trainees had to imagine working with Homer Simpson as a potential client. Listing

Homer's strengths proved a difficult task, as he is generally portrayed as a lazy, gluttonous, uncultured lager-lout. The trainee counsellors, however, quickly managed to identify many strengths and positive qualities in their imaginary client.

As part of the training, the counsellors were alerted to the importance of confidentiality. As well as ensuring the client's safety, it was made clear that the counsellors are required immediately to refer to us any serious cases (that is, where the client or somebody else is in danger).

In the following case study, the peer counsellors illustrate the empowering effect of withholding advice and encouraging the client to find his or her own solutions.

'Jack': case study by Katherine Sellar and Hannah Tait (aged 12)

Jack approached us in the playground and asked if we were ABC counsellors although, as we sometimes hang around with him, we got the feeling he already knew. He then asked if he could speak to us, so we arranged a time to meet.

In the session Jack said he was worried that he was a bad friend because he lost his temper with his friends. When he said this we were a little surprised, as we couldn't imagine him getting angry with anyone. He said he was not physically violent but lashed out verbally. He told us he found himself clenching his fists in his pockets and wanting to punch people. We thought it was great that he had enough self-control not to hit people and pointed this out to him. Jack thought he had few or no close friends and felt there was no one he could talk to. Jack appeared to always think the best of people even if they said horrible things to him. He forgave them, as he believed that these were just mistakes, and not the way they normally behaved.

Jack was our first client and we were nervous, but as he just marched confidently in and launched straight into what was bothering him, it made it much easier for us to talk to him.

We then moved on to scales and asked Jack what 10 would be if 10 was 'great' and 0 was 'terrible'. He said 10 would be that he controlled his anger perfectly, had as many friends as he wanted and never lashed out. We decided that we would set 0 as much worse than where Jack would probably place himself, so we said 0 was that he had no friends, and that he shouted at everyone all the time.

Jack put himself on the scale as a 7. We were quite surprised, as this was a high number and Jack still seemed to be very upset and distressed by the problem. We asked him why he was not a '6' and he told us that he still had a wider outer circle of friends and did not lash out all the time. He said he would be an 8 when he lashed out less and had more close friends. We talked to him about where he would realistically like to get up to, and he said an 8.5.

We asked Jack if he had tried anything already that had helped. He told us that when he was being bullied in a previous school he had made little clay figures of the bully and chucked them out of a high window. We found his answer interesting, as we had never heard of anyone using this method. He explained that this got rid of his anger when he got home, but not while he was actually speaking to the person.

We followed this up by asking him if he could think of any strategies he could use to calm his temper. He thought of:

- counting to ten before he lashed out;
- just walking away;
- breathing deeply;
- thrusting his hands into his pockets;
- keeping a stress ball in his pocket and squishing it whenever he felt irritated.

His favourite was the stress ball idea, as he felt that having something to squash would help him to release his anger. We also thought this idea sounded really useful and we were glad we had kept to ourselves all the advice we were aching to give!

It was really impressive that he came up with so many ideas that were helpful to him. He seemed happier now that he had thought of some possible solutions. Jack left the session smiling, having decided to try out the stress ball and tell us how it went.

We found it useful to counsel in a pair, because when one of us got stuck the other could jump in with something to say. Also, we could discuss the case together afterwards without having to worry about mentioning names.

I think the conversation between us flowed because we were all relaxed. This was probably because we had met and spoken to each other quite frequently in the playground.

When we spoke to Jack a month later, we asked him what in the session he had found most helpful. He said that by thinking of so many solutions it made him feel optimistic about controlling his anger and that he was able to look at the problem more clearly. Jack also told us that the stress ball was really useful as, although he still found he was getting angry, he now took it out on the stress ball and not the person.

Ongoing support and supervision

As co-ordinators we have undertaken a Brief Therapy management supervision course to provide supervision and support to our young counsellors. This is a vital part of the counsellors' development and welfare, as they often need to reflect upon and receive guidance with cases. They have inadvertently developed their own immediate form of supervision by counselling in pairs. This enables them to write case notes and support each other both during and after the session. Counselling in pairs also allows recently-trained counsellors to learn from those more experienced.

The language of solution-focused therapy has become second nature to the peer counsellors. Many have reported using phrases such as 'What would be different ...?' with both their friends and with other peer counsellors. They are constantly employing solution-focused theory and creating their own interpretations of the methods they have been taught.

The following description illustrates the way in which the peer counsellors seek to build their client's self-confidence. Applying their solution-focused counselling skills, they notice the difference that their conversation has upon the client and the way in which it provides him with a more positive outlook.

'Ben': case study by Emily Baron and Catherine Nieto (aged 15)

Ben is a Year 10 GCSE student. For the last three-and-a-half years he appears to have had no friends. We had both noticed Ben around the school, always on his own and, although we had not given it much thought, we'd been aware of how isolated he seemed from the rest of the year group. Initially he was referred by his Head of Year because he had come into conflict with a class-mate. This was our second meeting with Ben. During our first meeting we realised that Ben was more in need of a friend than anything else and decided to take an informal approach to Brief Therapy.

We began by chatting to Ben about the positive aspects of his life. However, Ben seemed reluctant to accept that there were any, or that there ever could be. He brushed away compliments with a negative comment and immediately changed the subject. For example, we commented that his idea of enrolling in a local cricket team for the summer seemed a good thing to do. He replied: 'It's unlikely I'll get in anyway and even if I do I probably won't have time to go because of school work.'

We tried another approach to looking at positives - the famous scale question. We asked: 'Imagine on a scale of one to ten, where 1 is being so unhappy you can't even get out of bed in the morning and come to school, and 10 is the happiest you can ever imagine yourself to be. Where would you place yourself now?' Ben replied that he was 'about a 4'. We asked him what had stopped him from being a three. He answered 'My interests out of school.' We then asked Ben to imagine being a 5 and what would be different about that. He said, 'I'd feel much happier and I would probably feel more confident.' Who would notice he was at a 5? He said his family and form teacher and maybe people at church as well.

We elaborated on these questions, and this helped Ben to leave the session on a more positive note and with some ideas.

By the fourth session we realised that a great improvement had taken place in Ben's self-confidence. Although still finding it hard to make eye contact, Ben sat facing us and chatted freely about the good things in his life. But most significant was where he now placed himself on the scale – at a 9. He was grinning when he said this. We were curious about what had happened and what had made this difference. Ben talked about the more positive outlook he had taken to life. We asked him whether anyone else had noticed the change in him. He said that his teacher had commented on how much more he had been smiling recently. 'That put me in a good mood for the rest of the day,' he added.

For the remainder of the fourth session we chatted on equal terms about his involvement with his local church, the summer holiday he had spent in France and the work experience that he proudly had organised for himself.

We felt very pleased about Ben's increase in confidence and how much more at ease he seemed with himself. We did not arrange to meet again, knowing that Ben knew where to find us if he wanted to.

Ben left the room, head held a bit higher, shoulders less hunched. He turned around and looked at us with a smile.

On reflection, we feel our method of drawing out the positive aspects of Ben's life was the most successful in building up his self-confidence. However, Ben would probably also have valued the informal style, which encouraged him to chat to us and to find his own solutions to problems. We feel the incorporation of the scale was a good starting point for helping Ben to see the good points and was effective in keeping track of the progress he was making. Furthermore, it was the scale in the fourth session that demonstrated to Ben and ourselves exactly how much we had achieved together.

The students' response to the training

The ongoing attendance of the student trainees was excellent and the levels of interest and participation were very high. Our colleagues from the Brief Therapy Practice were astounded at how enthusiastic and quick the students were to learn and adopt the methods taught.

The students felt very comfortable with the language used and related well to the structure of a solution-focused counselling session. The 'toolkit' of skills provided them with an anchor and removed the anxiety of 'saying the wrong thing' and the onus of having to give advice, common fears expressed by potential counsellors.

Scales were, perhaps unsurprisingly, the most popular 'tool' in the box and the students utilised these very creatively in their regular counselling sessions, as can be seen from their case studies.

Interestingly, the 'miracle' question posed a problem for the students. They found it unrealistic and worried that the word created false hopes for others, for example in the case of bereavement or physical disability. They felt more comfortable with the framework of an 'ideal' day and developed a revised question for the client: 'If you woke up tomorrow morning to an ideal day, where the problem had gone away, what would it be like?'

One of the most valuable lessons they have learned through the training is not to give advice, but rather to help peers to generate their own solutions and recognise their own strengths and personal resources. As Janica states in a most powerful analogy, the counsellor is 'simply the bridge to crossing the lake.' Evidently, solution-focused counselling has given them the tools to build the bridge!

In the final account included in this chapter, two peer counsellors outline many of the strategies used over several sessions to assist another student in overcoming her difficulties. The counsellors also reflect on the experience and give a vote of confidence to the approach they have adopted.

'Jess': case study by Janica Dennison and Clio Brown (aged 14)

My name is Janica. Over a year ago I went through the Brief Therapy training to be an ABC counsellor/peer supporter. When this piece of work took place I was a Year 9 student and had only recently trained.

My name is Clio Brown. I have also done the training. At the beginning I was pretty nervous and it was agreed I would work with Janica to help develop my confidence and to give her support. Janica would talk with Jess and I would observe. Afterwards, we would talk about what had happened and work out what to do next. It was a good way to think about what had worked and what we needed to change. Here is Janica's account of the sessions with Jess.

Session One

There was a knock at the door. I opened it and greeted Jess, my first client. So this was it – all my training and preparation put into practice. Was I nervous? Extremely. I'd never met Jess before. All I knew was that she was a Year 7 student having problems settling in. I soon found out there was more to the case than met the eye.

I began by introducing myself and explaining that I would respect and keep confidential whatever she told me unless she was in any danger, in which case I would have to report to one of my supervisors. I checked Jess had understood. She was nervous. I could barely see her face, as it was hidden behind her hair – her shoulders were curled and her head was bent, looking towards the floor.

I began by asking some general questions to break the ice: 'What tutor group are you in?' and 'What sorts of things are you into?' I found out that Jess was part of an acting class and enjoyed it greatly. However, she classed herself as an unconfident person. My immediate reaction was to comment, 'You came to see me and in my eyes that involves a hell of a lot of courage and confidence.' She smiled. I told Jess a bit about myself – my tutor group and what I was interested in, so in a way we were on mutual terms, knowing a bit about each other. And then the big question: 'What brought you here?' This is what I had been worrying about – the moment I would start to use my training. What if it all went wrong? Jess explained her situation. She was finding it hard to settle into secondary school. She had no friends in her tutor group and felt excluded from just about everything, especially PE, where there were nine girls and she was always left without a partner, always left alone.

By now I was full of ideas and advice to give her. However, I stopped myself because I knew that whatever I would have done in the situation wasn't what she wanted to hear. What I could do was to help her to find her own solutions.

I asked her the 'miracle' question – about how she would like things to be. I did not have time to develop this to my liking, as it was now time for both of us to return to lessons. My last words to her were to keep her head high. I also asked if she would like to meet again. She enthusiastically agreed and a session was set for the same time next week.

Throughout the session I had a prompt sheet in case I got stuck, but I didn't need to use it. Every situation is different and I had the basics and now had to develop my own style. I was pleased that Jess had wanted to meet again – it made me feel as though our session had been useful.

Session two

Jess started this session seeming much more relaxed. I asked her how the week was going and whether anything positive or good had occurred since the last time we had met. This moved onto a scale – in this case a 'feel-o-meter'.

Me: On a scale of one to ten, where would you put yourself in relation to how you are feeling in relation to the last time we met?
Jess: About eight … eight and a half.
Me: What makes this different from a seven?
(This helped Jess to reflect on her actions.)
Jess: Well, I've answered some questions in class, participated in drama activities …. Nothing major, but noticeable to myself.

It seemed to me that Jess was thinking more positively about what she wanted and how she wanted her life at school to be. By the end of the session she put her confidence on a scale at '5 and-a-half'.

I then had an idea that I thought was worth a try. It was to set a task for Jess to do. Jess later called it her 'ABC homework'. For the next time we met, I asked her to write down five positive things that were happening in her life and five positive things she wanted to achieve. This wasn't something we had been told to do – but I was learning with experience.

Session three

It so happened that the 'ABC homework' worked fantastically. One of Jess's positive points was her best friend Holly, whom she had invited along to this session. At first I felt a bit uncomfortable, wondering if her friend would be thinking, 'Is Janica doing it right?' But then, what is the right way?

Jess seemed much more relaxed and actually took her coat off and put her bag on the floor. She also had her hair tucked neatly behind her ears. School was still not going too well for Jess, as her classmates were still excluding her. However, Jess now had friends like Holly and this was really keeping her going.

We began by discussing the positive points and goals she had come up with, and Jess told me her ideas about how she was going to reach them. She decided she was going to set herself one goal per week, even if it meant improving her French homework! I checked out that this is what Jess wanted to happen and how it would be in relation to her work and confidence in class. I wondered if I was being a bit direct, but this approach seemed to agree with her. We also discussed how the situations were making her feel and what would make her feel better. Sometimes I would do this by running through her day plan – starting form the moment she woke up. I also asked 'What would be different when you move one point up the scale?' Her answers were often as simple as, 'I would have breakfast.'

Session four

Two weeks later, Jess came to see me, and it stuck in my memory as the most difficult visit. She came in crying. Not only was the bullying getting her down, but she was having family problems. One of her relatives was ill and she believed that this was partly her fault. We talked for a while, then she rated her confidence and general happiness – they were both zero. Where was I to go next?

What I did was to remind her what was good about her life and re-read her positive points. I asked her not to forget them.

After the session I decided I needed to seek advice, and a supervision session with the co-ordinators really helped. It highlighted what I had done that was helpful and it also helped me to think about leaving the case behind, along with the 'baggage' it carries. We also discussed how to approach the next session.

Session five

I saw Jess two weeks later. She had vastly improved. We recorded her scales:

Happiness: 3 and-a-half. Confidence: 6.

This was a short session. I learned that Jess was involving herself in more activities and so had less time to see me! This had been one of her aims on her positive list. She was now putting things into action – making her own goals and accomplishing them.

Session six

Six and-a-half weeks after meeting Jess, we had our final meeting. Well I wouldn't really call it that – more a 'self-assuring time'. For the last time we used the scales:

Happiness: 7. Confidence: 7 and-a-half.

I don't think Jess ever wanted to be a 10; it was unnecessary. Just knowing that only a few weeks ago she had rated her happiness as '2 out of 10', and now it was a 7, gave her self-assurance. Jess didn't stay long – she had places to go. I wouldn't describe Jess as hugely confident, but she was confident enough for her own liking. As long as she was happy with where she was, that was all that mattered.

Clio's observations

I thought that one of the most important things we did was to understand what Jess was going through from her point of view. From my own experiences as someone who has been a victim, just having someone to talk to who will listen to what you have to say can be a help; having someone who understands how isolating and painful being bullied can be, rather than just telling you what to do. Being able to discuss and unburden your anxieties and feelings makes a great difference.

In our solution-focused training, we were taught to search for positive things in people's lives, and this was done in all the counselling sessions with Jess. Although it seemed difficult at times, there were always positive things that had happened if you looked hard enough for them. For example, we helped Jess to realise that there were good things in school as well as bad, such as when she told us about doing well in her science test.

In all the sessions, Janica would refer back to the scales. These were really helpful in showing Jess her improvements and the progress she was making.

As I observed, I noticed that this seemed such a good way to focus on the direction in which Jess was heading. I think it also helped us to be clearer about the direction in which we were heading as counsellors.

From our point of view, was the case successful? Certainly. From Jess's perspective, she was able to get on with her life in her own way.

Reflections

We think Brief Therapy is an ideal structure for counselling. The positive focus allows us to empower our clients to look for their own resources and solutions. We are not there to advise people on what to do or how to go about it. We are simply their bridge to crossing the lake. But we can't cross the lake for them. This is what they must do alone; we are there to give support. Would we do it all again? We would and we have.

Final reflections

We envisage the ABC peer-support scheme in the form of a pyramid, with peer counselling at the pinnacle, supported by the strong foundation of the school community at large. The ongoing success of the scheme depends very much on its profile within the school community. It is important that the peer supporters become well known and that students feel it is safe to use the service. The peer supporters play a major role in helping to smooth the transition from primary to secondary school and take a proactive approach in raising awareness and promoting the scheme through drama workshops, assemblies, bulletins and various PSHE (pastoral guidance) activities.

ABC has received national and international media acclaim and we have been invited to disseminate our work, both in the United Kingdom and abroad. In 1999 the ABC counsellors were awarded the 'Camden Good Citizens' Award' for their contribution to the wider community. The DfEE has produced an anti-bullying resource pack, entitled 'Bullying: Don't Suffer in Silence', including a video featuring the ABC scheme as an example of excellent practice. The pack was made available to all schools in January, 2001.

The solution-focused training that was developed has reaped immeasurable benefits for the peer supporters themselves, and this is evident in their increased confidence, empathy and understanding of their peers, their families and themselves. Many have said that they have gained greater insight into the thoughts and feelings of others and consequently have become less judgmental.

Above all, the willingness to help their peers and create a more open, harmonious school environment is the latent force behind their tremendous commitment. As one counsellor so movingly commented in a recent interview, 'At the end of the day, if I can help just one person, it was all worth it.'

CHAPTER SIX

SOLUTION FOCUSED ANTI-BULLYING

BY SUE YOUNG

Introduction

Long-term bullying is often viewed as a difficult and intractable problem. As a result the resolution of bullying is generally expected to be difficult and long-term. Parents requesting help do not usually expect a totally successful outcome, and certainly not quickly – they are more likely to be hoping merely for some improvement in a desperate situation.

It was largely because of the success of this project's work, as compared to expected outcomes, that an evaluation was undertaken and the results published (Young, 1998). Our own expectations are high and this is inevitably conveyed to parents or schools asking us for help. The project expects to bring the large majority of referrals – over 90% – to a successful conclusion, within a month, i.e. the pupil is happy in school and both pupil and parent are satisfied the bullying has stopped.

For about five years, Kingston upon Hull LEA has had an anti-bullying co-ordinator working to help schools in a variety of ways, both preventative and reactive. The co-ordinator also provides a point of referral within the authority for cases concerning bullying that remain unresolved despite internal school anti-bullying procedures and policies. Referrals are almost invariably on behalf of the perceived 'victims' of bullying, rather than the 'bullies'. (These labels give the impression that we are talking about distinct and distinctive types of children, which is misleading and implicitly judgmental. But for the sake of clarity and to avoid cumbersome circumlocutions, I use these terms, albeit with misgivings.)

Referral routes

Parents frequently refer to the service through the telephone help-line. The number is in the local telephone directory and listed in the usual information booklets. In the first instance, they are given advice on how to approach the school and how to work with the school towards a successful outcome. Inevitably, a proportion of parents may have already tried to get help within school but the child is still having difficulties. In this situation it is a case of advising on the next move, which may involve the anti-bullying co-ordinator becoming directly involved in the school, advising or implementing strategies to resolve the difficulties.

Schools themselves also refer cases, usually when they have had support from the project in the past. On a few occasions, a solicitor's letter has prompted a request. School staff and parents often have conflicting perceptions of the situation and the anti-bullying co-ordinator can act as a relatively independent third party. Parents are appreciative of the involvement of someone outside the school, as they can feel intimidated by interviews with a head teacher, especially when there is open disagreement. Occasionally, heads are also glad, because an accusation that bullying is not being properly dealt with can potentially seriously damage a school's reputation in the local community. Schools have a duty of care for all their pupils and since the 1998 Education Framework Act, head teachers have legal duties with regard to preventing all forms of bullying.

Sometimes, an LEA officer may ask for involvement as a result of a parent's complaint. For example, a parent may request a change of school as a result of a child being bullied. A senior officer may also refer when a local councillor has had a complaint from a constituent.

Other local agencies, statutory and voluntary, request help for their clients, e.g. the Education Welfare Service and a local children's rights group.

Pupils can refer themselves through the anti-bullying telephone help-line, although this seldom happens in practice. We would encourage pupils to report bullying within their own school in the first instance, simply because that is how most bullying problems are dealt with and resolved. Pupils experiencing problems may be encouraged to tell either a member of the school staff or a parent/carer.

Rationale for using SFBT

The project uses two main approaches for individual referrals:
solution-focused support groups;
solution-focused intervention with 'victims' alone.

Initially, the 'No Blame Approach' to bullying (Maines and Robinson, 1993) was used, as suggested in the DFE guide 'Don't Suffer in Silence: an anti-bullying pack for schools' (1993). Differences developed in practice fairly quickly as a result of the influence of Solution-Focused Brief Therapy. At the time there was very little available about applying brief therapy in schools, with the notable exception of Molnar and Lindquist (1989) and Rhodes and Ajmal (1995), but neither included examples of anti-bullying. When I had my first formal training in SFBT with Ron Warner, a Canadian brief therapist, it confirmed the direction I was taking with the support group approach.

Every referral to the anti-bullying project is treated as urgent. The name of the pupil, school, parent, home address and telephone number (if there is one) is all that is needed. The most common type of referral is from the parent, phoning for support. Typically, they have already talked to the appropriate teacher and head of the school but they believe their child is still being bullied. Parents in this situation are pleased if someone will intervene on their behalf.

First of all, the school needs to be contacted to gain acceptance of our involvement. I think it is fair to say acceptance rather than enthusiasm is the normal response. Head teachers can be very wary when any allegation of bullying is being made. Usually, a home visit to the parent is arranged, followed immediately by a visit to the school. This would normally take place on the day following the phone call. Occasionally, the child is being kept off school and is at home with the parent. Treating referrals in this way sends out a clear message to parents and schools – that the matter is taken seriously, given urgent attention and, importantly, that action is being taken. Parents have reported later that the way the referral was dealt with from the start gave them confidence and optimism that things were going to be sorted out. I believe it lessens the time spent on any referral overall, and therefore is cost effective in terms of time.

Parents may be at the end of their patience because they believe, whether justifiably or not, that the school is not taking the problem seriously. Frustrated and unsure what to do for the best, they are often considering transferring the child to another school. The parents need primarily to be heard and reassured. They will also be given a summary explanation of how a support group might help. Initially, they may be seeking punishment for the 'bullies' because punishment is the only thing they know of that might work, even though it may have been tried in the past and failed. However, they are usually ready to accept an alternative strategy and try something different. What they want is effectiveness rather than retribution. It is also reassuring for them to know they will be kept informed throughout, something that schools may neglect.

The support-group approach

1. Interview the 'victim'

I try to begin with non-problem talk. I may start with a compliment about something they are wearing, or what they were doing when they were brought from their class. The idea is to avoid giving the impression that I only see them in terms of a problem. Then I ask questions that I know they will have no difficulty answering, such as 'What is your last name?', 'How old are you?, 'What is your class teacher's name?', etc. A couple of minutes spent in this kind of preamble can pay dividends for the rest of the session.

To introduce the main part of the session, I usually say something like, 'I have just been to see your mum – she's worried about you, isn't she?' It is well known that children feeling bullied often find it difficult to tell someone. It is easier for them to admit that someone else is worried. Then I might say, 'Do you think she is right to be worried?' Invariably, the answer is a nod or a quiet 'yes'.

Just three essential questions need to be asked. It may be necessary to reassure children that any pupils they name are not going to get into trouble, otherwise they may be reluctant to answer.

Who do they find it difficult to deal with or is making them feel unhappy?

In primary school, usually between two and five names are mentioned. There is no need to question how or why the child finds any one of these pupils difficult.

Who else is around when this is happening?

An essential ingredient in school bullying (unlike some other types of bullying, e.g. workplace bullying) seems to be the presence of bystanders. That fact alone suggests that it is important to include them as part of the support group. Usually two or three names are mentioned.

Who are the child's friends, or who would the child like to have as friends?

If bullying has been going on for an extended time, the child may have no friends left. It is not unusual for a child to give a name that has already been mentioned as a bystander or even a bully. Bully-victim relationships can be the result of friendship gone awry.

The support group is selected from these names. If possible, I would include all the pupils who are causing the child difficulties, plus a couple of bystanders and any friends or potential friends. I would be aiming at a group of five to seven pupils. I tell the child that I am going to ask these pupils to help me by making him/her happier at school. I end with the reassurance that things will improve, and I want the child to tell me the following week what they have noticed improving.

2. Convene the support group and establish the aim

The selected pupils are brought to meet me, often looking a little sheepish or nervous on entering the room. But I am smiling and welcoming – 'Can you sit here? ... Have you enough room there ?.... Can I see all your faces? ... Thank you for coming, I'm pleased to meet you all.'

I explain to the group that my job is to help children if they are not happy in school. Today, I am hoping that they will help me to help 'X'. The reason they have been chosen is because I know they can all help. I have found this the easiest and most accurate way of explaining the selection and articulating the aim without being at all judgmental. I would not say that X is being bullied in school, because this would probably make several members of the group defensive or resentful.

3. Raise empathy

In order to raise empathy with the target child, I ask if any of the group have ever been unhappy in school. There follows a very short discussion of occasions when they might have been unhappy. They always relate incidents of bullying – their knowledge of the situation is implicit. I may say something like, 'It's not nice being unhappy in school is it? That's why I am asking you to help me make X happier.'

4. Ask for suggestions

I ask them if they can suggest anything they could do to help make him/her happier? Some groups are full of ideas, some are not so forthcoming at first, but every suggestion is welcomed and complimented, unless it is clearly unacceptable. After the first couple of suggestions have been made, and reinforced as appropriate, the rest of the group can usually think of their own. Sometimes, there may be one or two at the end who cannot think of something different from suggestions that have gone before, so they may choose to help another member of the group. The essential point is that they make the suggestions and choose to do it, rather than my making suggestions while they pay lip service to agreement. I also check that they think they can do it – 'That's a good idea, would that be difficult for you to do?' They invariably say it would not be difficult, and this gives me the opportunity to compliment them on their kindness. I never give jobs; I never make them promise to do anything; I never ask them to be friends with the target pupil. I usually write down their names with the suggestions as we go along, but only as a means of valuing and validating.

5. Pass over responsibility and arrange to review

I end by thanking them for all their good ideas, and reassure the group: 'Your suggestions make a very good plan and I am sure you will be successful in making X happier in school over the next week.' I arrange to review how they are getting on a week later. I do not want to leave it too long before checking the child is happier, but on the other hand I want to allow a bit of time for things to settle.

6. Review a week later

First I meet with the 'victim'. This can be a very short meeting since everything is usually going fine and the pupil is happy in school. I congratulate the pupil – after all, they too have had to make changes and it is important for them that I assume they have a positive and instrumental role in the solution, e.g. I may ask, 'How did you manage that?' I conclude by asking if everything is going to be fine now or would it be helpful if I called again.

Next, I meet with the group. Again, this is usually not lengthy, but I give enough time so that each member of the group has a chance to tell me what they have done and I can compliment them individually as well as together as a group. I never refer back to the suggestions they made to check whether or not they have done them – that is not important. Sometimes one or two who were previously named as bullies are quiet during this session and I don't insist on contributions. It is as if they are standing back and just weighing up the situation. By the following week they usually have come on board and are eager to tell me about their contribution. Even if they don't, the important outcome is that they have not bothered the child any further and they can be fully included in the compliments for this reason alone.

It is not unusual for the group to report that there has been some bullying from someone not in the group. In these cases, the victim has usually not mentioned it. They usually take the initiative and sort out anything minor like this themselves. They may simply tell someone, 'We're not doing that any more.'

The future

I congratulate them as a group for a job well done and ask if they would like to continue for another week. They always say yes, and are often very enthusiastic – after all, they have not been persuaded to do anything too onerous, or that they didn't choose to do. When I make arrangements to review again, I do not ask them to watch out and report back any problems – I don't want them to be searching for difficulties and I do not want them to think that I like to hear about problems. Most often, all going well, I review the situation twice – in a minority of cases it may need continuing reinforcement for up to five reviews. It is very rare for it to go beyond this. After each review I phone the parents to gather their views and let them know how things are going.

When school staff are unaware of any further difficulties, the target pupil says he/she is happy in school, the group is happy with how things are and the parent is happy that the bullying has stopped, the referral is closed.

Comments/reflections

The way of working described above is not 'pure' SFBT. It is more an example of the application of some SFBT principles to another strategy, to create something new and even more effective. One of the roles of the anti-bullying co-ordinator is to help disseminate good practice in schools. I usually insist that a member of school staff observes the intervention, so that they know exactly what has been said and done and help to build a trusting relationship between the project and the school. The main advantage is that once they have seen it demonstrated, several teachers and teaching assistants have been encouraged to use the strategy very successfully for other pupils.

SFBT features integrated into this approach include:

The solution is independent of the problem

This apparent anomaly is clearly demonstrated in practice. All the details of what has happened, when and for what reason, are left behind. Not only is it not necessary, but when you apply this approach in practice it becomes clear that it is actually a hindrance to be raking over all the details. Although opportunity is given to pupils to say whatever they feel they need to say, generally they are happy, and maybe even relieved, to leave the past and associated bad feelings behind.

The skeleton key

It is a fact that one strategy, used to address a whole range of situations where bullying may have been taking place, is not a limitation but a strength of the approach. Steve de Shazer used the term 'skeleton key' for strategies that unlock a whole range of problems, even though there are potentially limitless differences between individual referrals.

It's fast!

SFBT is often described as a miracle or magic solution. Speed of change is one factor in this. Using the support group approach, we have found that in over 80% of referrals the problem is solved immediately. The vast majority of cases are solved within a month. This is a staggering success rate compared with traditional expectations for bringing about behaviour change in schools, traditionally thought to be slow and painstaking.

Reliance on the qualities and strengths of the participants

Observers often assume that I will be offering advice during the session, and are surprised that it doesn't happen. The precise opposite is the case – I am asking the pupils what is the best course of action. Moreover, I am validating their ideas and trusting that they will be right. They are given full responsibility on the assumption that they know the situation best, and so are in the best position to respond effectively. The power of finding their strengths and competencies and complimenting them is utilised whenever possible. When a pupils make suggestions, their ideas are immediately validated by warm appreciation. In this way the solution is self-reinforcing rather than imposed and therefore more likely to continue.

Longer term results

Although, unfortunately, I cannot say that I have never had someone re-referred for bullying, it remains relatively rare. I have also had the advantage of looking at the records of a school that decided to continue implementing this approach via a member of their own staff. The impressive records she kept showed that in approximately one year of over 50 children being supported by groups, only two were re-referrals.

On the other hand, this needs to be compared with all the referrals that come to me. In every case, other methods have been tried and have obviously not had long-term results. The most common strategy used in schools is punishment, e.g. the bullies are reprimanded, kept in for several break-times or parents informed. This may have been tried a few times. Now, clearly these strategies sometimes work. However, when the strategies already being used no longer work, the sympathy afforded the victim erodes and blame tends to shift to the victim. It is generally accepted that about 20% of bullied pupils are 'provocative' (DFE, 1993). This rather unfortunate perspective can only occur when a judgmental stand is being taken in the first place.

Non-judgmental

The title of the original 'no-blame approach', which was our starting point, has caused controversy. I soon learned not to use this title because it can give the impression that bullying is being condoned. That the support group approach is not punitive of bullies has occasionally been criticised by commentators, parents and teachers. However, many parents of long-term 'victims' of bullying are very grateful for this strategy that has enabled their child to regain happiness in school.

Case Study

Gary's mother telephoned the LEA offices to ask what could be done about her child being bullied at school. She was obviously distressed on the phone as she spoke. Although reluctant, the head teacher agreed to outside agency involvement. I rang the mother the same day and arranged to meet both she and Gary the following afternoon. I also arranged to speak to the head teacher.

Gary was in Year 6 at primary school. His mum explained that he had started school with speech difficulties, and although he had been making progress, he was still behind for his age in reading. He was also physically small and had unexplained rashes on his hands. He was wetting the bed at night. Mum was anxious to explain that she did not have the money to buy Gary expensive fashionable clothes, especially sports shoes, but she always made sure that he was clean and tidy for school. Both mum and Gary became distressed. Gary was particularly distraught when I was told about the bedwetting. Apparently mum had tried to reason with the mother of one of the 'bullies' and had mentioned it. As a result the boys at school had found out and taunted him about it. The bullying had become worse and had started to happen outside school time in the street. That is when she phoned the police who advised her to phone the LEA.

I outlined the support-group approach and said that this could be appropriate – it would not cause any resentment which might happen if the bullies were given a punishment. Gary was quite adamant that he did not want to return to that school. I put the point that changing school would not stop the bullying around the home. I suggested I check out how things were at school and return later.

When I visited the school I talked to the head teacher and the Special Needs Co-ordinator (Senco). They said that the family had given the school problems. The younger sister was very disruptive in class and the father was aggressive, having to be escorted off the premises on one occasion. They were aware that Gary had been the subject of some taunting but were also aware that he was 'no angel' himself. They did try to deal with incidents as they happened.

I suggested the support group approach would be an appropriate way forward, since no-one would suffer possibly unfair punishment. The school would be seen to be taking action that was included in advice published by the

DfEE. The children involved would enjoy doing it and it was, after all, the most effective approach that we know of.

The children were called out of class and seen by myself with the Senco. The group were aware that Gary was not happy in school, but we did not pursue any reasons why this might be so. A couple of the group said that they had been unhappy in school when they had been called names in the past. When I asked if they had any suggestions for how to make him happier they were quite ready to come up with their own ideas. They concentrated on playtime and lunchtime. One suggested he would sit with Gary in the dining hall. Another said he would watch for Gary at playtime to make sure he was not alone. Another girl said she would talk to him. After each suggestion I reassured the pupils that what they said was a good idea and praised them individually in various ways, e.g. 'That's a good idea! How did you manage to think of that? Have you done kind things like that for other people before?' When I had received suggestions from all of the group I thanked them, wished them luck and arranged to see them in a week's time to see how they were getting on.

It was difficult to persuade Gary to return to school. In the end, it was arranged that his mum would take him to school and only leave him when the whistle had gone in the yard. She would pick him up at lunchtime too. I said I would visit him at school in two days time. I checked with mum the following day that Gary had indeed returned to school. Mum sounded very worried on the phone about what he might be suffering at school, and what he would say at lunchtime. Mum warned me that if Gary had been bullied that morning she did not feel able to insist on him going back in the afternoon.

Two days later I saw him briefly in school. When he came in the room to see me he smiled and said tearfully, 'I never knew I had so many friends'. When I went back a week later, he said things were 'even better' because 'they weren't so fussy any more – it was just normal.'

I saw the group without Gary and invited them to tell me if they had managed to help, and if so, how. They told me, for example, how they had deliberately included him in games in the yard. After each report of how they had helped, I complimented them on how they had done it, e.g. the sensitive and careful way they had shown support. I asked them if they thought he was happier and how they knew that. They said because he was smiling and talking more and laughing. They were congratulated on their wonderful plan and asked if they would continue for another week. They were all very keen to continue.

I phoned mum to ask how she felt things were going and she reported that Gary was a different lad, enjoying school again. She said Gary had even insisted that he be allowed to stay at school for lunch.

The following week everything was settled and fine. I took a photograph of the group and Gary together – as I say I like to have photographs of the best groups. I also arranged for the Senco to make sure they all received an appropriate school reward for their achievement. About a year later I was asked to help with another case in the same school. The Senco watched again and now regularly uses this approach herself, with 100% success so far.

The support group approach to bullying is solution-focused, readily accessible to teachers, enjoyed by the pupils and can be used tomorrow if necessary with the highest degree of confidence. No other strategy has been demonstrated to be so successful in responding to incidents of bullying.

CHAPTER SEVEN

PROGRESS AGAINST ALL ODDS

BY BRYONY HOWE

Introduction

I trained as an educational psychologist (EP) in the late 1970's. Initially, I worked in an outer London borough for many years and then, in the 1980's, I moved to an inner London borough. During this time, I have always worked with schools for children with severe learning disabilities (SLD). This chapter looks at some of my work in this area.

In the beginning

In those far-off days, the emphasis was on the psychometric assessment of individual children, wherever they went to school. Even then, such assessments seemed to be less than helpful and often irrelevant, especially when applied to children with severe learning difficulties. However, as time went on, this impression increased and became reflected by changes within the profession.

The focus of EP work began to change, and EPs turned their attention to helping teachers apply learning theory and behaviour-modification techniques to children's learning and behaviour. There was also a move away from direct support for individual children to supporting those working with children in schools – helping them to refine the school and classroom systems in which they worked and to identify and follow practices that had been shown to be effective.

These changes were helpful. However, the teachers I was working with in the local SLD school were often highly qualified and increasingly experienced in assessing children's needs and using behaviour-modification techniques. I was not an expert on teaching children with severe learning disabilities and so I began to question more and more the ways in which I could be most helpful in this area.

Toward a solution-focused approach

One area of work, in which I found I did have something distinctive to offer, was in improving links between home and school. Poor communication sometimes led to inconsistent expectations, particularly when children had severe learning disabilities. Sometimes it led to conflict. However, I found that by listening carefully to both teachers and parents, it was usually possible to identify common goals and resolve conflict.

It was around this time that a couple of EPs in our service became interested in the solution-focused approach, and set up a series of training sessions. The ideas behind solution-focused thinking seemed to converge with my reflections on what I had found that worked in my role as an EP.

The approach emphasised listening but emphasised listening for solutions and strengths. This new focus helped to prevent the listener being overwhelmed by the problem. It helped to move expectations away from the EP as the expert, to the EP as facilitator. Even more positively, the approach seemed to be empowering to those presenting the problem, since they were also the ones who were indicating solutions which had worked. It was these positive features, together with a belief that there must be more I could offer – if I did something different – that really got me going.

Getting going

By chance, I was asked to see a mother with apparently overwhelming and intractable problems in her life. I found it difficult to know where to start. I asked her what she wanted from the session. She didn't know. Partly in desperation, remembering a question from my training, I asked her:

'If you could change one thing, what would it be?'

She replied that it would be her relationship with her daughter, something she had not mentioned so far in the conversation. I remember feeling quite taken aback as this had not featured in her long list of difficulties. It proved to be the turning point. Having identified her own starting point, she identified ways in which she could, practically, rebuild her relationship with her daughter, ways which had worked before.

This interview had a powerful effect on me. I felt that by allowing the mother to set the goals and making no judgements about how these should be achieved, this intervention had been successful. It had been empowering both to me and to this mother. It had freed me up to use the available time in a more creative and supportive way, helping this mother to look for solutions; and it had helped the mother to address what she saw as the central issue.

Support to carry on

Following that interview, I began to use solution-focused therapy more and more, particularly when faced with behaviour problems, and especially in the SLD setting. In this I was supported by my colleagues. A group of us regularly met in a coffee bar after at the end of the day to discuss our work – work we had carried out, both successfully and less successfully, and SF work we were planning to carry out.

I found increasingly that solution-focused therapy was becoming an indispensable tool to be used along with other skills and knowledge that I already had.

Finding solutions: shifting the emphasis from problems to solutions

Traditionally, faced with challenging behaviour, the most common starting point in relation to children with severe learning disabilities has been for the EP to consider the problem behaviour in considerable detail. EPs look for triggers to such behaviour and look for 'reinforcers' which maintain that behaviour. Often this is helpful, particularly where the behaviour has suddenly changed or consists of isolated incidents.

However, when the problem is long-standing and appears to those involved to be almost continuous, concentrating on the problem behaviour can have an adverse effect, making those involved feel even more trapped and helpless. This is especially the case when a range of strategies has already been tried, apparently without success. A detailed description of these failures, whilst revealing useful information for the EP, may make the teacher or parent feel even more hopeless. In the solution-focused approach, a greater proportion of time is given to the more positive activity of finding solutions.

Using exceptions and looking for strategies that work

The notion that there are always times when either the behaviour is absent, that it is less severe or it bothers people less, is extremely empowering, both to those I work with and to myself. This is particularly the case with behaviour difficulties. If the problem involved is behaviour, my aim is to extract exceptions. Next, to tease out, through careful questioning, why these exceptions may have occurred. Then to examine in detail what was different, in order to reveal possible solutions.

This is not to say that one can, or should, avoid listening to the difficulties. Expressing their views and feelings about the impact of the difficulties is part of the process for the problem owner. However, the listener is less likely to be overwhelmed if he or she is listening for exceptions.

At times, it is true, one has to listen long and hard. At a meeting in a primary school I listened for about 15 minutes to a description of a child's extremely difficult behaviour presented by both the head teacher and parents, before I was able to identify a possible exception. This occurred when the head teacher described how the child's behaviour had now reached the point where the school had been forced to assign him his own helper. This comment implied that his behaviour had not been as difficult before, and this indeed turned out to be the case. From there we were able to consider what had been different at these times.

Using solution-focused thinking to reveal and address underlying systemic issues

Many problems cannot be resolved immediately. Sometimes there are underlying issues that need to be addressed. As time has gone on, I have experimented with using solution-focused therapy as a way of challenging beliefs and addressing systemic issues which need to be tackled. The following example provides an illustration.

Mark was a boy of 10 who had been diagnosed autistic and who had, in addition, severe learning difficulties. He was unable to communicate verbally. Mark was discussed with one of his teachers because of concern about his lack of motivation, which had decreased on a scale of 1 to 10 from 5 to 1. Through solution-focused questioning, it became clear that there were times when Mark's motivation was greater, and in fact he had quite a range of interests, albeit more typical of a much younger child. None of these was group activities. Perhaps unsurprisingly, Mark positively disliked and avoided group activities. Yet this teacher was time-tabled to teach Mark in groups for the first half of the week.

By focusing on exceptions, Mark's teacher was able to understand what might have contributed to his lack of motivation and felt able to address the problem. She redefined her goals for Mark, so that they were more realistic and achievable. Instead of joining in with group activities, Mark's target behaviour was to sit near to the group and join in with just one activity.

The significance of his having two teachers was brought home to me when the second teacher joined our meeting. She rated Mark's motivation as 5. Why the difference? It emerged that the second teacher taught Mark during the second half of the week when Mark was time-tabled to be involved in individual activities.

Following on from our discussion, the two teachers decided to look at the timetable together in order better to mix group and individual work through the week and between themselves; and to increase his motivation by building on his interests. However, during our discussion it also emerged that many of the resources that Mark might find interesting were held in cupboards in other teachers' rooms. All teachers in the school had their own set of resources which was perceived as belonging to them rather than to the school. This issue was later addressed with the head teacher.

Using solution-focused thinking in a school for children with severe learning disabilities: a case study

I was asked to meet with Joe's teacher to discuss his problem behaviour. Joe was 8 and had a severe learning disability.

This example illustrates how I used solution-focused thinking to help Joe's teachers and parents move forward in what appeared to be a very stuck situation.

Joe's teacher began by discussing the significant progress Joe had made, but as she focused on the many problems, she quickly lost sight of this progress. The situation seemed overwhelmingly hopeless. The challenging behaviour – throwing, hitting and hurting adults and children – continued. However, while we were talking, I commented on my observations of Joe in the classroom. I remarked that Joe had been quiet and occupied during this time, for more than 20 minutes. She agreed and commented, ' It feels like he's difficult all the time but I know he's not. Sometimes he can be as good as gold.'

In this way, Joe's teacher took up and developed my comment on Joe's behaviour, turning it into an exception. If she had not related to what I had said, I would have left it. The power of an observation depends on the meaning it has for the listener.

This proved to be a turning point. On reflection, she acknowledged that previously she had managed Joe well but his mother was very critical about her methods and she now felt unable to use these effective strategies. As a result, she felt helpless and de-skilled.

Hoping to build on the positive aspects of this situation – Joe's teacher's effective strategies and the fact that Joe's behaviour could be very good – I suggested that she should keep a tally of the times when Joe was taken out of class for throwing heavy objects or hurting adults and children. This proved to be unhelpful. By the time I returned, the list of unacceptable behaviours had lengthened and had once more become overwhelming.

In retrospect, it might have been more helpful to have asked her to note the times when things were going well, and to think about what was different about those times. In practice, I had followed the more traditional line of enquiry looking for precursors and reinforcers. This had not been helpful.

Meeting with Joe's mother

In the meantime, Joe's teacher asked me to see his mother, to persuade her to agree to the school's management plan. I agreed to see Joe's mother but not in the first instance to persuade her to agree to the plan; rather, I would try to understand her objections to his teacher's management and find out what effective strategies she was using at home. I was interested in finding out whether any of these could be used in school. I made two assumptions:

that Joe's mother had good reasons for objecting to some of the school's strategies;

that she had found strategies that worked at home.

In the past, I would have begun by asking Joe's mother about her objections at the outset, but on reflection I felt this was likely to become not only counterproductive, but would convey the impression that she herself had no effective strategies – something that seemed most unlikely. I wanted to start in a positive way by asking her what she did that she had found helpful.

Tracking down what works

Initially, it seemed she had found no answers. She described how at home Joe was 'hyperactive and out of control' and how she wanted help in managing his behaviour. At home, he would demand attention and an adult with him all the time. If this did not happen, he would turn beds upside down and generally trash everything he came across. If restrained, he would hit back, kicking and throwing objects at anyone who came near.

However, I persisted, working on the assumption that Joe's mother was managing somehow, at least at times. I asked her, 'How?'

Sometimes, it seemed, she left him alone in his bedroom and recently, he had started to look at a catalogue for a few minutes. I commented on this sign of progress. I asked whether anybody else was able to manage Joe better but this seemed to lead nowhere. It did, however, reveal that a large number of older children and adults lived in the house. It seemed, also, that despite Joe's mother's statement that nothing was working, she was able to give advice about what made things worse. These things were getting angry, shouting and becoming physical.

If Joe's mother knew what made things worse, she must know what strategies were helpful. I returned to my original question, phrased in a slightly different way:

EP: What does work with Joe?

Mum: Talking to him in a calm manner, finding anything he's interested in, like having drinks or sandwiches made. In fact, he's best with his sister.

It seemed Joe's sister might have found a way forward. We looked in some detail at what Joe's sister did with him and how this was different to what other people did. Following on from this now much more positive description of Joe, his mother reflected that his behaviour had in fact improved significantly over the last year, and that she had found a number of strategies that seemed to work.

EP: How have you managed this?

Mum: I let him go to his room when he gets home from school, and let him do what he wants. I just watch him from the doorway. At first he's very active but then he might sit down for a little while. I bring him something to eat and drink and after that his behaviour's a lot more settled. This is the improved Joe.

E P: What have you done to make the new improved Joe?

Mum: I'm more relaxed. I don't shout as much. I talk to him more and I insist on eye contact. I've started taking him to the shops. I'm not as terrified of him as I was.

EP: What's changed for you, as a result?

She spoke of the positive effect this had had on her relationship with Joe and then, quite spontaneously, talked about her relationship with Joe in early childhood; about how close they had been and about how things had gradually deteriorated. Joe had been in and out of hospital until the age of about two-and-a-half. One night, she recalled, she had been unable to be with him and on this night he had almost died. After that, he had seemed different, very angry and difficult to manage.

I was surprised that Joe's mother spoke so spontaneously about these events which were clearly distressing for her. I would not have felt comfortable investigating her early relationship with Joe in this detail at this point. In my experience, when parents of older children are asked about their children's early childhood at the outset, they often become angry as they cannot see the relevance of the questions. Joe's mother had been receiving therapeutic support and perhaps it was this that made the difference. However, she must have judged for herself that it was important for me to have this information; she told me as much as she felt I needed to know. This included the fact that there had been a time when her relationship with her son had been more positive. Once she had identified that, it gave her the determination and hope that things could change.

Building on this, I continued:

E P: Who else has noticed the difference between you and Joe now?

Mum: His dad and his carer. They've noticed that Joe wants to be with me more and do more things with me. And the carer's noticed that I am sharing Joe's care more with her.

Building bridges between home and school

I felt I now understood why Joe's mother objected to his teacher's use of shouting as a technique. At home, she had found it counterproductive. However, it was important for Joe that he was treated the same way, as far as possible, both at home and at school; and it was important for his teacher that she had his parents' support for what she was doing.

I asked Joe's mother whether we could discuss her views about his teacher's management of his behaviour.

Some of the issues had been resolved, she felt, but she still felt strongly about Joe's teacher's use of shouting as a technique. (So, incidentally, did Joe's head teacher). She had no complaints about previous teachers, who had managed Joe as his sister did, quietly and calmly. Moreover, she actually felt strongly about Joe's teachers setting limits at all.

Using solution-focused therapy to challenge beliefs

It was clear from what Joe's mother had said that her views about limit-setting were based on her experience as a child. She saw limits as punitive. She was terrified of setting limits in case Joe became more aggressive and in case she lost the relationship she had begun to build again with him.

To challenge this belief, that she herself did not usually set limits (something I did not believe) and that when she did, Joe reacted in the way she feared, I explored times when she had set limits to keep Joe safe, e.g. on roads. Then I asked about Joe's response. She admitted that when he ran towards a road and she chased after him, he usually found it very amusing.

Reflecting back progress and strengths and finding more ways forward

At the end of an interview, I like to reflect back the strengths of those parents and teachers with whom I have been meeting, as well as the solutions that they have identified. At the end of this interview, I was able to comment on the progress Joe had made and the amount his mother had achieved – both in finding ways to manage Joe and in improving their relationship.

We left it that she would observe more closely how Joe's sister managed his behaviour, whether she set limits and how he reacted. Did he appear angry or did he find it comforting and containing? We agreed to meet at the beginning of the next term, after the Christmas break, to talk about how things were going.

Bringing Joe's teacher and parents together through a written report

Following this meeting, I wondered how I could bring teacher and parent closer together; if not by agreeing to use exactly the same approaches to deal with Joe, then at least to support each other's methods. I felt I might be able to do this by focusing on what worked, since both Joe's teacher and his mother had identified effective strategies.

Following a piece of work like this, the EP traditionally sends a report to teacher and parent, including a detailed description of the problem behaviour and the implications for teaching and learning. The EP might make recommendations about management based on observation of the child and discussions with teacher and parent.

I decided to change the format and focus of the report. The report was set out on one side of A4 in four sections, with more detailed EP observations on the reverse (see Appendix 1).

I outlined the problem behaviour, very briefly, in one section, emphasising that a feature of Joe's behaviour was that it seemed so overwhelming that at times both teacher and parent were unable to remember the progress Joe had made. I then made a much longer list of Joe's strengths and areas of progress. In another section, I detailed the strategies that seemed to work, based on my discussions with mother and teacher. In the third section, I summarised the strategies that worked at home and at school. In the fourth, I listed the tasks that could still be carried out:

– looking for strategies that work at home and at school;
– agreeing a common behaviour programme.

The thrust of the report was the areas of progress and strategies that worked. I sent a copy of the report to Joe's mother, teacher and head teacher and then waited.

Follow up

Joe's mother requested a meeting with myself and Joe's teacher a few weeks later, at the beginning of the next term. Joe's mother brought her partner, who had never before been to the school.

The holidays had gone well. The family had thought carefully about presents for Joe which he would want to play with, and for much of the time he had occupied himself well. Lately, he had begun to tear out pictures and stick them to his walls and windows. To me, this seemed a sign of progress. I checked it out with Joe's parents who agreed. There was a feeling that the family members were working together to find solutions that might work.

Joe's teacher joined us. One of the most important developments was that Joe's teacher and mother now agreed with the behaviour programme and limits it set. Joe's teacher agreed to limit her use of a loud voice to a 'No, Joe!' in dangerous situations.

It seemed that Joe's teacher's use of a loud voice no longer presented the same problem to Joe's mother.

However, I was concerned at the lack of any explicit reference to praise and rewards in the behaviour programme, particularly as an important part of it was the emphasis on listing the activities Joe found rewarding. Joe's teacher had felt these did not need to be stated but agreed to put them in. This allowed her and Joe's parents to list those activities they had noticed that Joe enjoyed and, by doing so, reflect on the positives together.

Following this meeting, I again wrote a brief summary for all those present, highlighting the strategies that had worked and things that Joe found rewarding. His mother had commented that she had liked the previous report. Unfortunately, I omitted to find out more details about what she had particularly appreciated.

I am sure this will not be the end of the matter. Joe's teacher still finds it difficult at times to focus on the progress he has made and can return to recounting his latest exploits. However, her confidence about being able to manage his behaviour has returned. Similarly, there are bound to be lows as well as highs for Joe's mother. As Joe begins to respond to his mother, though, so she will feel more in control and her relationship with him will grow.

Final thoughts

I find myself using solution-focused techniques more and more, particularly when faced with challenging behaviour. In the SLD school, where many pupils are unable to communicate except through their behaviour, it has for many years seemed appropriate for teachers, in particular, to look more closely at what those pupils are doing. However, the traditional emphasis on looking at the problem in more detail can sometimes lead to an increasing sense of powerlessness and despair. By contrast, focusing on those times when the problem behaviour does not exist or is lessened has almost always resulted in a renewed sense of hope, together with an observable change. Even more importantly, perhaps, focusing on solutions has helped to build active partnerships between school and parents, since parents and carers clearly have much to offer in looking for solutions.

And this, I believe, is where the strength of the process lies – in the belief that parents and teachers are, for the most part, problem solvers; that they have the resources and skills needed to solve their own problems and that for the most part, they do so all the time.

Focusing at the outset on parents' and teachers' strengths and achievements, on what they do well, shifts everyone's view. Whilst they may be presenting a problem now, they are also people who have solved many problems in the past and who have the resources to continue to do so. The EP is there just to help them find their way.

Appendix 1

SUMMARY OF EDUCATIONAL PSYCHOLOGIST'S INTERVENTION

Pupil's name: Joe.. School: ....

Dates of involvement: .... Date of Birth ....

Date of report:.. Age: 8

Name of Educational Psychologist...

Areas of strength and progress

• Joe is able to make choices, i.e..

....

• Joe has made significant progress in language development, i.e ....

....

• Last year, Joe's behaviour improved, i.e ....

....

Nature of difficulties

• Increase in challenging behaviour. In particular, throwing hard objects and hitting other children and adults.

In school, this behaviour can seem overwhelming to the extent that to staff in class it seems to be happening all the time.

• Mother's concern about some of the school's strategies for managing Joe's behaviour (in particular, shouting and physical restraint) has led to disagreement about the Individual Behaviour Programme.

Aims - next steps

• To develop a small set of strategies for managing Joe's behaviour which are effective, consistent with strategies used with other pupils, easy to follow and acceptable to all those involved with Joe – both at home and at school.

• To ensure that all those involved know them and use them consistently.

Effective strategies and areas worth investigating further

- Observe closely how Joe's sister manages his behaviour and adopt her strategies (see EP's observations)
- Observe Joe in class when things are going well. What is different about those times and how can they be built on?
- Note those occasions when Joe finds limit setting containing and comforting.
- Limit the use of shouting as a strategy and use another strategy alongside
- Build on the excellent principles outlined already in Joe's school support plan, i.e.
  Structure and clearly defined boundaries.
  Calm, firm handling.
  Warning and support when faced with change.
  More attention when behaving well.

EP's observations of areas of progress and effective strategies

- Despite the increase in frequency and intensity of challenging behaviours, there are still times in school when Joe is 'as good as gold', and his Mum describes him as 'a new improved version' this year.
- Both at home and at school, there are strategies that work at least some of the time.
- Joe responds to being talked to and to eye contact.
- Displays of anger and shouting (by his brothers) make Joe worse. Hence his mother's concern about the use of shouting as a strategy.
- Joe is most responsive to his sister. She accepts him as he is, is gentle, calm and gives him lots of cuddles.
- At home Joe responds better after a day at school if he is allowed to act out in his own room for an hour or so before going downstairs. (His mother watches him from the doorway).
- Joe's relationship with his mother has improved significantly since last summer, i.e. ....
- Joe's mother tends to see the setting of limits as unhelpful and potentially undermining of her improved relationship with Joe. However, she accepts that some limits are necessary, e.g. to keep him physically safe.
- Despite previous reservations about Joe's teacher's strategies for managing his behaviour, Joe's mother now trusts her judgement. It should therefore now be possible to agree some consistent ways for managing Joe's behaviour at home and at school.

CHAPTER EIGHT

CREATIVE SOLUTIONS TO EMOTIONAL & BEHAVIOURAL DIFFICULTIES IN SCHOOLS: WORKING TOGETHER FOR CHANGE

BY SUZANNE LOGGIE & JEAN DAY

Introduction

As qualified teachers and counsellors on the behaviour team for a local education authority, our work is with families and children experiencing emotional and behavioural difficulties. We believe that Solution-Focused Brief
Therapy ideas have led to a way of working which harnesses the skills and
strengths of all parties, opening new possibilities and overcoming the cycle of
blame that can occur, particularly in very difficult cases.

In 1994, inspired by teachers from the Marlborough Family Unit and a
two-year course in systemic family work at the Institute of Family Therapy, we
decided to work with families with children experiencing behavioural difficulties, on one afternoon a week. We worked with whoever wanted to come
along and were surprised at the eager response.

Initially, we followed a Milan model (Boscolo, Cecchin, et al 1987) but
were soon attracted to solution-focused ideas (de Shazer, 1982, 1985). We
liked this client-centred, highly respectful approach which highlighted
people's strengths, resources and competencies. Many of the children we
worked with were branded as 'disruptive', 'deviant' or a 'waste of space'. Also,

because of the human tendency to look for causal explanations to account for behaviour, the children's families were often stigmatised with similar descriptions and regarded as dysfunctional by teachers and other professionals. The families in turn blamed the teachers or often blamed themselves! There seemed little hope for change.

A format for working which stopped pathologising people or regarding them as inferior not only sat comfortably with our beliefs but also encouraged a collaborative approach between families and schools. When people were viewed as competent and resourceful it appeared to have a remarkable effect on their ability to overcome their despondency and despair and increased their motivation to change.

Working together - where, how, why?

We now work together for one day a week, offering solution-focused family sessions to children and their families who have been referred via the Education Service. We usually see three to four families a day, either at our work base or at the child's school. Although working together can seem a luxury, we are aware of the great benefits that this approach affords. As this work has developed, we can see clearly that working with the whole family helps the child concerned to change and improve his/her behaviour at home and in school and it supports them all in dealing with the issues they are facing. A brochure (Appendix 1), explains how we work and is sent to schools and parents prior to the first meeting.

Partnership work greatly reduces the feeling of isolation one can experience when working with troubled families and the burden of having to take sole responsibility for cases. We feel more empowered and creative on our partnership day. We find that the different perspectives each of us contributes, increases the likelihood of families seeing their difficulties in an alternative focus and developing ideas for change.

Families are referred to us in various ways; from a head-teacher or Senco (Special Educational Needs Co-ordinator) or from an Educational Psychologist or other support teacher working in the school. Sometimes, parents will ask for help with a problem that they are experiencing at home, which is not initially manifest in school. We ask the Senco or another senior pastoral member of the school staff sensitively to discuss the support we can offer with the family before referral – our information leaflet is also given to them at this stage. We stress that it is the family's choice to see us and so we are fortunate in not dealing with reluctant clients. In fact, a number of the families who come to see us are often feeling quite desperate about their situation and are pleased to be offered an appointment within a few weeks of referral, especially as there is often a wait of many months for a similar health service based appointment.

Following referral, we make contact with the family by letter or telephone. In this initial contact, and at the first session, we stress that our meetings are confidential (unless we have concerns about anyone's safety) and that we do not share the content of the session with the school. This gives a sense of security to the session and can often reduce the feelings of defensiveness and disempowerment that parents with children in difficulties can experience within the school system. We do not usually invite school staff to any of these first meetings but pass on compliments and positive feedback to them with the parents' permission. This can often be the start of a new partnership when relationships have broken down. In later sessions we have found it extremely beneficial to invite teachers, personal tutors, classroom assistants or any other appropriate member of school staff to attend and make their contribution if the family is in agreement with this. We are always aware of the need to maintain the family's confidentiality from earlier sessions. We tell families that we may repeat past questions so that they may choose what they wish to share in the larger group.

We base our way of working on Tom Andersen's 'Reflecting Team concept' (Andersen, 1987). One of us adopts the role of observer, sitting a little apart from the group and taking our confidential notes (with the permission of the family), while the other conducts the session. About three-quarters of the way through the hour's session the observer joins in, discussing with a colleague their observations and reflections. This is always done in a respectful way, noticing the strengths, resourcefulness and resilience in the family and its relationships, identifying any steps to success that they have already made and complimenting them on the way they are dealing with their dilemmas. The family shares in this discussion and comments on the ideas and links that have been made. A task may then be agreed upon, such as to look out for the positive happenings in their lives which they wish to continue.

When a home/school relationship has become rather strained, these joint sessions afford an opportunity to form a new co-operative partnership. We have seen individuals' unhelpful perceptions about others disintegrate when they hear about the struggles in peoples' lives and witnessed how quickly participants in our sessions engage in solution development when they realise their views and opinions are going to be treated with respect and seriousness. The presence of a teacher who has given up a lunchtime break, or been given cover to attend the meeting, is often an indication to the family of the school's level of care and commitment to their child. As such, it can be a powerful force for change. In a recent meeting, a positive comment from a head teacher seemed to be a significant turning point for a nine year-old boy; when we asked this pupil how he was able to give such a high score to his level of confidence about maintaining the changes he had made he replied 'Because Mr. K. has said that he believes I can do it!'

The number of times we see a family varies. Sometimes, a single session is sufficient to identify and reinforce the positive changes that are already happening but, more often, we see families for three or four sessions and some for much longer. This is always decided in ongoing discussion with the parents and children. There is normally a three- to four-week gap between appointments, although occasionally we will arrange to meet more frequently. Though we would like the families themselves to decide the interval time between sessions, it is not always possible since we find it more practical to arrange several appointments on the same date when we are seeing a number of different families in the same school.

We seek to empower the family as much as possible and so offer them the choice as to who attends the sessions. Sometimes the room is full; a recent family brought the father's three children, the mother's two, their baby, and Grandma. On another occasion we had one session with the parents of a child who was regarded by the school as becoming a 'school refuser'. Within a couple of weeks she was happily attending school regularly. We did not ever meet the child!

Solution-focused thinking is a goal-orientated approach that fits comfortably alongside the Special Educational Needs Code of Practice (DfEE, 1994) and places emphasis on the children creating and developing their own solutions and strategies for success. Some of the underlying assumptions which lie behind the approach, such as the idea that it is not always necessary to search for causal explanations in order to develop solutions, or the idea that successful solutions may not be even logically related to the problem, invite all those involved – children, parents and teachers – to join in a new and collaborative endeavour which can result in creative and exciting outcomes.

Helpful and unhelpful explanations

We have found that the human tendency to look for the root of the problem in order to get a clue on how to fix it has been the biggest stumbling block to collaboration between families and schools. It is still not unusual for us to hear criticisms such as 'Those parents have inadequate parenting skills' or 'That teacher can't control them.' Parents, teachers, and other helping professionals sometimes get tied up with a lot of unhelpful explanations that encourage blaming and shaming and discourage creativity and change. Senge et al. (cited in Selekman, 1997, p. 155) describe self-generating beliefs that block collaboration:

our ideas are the truth;
the truth is obvious;
our beliefs are based on real data;
the data we select are the real data.

We are all apt to forget that the answers we give to the question 'Why?' are merely hypotheses made to fit the facts. They are constructed, made up and yet we often treat them as though they are written in stone. It is quite easy for all of us to develop a sort of tunnel vision and fit people to our theories. Palmarini (1994, p. 119) states 'We need to be wary of our over-confidence which tends to be greatest in our own areas of expertise.' Even solution-focused therapists can fall into the trap of being so overbearingly positive about the future that they fail to acknowledge and validate people's experiences of real suffering and despair. Bill O'Hanlon (1994, p. 9) describes how people have often fought long and hard to construct sets of ideas or labels to give meaning and dignity to their experiences, and it is important to respect this.

When families come to us for the first session, they are either ready with explanations as to why their children are behaving in the way they are or they are looking to us as the 'experts' to give them explanations. In the latter situation it is often quite easy to explain that because human beings are so complex we might search for years and come up with some sort of explanation but it might be more useful to concentrate on how they want things to be. In the former circumstance we feel it is vital to acknowledge and hear every family member's explanation so that we can begin, through our questioning, gradually to shift entrenched and unhelpful explanations that preclude the possibility of change taking place. Since the urge to have explanations is sometimes overwhelmingly strong we look to develop explanations that:

encourage creativity and collaboration;
value clients'strengths, resilience and resourcefulness;
open up possibilities for change

In other words, to normalize the difficulty without trivialising it.

When we get locked into one way of thinking we immediately cut off all the creative, imaginative and playful ways to solve difficulties. We enjoy working with young children so much because they so often find extraordinary and inventive ideas to solve their dilemmas.

Creative strategies: four case studies

Darren: playground videotapes

Darren is a nine year-old boy who was having some friendship difficulties and getting involved in fights on the playground. When we asked Darren to describe a really good day at school he poignantly described one when other boys allowed him to join in their games and stopped saying nasty things to him. However, he quickly, if somewhat accidentally hit upon the solution to his difficulties when he caught sight of the end of a piece of filming we had made on another boy in a different school whilst he was viewing a video tape of himself in a previous session. He immediately asked if he could send a video-taped message to the boy, telling him about himself and what he liked doing. The following week, with the permission of both boys' parents, he made a short three-minute videotape that we played to the other boy in school. This began a videotape dialogue between the two boys over several sessions and although their enthusiasm gradually petered out, they both seemed to benefit enormously from their communication with each other. Darren particularly began to change his perception of himself, realising that he did have an ability to make friends. He initiated a new friendship in school and when we asked him how he knew he could be a good friend he said 'Because Jay [his 'videopal'] likes talking to me and listening to my jokes.'

Sara: the shop-to-shop run

Sara developed a solution to her difficulties without needing to find out why she was in her current situation. She was a sixteen year-old with a serious gambling problem that was controlling her life. She was spending all her weekly earnings from her part-time job on instant scratch cards and had started stealing money from other members of the family in order to pursue her obsession. She felt miserable most of the time, the exceptions being when she experienced the buzz of excitement before she scratched the cards. She was allowing her schoolwork to slip and was putting on unwanted weight from eating too much. She was regarded by the school as a promising athlete but had given up her daily training and was feeling unfit.

By exploring her preferred future through the miracle question (de Shazer, 1988, p. 5) we were able to work out together a solution which put her in control of the gambling as well as the other aspects of her life. She was able to offer a very concrete and detailed description of her life after the miracle and saw immediately the ripples of positive effect that getting in control of gambling would have on herself and her relationships. Inspired by some of the cases of Milton Erickson (as cited in O'Hanlon and Hexum, 1990) that I described to her, she decided that she would combine her training with her gambling by only purchasing one card at a particular newsagent and not allowing herself to scratch it off until she had run half a mile to a second newsagent where she would allow herself to purchase another card. This way she could prolong the excitement of imagining she had won, get her training done and spend less money in the process. She carried out her solution the following week and was pleased with the results. In three sessions she had paid back the money she had 'borrowed' and had put some money aside for a summer holiday.

Mary: a lesson in patience

Sometimes it is very tempting to look for explanations; Mary is an example of a case where school staff were keen to get to the root of the problem in order to solve it. Mary was referred to us, with her family, after she had been in primary school for two terms. She had not spoken to anyone since entering school despite the best efforts of her teachers and other staff. A behaviour-support teacher was called and although this teacher had made very positive and imaginative efforts, Mary still did not speak. She was progressing well in all her written work and was able to communicate her basic needs, such as needing to go to the toilet. She appeared to be happy and was forming relationships with other children. However, her refusal to talk was creating an atmosphere of anxiety and frustration around her. When she was referred to us by her behaviour-support teacher we decided to meet with her family at our work base, away from Mary's school. We also decided not to refer to ourselves as teachers. The whole family, Mum, Dad, Mary and her three older brothers came to the first session. When we collected them from the waiting room we could hear Mary chatting happily and she talked and played with her brothers throughout most of the sessions, although she was sometimes quiet when asked direct questions.

As we began the session by finding out about the family – their strengths, abilities, and interests – we found that they were a musically gifted family, that both parents had coped courageously with a number of tragedies in their adult lives and that, perhaps most importantly, their main concerns were not about Mary. In fact, they were most worried about their sons, who were experiencing problems with communication and self-confidence.

It would have been very easy at this stage to pathologise this family. Sometimes we both find that earlier psychodynamic training hits us like a recurrent bout of malaria and we could see all sorts of reasons and explanations as to why Mary might not be speaking in school. However, by working together as a team and staying solution-focused, we resisted this tendency to look for reasons as being unhelpful. We were also aware that previous work had been done in trying to persuade Mary to talk without success. We therefore chose to follow the family's agenda and looked to the issues they presented, noting and supporting their strategies and abilities in dealing with them.

In separate meetings with Mary's teacher and head teacher, we made efforts to lower their anxieties and to reassure them that our work with the family was going well. We complimented them on their commitment to this pupil who was clearly happy and experiencing success. They seemed relieved that they did not have to worry unduly any more and relaxed their vigilance over Mary. In terms of the presenting problem, we were not sure where we were going, but felt convinced that ignoring Mary's silence in school was the best solution. As the other issues in the family began to be resolved the parents grew in confidence and hope about the future. After several months the only issue was that Mary was still not speaking in school, and her parents were still not particularly worried about this. So we agreed not to meet with them unless they requested it.

A year later one of us was in the school to see another child and asked about Mary. She was still a quiet child, but would now read to her teacher, answer questions and was working well. She also had a small speaking part in the class Christmas drama.

This could be seen as a creative non-solution! We felt that by working in a solution-focused way, to the parent's agenda rather than the one we were given, we were able to create an atmosphere around this child that was accepting and stress-free. This enabled her to change in her own time. The parents were appreciative of the sessions we shared with them and seemed to grow in their own self-confidence. This was reflected in their developing trust in their own skills to raise and support their children.

David: puppets and tapes

The case of David is another example of how inventive explanations can open up opportunities for changes in self-perception and concomitant behaviour change. David was an eight year old who was causing great concern at school. At the time of referral David's teacher reported to me that he was finding it very difficult to motivate David and, although he had spent a great deal of time in positive encouragement and reassurance, David would often flatly refuse to tackle set tasks or become very upset when requested to start an activity. On a one-to-one basis the teacher was sometimes successful in getting David to work but the output reflected poor effort and little interest. That David achieved anything at all seemed a result of the dedication, energy and clear commitment that this teacher showed.

David's teacher was also concerned about David's poor social skills and his lack of real friendships within his peer group. David often made inappropriate comments to peers that provoked angry responses and he also received more than his fair share of cruel comments in return. In the playground it was observed that he had little interaction with other children, often playing on the edges of groups or temporarily attaching himself to perceived 'naughty' boys by trying to impress them with anti-social behaviour.

David's emotional well-being was of very serious concern since he had expressed a seemingly serious wish to be 'dead' in response to a question about what he wanted to be when he was older, and had also told a colleague of mine that he wanted to crash into a car and be taken to hospital.

From the outset David trusted me with his feelings in a very open and articulate way. He told me that he liked football and swimming and he liked playing 'policemen', but that he didn't like being at school because the other children were horrible to him. In fact, he wanted to be a policeman because you could arrest people, handcuff them and send them to prison!

When I am working with young children I often take different play materials to the session and use a set of six animal hand puppets in different ways according to how the children want to use them. These puppets rapidly became David's friends and supporters and came out in every session we worked together. Sometimes he just used them to express all his sad and angry feelings about his current situation, but he would take in their compliments and comments and answer their questions in a thoughtful and serious way. They became my reflecting team and it was their 'diagnosis' of David's 'problem' that started a change in David's feelings about himself.

One day while we were working, he told me that he would never have any proper friends because he was stupid. The teacher set him easy work because he was stupid and the other children did not want to be friends with someone who was stupid. The puppet team immediately went into conference and told David they could not agree with what he said since everyone was clever in some way and that he must be suffering from 'hidden cleverness'. David just needed a way to show this cleverness to other people. David seemed to like the idea and suddenly invented a twin brother who was clever. When I asked how he knew he was clever, he said he knew lots of stuff and illustrated this in great detail by telling me about the Ku Klux Klan and vegetarianism. When I asked him how his twin brother knew all that stuff he informed me 'Because his mum makes him watch all sorts of boring things on TV'!

In the following session David came up with the idea of making an audio story tape for his sister's birthday which would show his cleverness. In three sessions he had painstakingly put together an amazingly imaginative and humorous tape which told the story of the capture and rescue of two children in the enchanted forest. It was a masterpiece of which he was justifiably proud.

He created all the different voices for characters in the story and used musical instruments to make the sound effects. My own contribution was little more than turning the tape recorder on and off, although I couldn't resist joining in with the sound of the wild pigs!

David's family was astounded when they heard the tape and David's teacher agreed that it was such an excellent piece of work it should be played to the class. Several members of the class told David how good it was. I was rewarded by David saying to me, 'I think I might be clever after all!' This was a pupil who had been described a few months ago as having poor motivation.

A year on from this, David is doing very well and is actually planning to make a sequel to the Enchanted Forest story for his sister's next birthday. He was recently presented with a golden award in assembly for effort and achievement in his work and proudly described how he had made a model of 'The Iron Man' and shown it to the whole school. Of course I cannot claim that this progress is entirely due to a solution-focused intervention, but I feel that it had a significant part to play in contributing to David's success. David's teacher and support assistant were extremely dedicated and committed to supporting David and to using a solution-focused approach. I was fortunate to be able to liaise with them a great deal and was keen to hand compliments back to them for David's achievements. I also met with David's mother on two occasions to thank her for her contribution to David's progress.

Solution-focused work with children, adolescents and families: a quick fix?

We both feel that there is one major disadvantage of working in a solution-focused way. We receive so many referrals these days that we have become victims of our own success. Several of the families we are working with have been recommended to come for help by other families we have seen previously, and many schools have stated that they could do with our services on a full-time basis. Our evaluation forms are returned to us with encouraging comments from parents, children and school staff, and although we do not claim that the successes we witness are attributable to our interventions, we feel sure that this way of working inspires everyone to come together in a collaborative endeavour for change.

We believe that people are able to make changes in their lives when they are seen as competent and resourceful human beings, experts in their own lives. Many prescriptive interventions may work temporarily but long lasting change is achieved by people finding out for themselves what works best for them. If you tell people what to do, or how to be, it rarely works and more often makes them feel inadequate and disillusioned, reinforcing the feelings they had when they first came for help.

We feel privileged to listen to the stories of people's lives and hear about their courage and resilience in the face of adversity. Their stories often impact on our own lives and relationships in a positive way, making every encounter a new learning experience.

Appendix 1

What kind of families use this service?

All kinds of families – those with two parents, families with divorced parents, single-parent families, families where relatives are bringing up children, or those where children are adopted or fostered.

How old must the children be?

Of school age from 4–18 years.

What kind of difficulties do you help with?

We normally see families where there are school-related difficulties. Either the school or family may be concerned about the child's feelings or behaviour or relationships.

What does 'solution-focused' mean?

In solution-focused work, our aim is to help families recognise their strengths and abilities and to look for and develop their own solutions.

Is it confidential?

Yes. We keep our own records only to remind us of details of our work and to help us plan ahead. You can always discuss this with us. Should we need to contact other agencies we will always speak to you first.

How do we get an appointment?

Schools or their Educational Psychologist will normally ask families if they would like an appointment with us. We normally arrange a first appointment within a couple of weeks of being contacted.

What happens when we come?

It is helpful if, for the first session at least, the whole family can come, although this is not always possible or necessary. There will usually be two of us in the session. We like to talk with the family in order to gain a better understanding of the difficulties and to look at all possible changes and new ways of dealing with dilemmas.

How many sessions will we need to attend?

The average number of sessions is four to six but this varies depending on individual family's needs. Sessions are usually fortnightly or monthly during term-time.

Who are you?

Mrs. Susanne Loggie and Mrs. Jean Day. We are qualified teachers and counsellors with family therapy training. We provide this service within the Education Support Services.

CHAPTER NINE

WRAPPING NEW NARRATIVES IN GOLDEN PAPER:

SOLUTION-FOCUSED WORK WITH PUPILS, TEACHERS AND PARENTS IN MAINSTREAM PRIMARY SCHOOLS

BY CATHERINE MCGLONE

Introduction

The Primary Behaviour Support Service was set up in 1990 by Strathclyde Regional Council following recommendations made by the Warnock Report (1978) and the 1981 Education (Scotland) Act (as amended) in order that mainstream support be given to those pupils who were categorized as having EBD. The task of supporting pupils whose behaviour was considered extremely challenging was a daunting one. A particular challenge was that of establishing collaborative working practices with mainstream teachers so that support plans could be developed. I was an original member of the team and it is encouraging to note that ideas, which at one time seemed peripheral to education, are becoming so widely known. I hear less frequently 'Solution-focused what? Never heard of it, Cath!'

Solution-Focused Brief Therapy was introduced to the team and developed by Frank Watters, a senior educational psychologist who had a specific role in staff development. His training was subsequently augmented by training from the Brief Therapy Practice in London. Watters (1988) emphasized systemic approaches to behavioural problems over the more mechanistic behaviourist models, the limitations of which are recognized by many teachers who work with pupils who have EBD. Ecosystemic approaches to behavioural problems were being adopted in other British schools and Grey Miller and Noakes (1995) claimed that by the mid 1980's behaviour support teachers were adopting systemic approaches which:

> 'Concentrate on stories used to explain events, and the construction and reconstruction of explanations as the model of behaviour change.'
>
> (Grey Miller and Noakes, 1994, p.56)

Although support teachers recognised the value of adapting the ideas, which had their origins in therapy, they were also conscious of the stresses facing professionals who were 'initiative weary'. Watters (1988) cited Stern and Keisler's (1977) findings on factors which influenced positive uptake from teachers of innovation among which were:

– involvement in planning and decision-making;
– the creation of an atmosphere which encouraged reflection and encouraged teachers to express their doubts and fears;
– acceptance of personal responsibility or ownership of the innovation.

His commitment to the development of solution-focused ideas provided a framework for staff who wished to work with their colleagues, pupils and parents in ways which emphasized mutual respect. Our understanding of the process was strengthened by listening to those therapists (Iveson, Ratner and others) who, over the years, journeyed north from the Brief Therapy Practice in London in order that we might develop our skills. My interest in the process deepened and I have been involved in a research study (Ph.D.) which seeks to illuminate how pupils, parents and teachers evaluated the process. Their contribution to my own understanding of the process has continued to prove most valuable and insightful.

In this chapter I have chosen to illustrate my work with imaginary texts, as it is my preferred option that if real cases were used then they would be truly co-authored. A major theme of the research study was an exploration of the process of cooperative work which is considered a prerequisite of effective support. To view solution-focused approaches to problem behaviour as a quick fix or another strategy to be used from a 'bag of tricks' undervalues the contribution of language in the deconstruction of a 'deviant' identity and its role in creating more hopeful alternatives. I agree with Efran and Clarfield, (1995) who view psychotherapy as a form of education. They state:

> 'The natural medium of therapy – as in most other educational
> pursuits – is language. The context is basically philosophical
> rather than medical and constructive rather than simply reme-
> dial.'
>
> (Efran, J. S. and Clarfield, E., 1995 .p.212)

At a time when schools and teachers are increasingly being criticized for their supposed deficits, I continue to find that working with pupils, teachers and parents in a solution-focused way generates hope and possibilities for the future. Michael White (1995) believes that schools could become 'Communities of Acknowledgement' and recognizes that the voice of the teacher is significant in helping pupils challenge a dominant story of failure. The next section explores how the ideas, which were originally forged in the context of therapy, came to be applied in school. Space does not permit me to discuss in full how the application of solution-focused thinking has influenced my work, so I have chosen to illustrate some aspects of my work which have changed as a result of my adopting a solution-focused perspective.

Key aspects of practice

Observations rescripted

A recognised part of a behaviour support intervention is the period of observation during which the teacher observes the referred pupil in different contexts and which traditionally implicated the observer in assessing the extent of the problem and its impact. Approaching the task of observation from a solution-focused perspective, I was influenced by Berg (1994) and Durrant (1995) who contend that assessment and intervention are interconnected. Durrant (1995) cites Berg, who warns that assessment often results in a 'laundry list of all the things that are wrong with the client.'

My usual practice, before observing the child in class, is to converse with the member of the staff concerned. I make a point of distancing myself from the role of expert/advice giver/interpreter and hope that I will be able to establish a relationship where I am perceived as a co-worker.

In practice, this means that I do not emphasize the value of my supposedly 'objective' observation over the description which comes from the teachers or parents. I explain that I have no reason to doubt the validity of their experience and thank the teacher for the detailed documentation which has been completed before meeting me. I assume that she will go on collating information about the difficulties she faces.

I explain that my approach is a solution-focused one which emphasizes the role of language and stories in helping children, teachers and parents arrive at solutions to problems. This invariably intrigues my colleagues, as focusing on language is an integral part of the curriculum. I ask that, during the observation period, I am permitted to focus on those times when the child is behaving in a way which differs from the problem description so that I may share it with the child and their parents. I emphasize a pedagogical perspective in relation to observation, rather than a psychological or medical one. This enables the teacher and I to collaborate in a linguistic or narrative experiment by focusing on language and stories rather than symptoms and causes of problems. Teachers are generous in their sharing of ideas and I hope that our conversations are about mutual exchange of ideas. I have often found that I learned much in my teaching career from teachers who 'talked shop' over coffee and cake. Unfortunately, as Gitlin (1992) noted, 'teachers were often discredited as experts.' I believe that using solution-focused ideas in schools will go some way to countering such a view.

Golden book: challenging the problem story

I introduce the teacher to the idea of the Golden Book, which aims to transform the traditional observation with its emphasis on diagnosis/cure, to one characterized by curiosity and collaboration. Traditionally, observation records were mainly problem-focused and used language which Rom Harre (1985) calls 'file speak' and which focused on apparent deficits. My preferred approach is to begin a story which describes not just the strengths and competencies of the pupil, but includes a story which challenges notions of schooling being a process which excludes.

Miller, Duncan and Hubble, (1997) have noted the similarity between the use of de Shazer's 'exceptions' and that of White's 'unique outcomes'. In the literature of Narrative Therapy, the latter emphasizes the process whereby the therapist and client build a story around those times when the problem is either being challenged or is not dominant. The Golden Book, influenced by the work of Michael White (1995), whose use of documents and letters to clients contributed to them becoming stronger at challenging their problem-dominated identity, hopefully illuminated what is hopeful and respectful in the day-to-day life of pupils and teachers at work in school. White states:

> 'These documents are grounded in hope; for example, they often include details about personal qualities and other characteristics .... These documents can also include details about any recent developments in the person's problem- solving skills.'
>
> (White, 1995, p.143)

The Golden Book was an exercise book (covered in Golden paper) which I used to document an alternative to the problem story. Parents and teachers often reported that their value lay in the fact that they were grounded in actual experience and testified to the way in which apparently simple things could help the child to overcome difficulties.

The book was used in the following ways:

– it was a record of those times when the problem was not present and the child was witnessed challenging difficulties;
– significant people could become involved in co-authoring the story;
– solution-focused conversations with the child were written in the book thus making known their preferred alternatives;
– the voice of the child was respected and their need for support validated.

Stance of curiosity

When there is agreement that my time may be more profitably spent recording exceptions to the problem story, I might inquire:

> 'I am wondering about N, you know, those qualities which he/she has shown that will and help him/her challenge this problem.'

Anderson and Goolishian (1995) claim that the therapist, by taking on a not-knowing position helps open up new spaces in a conversation from which 'newness' can occur. Adopting a dialogical position can lead to mutual exploration, but explorers have to be intrepid! Expect responses from the teacher which vary from amazement to hilarity. It should be remembered that by the time the pupil has been referred to the behaviour support system, things are at a critical stage. Teachers are usually tired or stressed and it is a measure of their professionalism and sense of optimism in the educational process that many of them are able to continue to converse with me. During a workshop which was given by de Shazer in Glasgow (1995), I learned the value of remaining quizzically quiet for as long as possible. The teacher, given time, is most likely to respond with something like:

> 'You know, he does not give up easily, he is a joker ... at times he makes me laugh – at times I could cry.'

Crucial to the process of re-storying is an acceptance that the documents of support are distinct from the prompts to achieve associated with positive behaviour strategies. To use this book as a 'Positive Behaviour Book' book fails to capture the power of the narrative and the role of language in challenging a deficit view of the child. An example of how a first page might appear is shown below and I request some time with the class teacher and the pupil so that my 'observation' can be read:

> Today I met Miss B, and she said N works hard at maths and

likes to complete his work. She also said he tells good jokes. I
visited Class ... and I enjoyed watching Group B making a model. I
noticed that N passed the scissors safely to J. It seems to me that
he respects other people because I heard him say thank you to me
when I offered him one of my pencils. Before interval I noticed
he listened to the teacher who was telling the pupils where to put
their models.

Continuing the story: exploring life without the problem

I request time with the child and his/her teacher so that subsequent conversations can be scripted in the Golden Book. The notion of 'preferred futures'
is helpful in negotiating a plan of action.

This can be a light-hearted encounter exploring life without the problem.
It also involves my conversing with my colleague and incorporating elements
of a solution-focused conversation, as appropriate. Important in this exploration of the problem-free future is the use of the word when instead of if. When
denotes notions of belief and hope. If on the other hand may suggest notions
of contingency, incertitude and scepticism. It has long been recognised by
those who educate pupils who display extreme behaviours that saying 'if you
do... then ...' can lead to an escalation of difficult behaviour and conflict.
Future-oriented questions should convey a genuine interest and a real curiosity about the preferred future. I avoid trying to get the 'right' answer.

> When things change what will be happening
> Who will notice?
> Who else?

In school, significant people can be enlisted to notice and document the
changed story. Each member of staff will have a unique relationship with the
child. Headteachers often represent certitude and security, janitors and
administrative staff often 'look out' for the child. On occasions, the stories of
janitors and clerical staff have proven powerful in countering the 'bad name',
which some children acquire.

> Whose words will you enjoy reading in this book?
> Why?
> What do you think she/he will say?
> Draw a picture/cartoon of what it will be like when things have
> improved.

The use of drawings, especially cartoons, is helpful at this stage and provides
a focus for further discussion. White (1995) cautions us to be alive to the
dynamism of language and adopts a social constructionist approach, which

emphasizes the creative elements of language. Once the child voices his/her description of life without the problem, it seems that there is a subtle change in the relationship between the child and the teacher. In some cases the teacher becomes an advocate for the child and the pupil enjoys listening to the words of the teacher, as the changed story is co-authored.

> When, this week have you noticed ... behave in a way which tells you that things are changing for him?
> When else?
> Who else in the school will have words to say about ... which he will enjoy hearing?

These conversations provide a basis for future planning and are significant in helping the child challenge problems, which may have seemed intractable. The use of IEP's is currently being advocated in education and I believe that the Golden Book may provide a useful way of exploring how better to support a pupil and teacher in educational planning.

Externalizing conversations

This work derives from the work of Michael White (1995) who claimed that by engaging pupils in externalising conversations:

> 'They are introduced to ways of speaking about their lives that don't implicate their relationship with the problem. These externalising conversations are a powerful antidote to contemporary 'problem speak' and to the 'modern problem-identity practices.'
> (White, 1995,p57)

Generally, descriptions about a pupil's behaviour usually take the form of locating the problem within the child .The child often describes himself as being bad tempered or lazy. Some pupils describe themselves as 'big trouble'. Externalising conversations locate the problem outwith the child by asking that the pupil consider opposing the problem, which is named.

W:What will you call this problem?
C: Temper.
W:When you are challenging Temper what is happening?
C: Well I can feel jumpy but I don't throw my books about.
W:Whose words help you when you are challenging Temper?
C: My teacher says 'You are beating temper again - look at your work, it's great.'
W:Draw a picture of YOU when you are challenging Temper.

When speaking about temper/anger it is important that the child is given sufficient space to explore those circumstances which contribute to anger becoming stronger. This affords the pupil the opportunity to give voice to any circumstances which are having an adverse effect on his/her life, and enables those who have responsibility for the child's welfare to examine how the child could be better supported.

Consulting with children: problem solving and support

Conversations with pupils can often be light-hearted and hopeful, emphasizing the idea that learning and problem solving are lifelong activities. I sometimes introduce children to a problem which I face called 'messy handwriting'. As a teacher I know the value of good formation of letters when working with primary school pupils. Admitting that my handwriting in their Golden Books falls short of their teacher's expectations of good handwriting has had unexpected results. Subsequent support from the children has taken the form of pupils lending me pencils or re -writing my words. Many became interested in my pencil collection and have given me advice about where to buy pencils. When they notice my writing has improved they say kind and supportive words. Their teachers also support my efforts to do something differently. The teachers and children have acknowledged that the problem which I face – messy handwriting – is affected by factors such as being in a hurry or forgetting my pencil case. Their stories of challenge have similar elements to mine.

Matching language

A teacher or parent may, in the course of conversation, describe the pupil as defiant, wilful, or disobedient. In response, I aim to use language which mirrors the feelings of those involved, but which opens up possibilities for the emergence of alternative descriptions. Thus, I may become curious about other words which are similar and yet different. Speaking about defiance can become a conversation about showing qualities of strong-mindedness. Taking this position can turn the therapeutic conversation into a 'linguistic event' as described by Anderson and Goolishan (1995):

> 'The therapeutic conversation is a mutual search and exploration through dialogue, a two way exchange, a criss-crossing of ideas in which new meanings are continually evolving toward the dissolving of problems ...'
>
> (Anderson and Goolishan, 1995, p126)

Coming from a pedagogical rather than a psychological or medical background helped me engage parents and children in conversations, which usually began with, 'I'm wondering about ....' Schools are places where people should be encouraged to wonder. Perhaps solution-focused thinking will provide an antidote to approaches which, because of their prescriptive tendencies, have contributed to the silencing of the more creative voices in education.

Scaling Questions

Scaling questions can be useful at the end of a session with both pupil and teacher.

> 'On a scale ranging from 0 – 10, where 0 is when interval times
> are not good and 10 when you are having fun with your friends
> playing safely. Where are you now?'

The scaling questions can be used to ascertain the differences in perceptions about how the pupil is managing, to clarify the next steps and to enlist support. The following questions can be used after this has occurred.

> 'What will you be doing when you are at ...?'
> 'Will you notice those times next week when you see ...doing
> this?'

Scaling questions can be helpful because:

- the differing perceptions of the teacher and pupil can be ironed out;
- a plan can be negotiated and re-negotiated – noticing tasks being incorporated;
- other supports can be enlisted, (parents, janitor, other pupils).

I seldom use the scaling question with pre-five pupils, preferring to use it with the significant adults in their lives and incorporating their changes perceptions into the re-storying.

Reflection

Working from a pedagogical perspective encourages teachers and pupils to become involved in a dynamic process of learning; the stories and solutions in one case may contribute to more innovative work in others. Schools are creative places to work in and it is my experience that when teachers are asked for their advice with regard to helping a child access the curriculum better, collaborate on a playground game, etc., the results are often wonderful. Giroux (1997) argues that schools have fallen short of 'developing a language that engages schools as sites of possibility' and he stresses the inter-relatedness of student and teacher voice, contending that account must be taken of the constraints which hinder the process of what he calls a pedagogy of hope. He views those educational theories which seek to compensate for deficits as contributing to the silencing of dissenting voices.

Such theories are embodied in some educational approaches which are more prescriptive and which seek to emphasize control rather than dialogue. His hope is that schools can be:

> 'Places where students can be educated to take their places in society from a position of empowerment rather than from a position of ideological and economic subordination.'
>
> (Giroux, 1997, p.123)

He acknowledges the contribution of teachers to this process. It is to be hoped that ideas, which have helped families resolve conflict, may prove useful in the context of school.

Challenging behaviour in nursery – a changed story

These brief outlines of the case illustrations are fictional but they represent summaries of accounts of work done, reflecting a general pattern of events and experiences. The first case illustrates how the staff of a nursery and a parent can become involved in a behaviour support plan which represents true 'joined-up working'. Four-year-old N, described as defiant and uncooperative by his teacher and parent, was referred to behaviour support. When asked to sit in the story corner, N typically refused and threw a tantrum. The key worker was both skilled and experienced. The parent reported feeling anxious.

A meeting was convened with the behaviour support teacher, the parent and the teacher. There was agreement that they had tried everything. Typically, N responded to the words 'Tidy up time, N. Will you please help?' by refusing to do as he was asked and sometimes throwing a temper tantrum. Rewards and coaxing had been tried to no avail. It was thought his behaviour was getting worse. His mother was fearful that because he was so uncooperative he would run away from her when they were going to nursery.

Solution-focused response

The main focus at this stage is to converse with those in the problem situation in order that space is created for alternative stories to emerge, which in turn can lead to the planning of different ways of acting, i.e. 'doing something different' (de Shazer 1995). In my work I always attempt to introduce the idea of wonder, about which Dahlberg (1999), who is involved in an Early Education project in Stockholm, said:

'Wonder is the primary prerequisite for experience and learning, as many philosophers from Aristotle onwards have recognised, so we must take care of children's wonder about the surrounding world.'

(Dahlberg, 1999)

In order that children are encouraged to wonder, parents and teachers too have to be able to become curious. Solution-focused approaches can facilitate this process. With this in mind I say 'I am wondering about N [pause] and this quality of strong-mindedness that he shows.'

The conversation led us down a path of wondering about the strengths of this quality. The conversation about strong-mindedness and the different types of responses which can be expected from people, opened up the possibility of re-scripting a different story for N. Given an opportunity to reflect on their unique experience, staff and parent were able to begin a process of collaboration, which impacted on the child. When asked if people of their acquaintance who showed this quality like to be told what to do without being prepared, laughter ensued, followed by more stories ....

Experienced teachers who work with pupils who have EBD know the value of preparing children for change of activity. This is known as sign-posting. Subsequently, the idea of perceiving N as showing qualities of strong-mindedness and preferring to know things in advance (sign-posting), involved the parent and staff in changing their thinking and language. The story of N changed. The language of the parent and staff changed. In practice this meant that when the child was expected to change activity, the teacher and parent, in recognition of his possible preference to be prepared, experimented with language which accommodated this preference.

'When it is tidy-up time, N, will we see you helping Melanie or fixing the books?

'When you are going home safely and holding mum's hand, will you be skipping or hopping?'

The work can be further developed by the use of the Golden Book, which consolidates the collaborative work already established with the staff and parent. The staff, on hearing the concerns of N's mum about walking home safely, listened to the story of his mum's preferred future and incorporated elements into their drama and storytelling activities. Thus, nursery staff and parent devised stories which were relevant to their local situation, using familiar language and a local landscape. Stories and songs about going home from nursery safely and going shopping were integrated into the curriculum. The language of the school and the home fused in a way which was wonderful.

Parents, once included in this process and encouraged in their natural story telling abilities, can become adept at solution-focused work and provide an opportunity for professionals to work in partnership with them. It has been my privilege to work with parents who, when encouraged, filled the Golden Books with celebratory stories of their days with their children. One mother said that the Books meant so much to her that even several years after the work, she still finds it enjoyable to re-read them.

Instead of writing a commentary/critique on the work done I tend to wonder about the possibilities for future work. I wonder about ways in which solution-focused work in the nursery could enhance parent partnership, about the possibilities of the nursery nurses and the parents whom I met developing their interest in solution-focused approaches. The way in which nursery schools already work with parents in respectful ways means that their adoption of solution-focused work would go some way to preventing future exclusions.

Solution-focused group work in schools: maths meets therapy

A major problem facing class teachers with a pupil categorized as having EBD was related to group work. A common complaint against the consultancy model of support is that it relies on advice-giving and fails to take account of the reality of the classroom situation. An accepted role of the behaviour support teacher involves working with pupils in areas of curriculum so that the referred pupil learns 'more appropriate ways of behaving.' This ordinarily engages support teachers in processes of curriculum hurdling, i.e. helping pupils to become more proficient at a particular task or social skills training. A solution-focused or narrative approach celebrates difference, curiosity and multiple perspectives. Applying such principles to the learning situation requires the powerful to become more uncertain. The learning situation is seen as a collaborative venture characterized by consensus, curiosity and respect. 'Rules', rather than being pre-ordained from on high become co-constructed and attempts are made to accommodate different perspectives. How we learn becomes as important as what we learn and respect for each other is given a strong emphasis, as is the notion of different ways of approaching learning.

The group work which I do involves a referred pupil working on a curricular task such as maths games or problem-solving activities. Before beginning curricular work I become involved in a discussion with the group about the class rules. The discussion centres on the word 'respect' and its meanings for us in relation to our preferred way of teaching and learning. Thus, I might say:

'When I am working with a group I respect the voice of every child in that group. Which class rule will help me in my work?'

In general, pupils respond favourably to the notion that teachers wish to respect them and encourage their learning. The role of language in relation to fostering respectful ways of working is highlighted.

'What are you doing when you are respecting the other pupils' right to be heard?

'When someone makes a mistake what will you do that shows you respect them?'

With permission from the referred pupil, I write in the Golden Book an account of how he/she learned something new. I also document how the pupil respected the rights of others to be safe and to work. I have found that when children are consulted in ways which are respectful and which celebrate their unique contribution, then the results can have profound effects. The contribution of schools to fostering resilience in children is widely accepted and it was my privilege to work with others who have a duty of care for children. They became interested in using solution-focused language in contexts other than school. I refer to social workers and foster carers who support those pupils who are looked after and accommodated by their local authorities. We worked with the children in ways which put their views at the centre of the agenda. I agree with Marshall(1999) who notes,

> 'We need to engage with foster children to ensure that their real
> needs are taken account of. We need an agenda set by them.'
>
> (Marshall, 1999, p.371)

In the natural setting of school, the voice of children can be acknowledged and adults can become involved in supporting their efforts to challenge difficulties.

Commentary

Given that school is recognised as having an ameliorating influence on children who are facing difficulties in their lives, I wonder about the possibility of using solution-focused approaches to foster collaborative work with other agencies which have responsibility for children. It is my hope that parents, teachers and others who are interested in justice for children will be afforded opportunities to learn from each other so that those children who are in danger of being excluded are given a voice about their 'preferred futures'. The possibility of schools becoming 'Communities of Acknowledgement', as Michael White envisaged them, may indeed become a reality.

CHAPTER TEN

'A THOUGHTFUL PROCESS'

BY MARGARET KAY

Introduction

This chapter sets out to describe solution-focused approaches to working with children of primary school age who are seen as troubled or as having social, emotional or behavioural difficulties (SEBD). These difficulties will normally be perceived to be of an extreme nature by the time the child is referred to our service as, through the educational psychologist (EP), other interventions will already have been tried. The work of our team has been to maintain the SEBD child in mainstream education, and in the past ten years this has proved successful in that most of the children referred to our service, often with a history of exclusion and permanent exclusion a possibility, are maintained in mainstream schools.

The EP, having worked with the school, refers the child to a consultative group of psychologists and, when appropriate, the child is referred to our service. There is a referral meeting at which the EP, head teacher, class teacher and perhaps social worker are present. They present the current situation regarding the child in school.

Many children with whom we work have either compulsory or voluntary social work support and some have been referred to the Child and Family service (Child Psychiatry). This makes links with our colleagues in other agencies an essential part of our work. The members of the team have in common the fact that we are all teachers who have developed eclectic ways of working. Some have developed holistic approaches, others are trained counsellors, while my colleague, Catherine McGlone, and I have an interest in and have attended numerous courses in solution-focused and narrative ways of working. This work is of a systemic nature; I work with the parent/carer, the teacher/school and the child.

My work is peripatetic and typically I will be working with between six and nine children while monitoring the progress of a few others. Initially, most of the children who are referred to our team have little choice, as it has often been made clear to their families that if this intervention does not take place then the child will not be able to remain in his/her present school. However, we also work with children when a school or a parent is concerned about withdrawn or other behaviours which are not necessarily disruptive.

Developing practice

While studying psychology I became aware of various schools of thought and although I have seen very interesting work done using a behaviourist approach, this for me has proved fairly unproductive, since I am interested in giving voice to the child and am wary of setting up rewards which can serve further to label an already well-highlighted child. The children I work with are often very hurt and when I give them a biscuit it is not contingent upon behaviour but because we are having a chat and drink of tea or juice.

In the course of completing a counselling qualification which was largely informed by psychodynamic theory, I found the process of interpreting what is going on in someone's life to be intrusive and decided not to pursue this in my work. The Humanistic, Person-Centred approach of Carl Rogers fitted best with how I wanted to work and led to my interest in solution-focused work and in the post-modern collaborative approaches to working with others which developed in the later years of the twentieth century. This coincided with my interest in Liberation Theology and the work of the South American educator Paulo Freire.

My practice of solution-focused work has been informed by my reading of the American Brief Therapists de Shazer, Berg, Miller, Durrant and Dolan and by the London Brief Therapy Practice (BTP). It has also been influenced by the many workshops run by the BTP which I have attended, where I listened to visiting practitioners from the US and to Michael White.

I am aware that the reader may be looking for a formula but I would emphasize that this is not a formulaic way of working.

> 'From a position of true respect, techniques per se become superfluous, as action appropriate to the situation is generated from the simple act of paying attention to what is needed.'
>
> (Simon 1996).

The quotes used in this chapter feature the words 'therapy', 'client', 'treatment' etc. These are not words I use in an educational context, but were relevant to the points being made in this chapter.

Practice

When a child is referred to us and we make an initial visit to the school, the worker will listen to the head teacher's story and make arrangements to interview the class teacher. Regular interviews with the class teacher, perhaps monthly, are an integral part of this work and teachers have evaluated this as very beneficial to their work with the referred child. These interviews give both worker and teacher the opportunity and time to reflect. Reflection time is at a premium in today's classrooms and in a class with an EBD pupil it can be impossible. At this point an arrangement may be made to come and work with the referred child in his/her class or group . The parent or carer of the child will be invited to the school. When I meet the parent I will seek an agreement on working together, usually on a weekly basis for no more than six weeks to begin with. My opening question is often, 'Why do you think we are here today?' and I listen carefully however long it takes. I explain that I will not be asking about the problem. We set out where we will work and who will be present (I prefer to work in an open area). We discuss the different tasks involved in recording success and then I begin usually by looking at exceptions. This is based on a theory:

> 'First, if it works, do more of it; and second, if it doesn't work, do something different.'

> (de Shazer 1991)

I may say:

> 'When are things going well?'
> 'When do you not get phone-calls from school?'
> 'When do you see X smiling?'
> 'Tell me about that.'

Perhaps at this point I will ask a miracle/dream question to direct the conversation towards a hopeful future, or I may use a scaling question for that purpose. If a mother is coping with an active toddler while with me, I would opt for a scaling question which would perhaps need less time to respond to and talk through.

During interviews with significant adults, I will listen respectfully to the person's story, because not to do so will invalidate their often painful experiences. This is also true of the child. I will listen, but I will not ask about the problem. I will know who the significant adults are when the child tells me, perhaps in response to these questions:

'Who will notice when things are better?'
'Who would you like to read about what you do well?'

I explain my role as working with people who are having some trouble. I usually ask about pre-session change and record this.

'The client can always be "blamed" with confidence for improvement before therapy has started.'
(Kral, R.& Kowalski, K. 1989)

I always show my notebook and explain that it is a memory aid and is not secretive, they can read it or have it read to them at any time. As well as my notebook I always have some method of recording success. It is usually a little half-jotter. Sometimes it is covered in shiny paper, especially with younger children – a Golden or Silver Book.

At the beginning I write 'This is X's book. In this book you can read kind words about what X does well.'

I do not use word praise. This work, in my opinion, has to be real. When a child completes a piece of work, it is real, in Scotland, to say 'Well done Thomas, you finished your Maths.' I do not use superlatives and never say or write 'Wow!' although I admire the work of Insoo Kim Berg, who uses 'Wow!' most effectively in an American context. This is important because a child who knows me knows that I am not a 'wow!' person and will know that, when I say 'Well done', I mean it.

When the teacher says 'Well done' and writes this in the book, it is the adult at home's homework to read this, in the child's hearing. This adult then writes about successes at home.

You can see from this that the child's story is already changing.

Again I am looking at exceptions:

When does Thomas sit calmly?

When does he respond to your instructions?

In the interest of the work being real, I think that when language is respectful and the recipient is taken into consideration, then matching language is not a problem. When asking future-orientated questions, e.g. a miracle question, I will ask:

'What words will you say when you see Thomas smile?'

Then I write in the Golden/Silver book 'When Thomas' mum sees him smile she will say "That's lovely Tom."'

When work is about people's ability to solve their own problems, it is important to validate their ways of telling their story – this makes it easier for them to believe that they know what will work for them.

Paulo Freire tried to resolve this issue in the following way:

> 'When giving a talk among poor people of Chile it came to question time and he faced a dead silence. He, who believed in empowering the poor, had reduced them to silence by the sheer weight of his own learning. So he challenged them to a game. He would first ask a question, and then they would ask him one. They would write the scores on a board: if one side did not know the answer the other side would score.
>
> 'First question: "What is the Socratic Maieutic?"
>
> ' General Guffawing.
>
> '"Score one for me. Now it's your turn to ask me a question," I said. There was some whispering, and one of them tossed a question:
>
> '"What's a contour curve?"
>
> 'I couldn't answer and marked down one to one.
>
> '"What importance does Hegel have in Marx's thought?"
>
> 'Two to one.
>
> '"What is soil-liming?"
>
> 'Two to two.
>
> 'And so it went on until the score was ten/ten. By this game the peasants began to realise that they did know lots of things. But they were not convinced that their knowledge would be real, valued in the academy, and they would be right.'
>
> (Freire 1996, cited in Grey 2000)

Working with girls

The children referred to us are usually boys. This is not to say that there are many less girls in the SEBD category, rather that boys with such difficulties tend to be disruptive and girls on the whole tend to be withdrawn. So in the tradition of the Scottish expression 'the greetin' wean gets fed first,' we mostly work with boys.

In our society, it still seems less acceptable for a girl to act in an aggressive or violent manner than for a boy. It has, therefore, been our experience that it is more difficult to find a group or community for troubled girls in their own class or school than for boys.

We brought these girls together one afternoon per week and we decided to make this work completely solution-focused with a narrative bent. That is, we combined our already developing solution-focused approach with Michael White's telling and re-telling of the preferred narrative. We came together and we told our stories or listened to others, and I hope to describe how this developed into a community of support where girls supported one another and the product generalised into the school context.

When working with a group of girls we found that they were experts in encouraging one another when a difficulty was expressed.

'That happened to me, it's horrible.'

We would ask questions such as 'What words will you say when someone is unkind?' as part of a child's plan for dealing with difficulties in school. The other members of the group would be part of this and would offer suggestions. The aim of this work was to make the child aware that she had a voice. However, we were also aware that building the voice of the child could have implications for her safety. This will be discussed further in the chapter. In the work we did with this group, we became very interested in the voice of the child or teacher or parent and in the implications for interactive work in keeping the child safe. There was much humour in this group, e.g.

Child: 'Knock '
Me: 'Who's there?'
Child: 'Disease'
Me: 'Disease who?'
Child: 'Disease wee trousers fit you?'

> 'Narrative practices not only provide options for therapists to join in the identification and the exploration of the little events and acts that contradict the problem-saturated stories of persons' lives, but also provide the opportunity for therapists to join with these persons in celebrating the significance of these events and acts. The joy that is had by therapists in doing so contributes directly to their experience of their work, and invariably flows into other domains of their lives.'

(White 1997)

Words

This group became a community of support in which the girls used kind words to commend and compliment one another. These words were written in the individual child's Golden Book as another example and reminder to that child and to others of her success. e. g. Angela said, 'I'm glad you managed to get your work done yesterday Karen and I'm glad your teacher liked it,' or Jane said, 'Good luck with your plan for this week, Helen .'

The words used in developing solution-focused interactive practice, where we looked at co-authoring the child's success along with that of parents, carers and teachers, become increasingly important. For example, in looking at a hopeful future it is important to make the language unconditional. In asking a miracle question our practice was to move away from the 'if' to 'when':

> 'When you waken up, who will you see?'
> 'When you see Mum what will she be doing?'

Or in a scaling question:

> 'When you get to four and a half, what will Mum write in your book?'

When a child's name is first given to me I am sometimes asked by the school, 'What will you do?' Truthfully, I must answer 'I don't know.' There is no recipe and as I write I am aware that there would seem to be a number of techniques which would ensure a solution-focused approach. This is not the case. Berg (1994) calls solution-focused questions 'expressions of an attitude, a posture and a philosophy, saying that no amount of technique will disguise the therapist's lack of listening skills, lack of faith in the client's ability to know what is good for him, and miscomprehension of the philosophical thinking that generates questions.'

A systemic approach

The child does not exist in a vacuum. He/she is part of a system in which change in one part will have implications in others. The system I work with consists of the child, the parent and the teacher. I have a choice of working with the parent, the teacher and child separately or together or a in combination of both. It has often proved successful to bring the parent and teacher together, sometimes with the child. I would, however, caution that while there is any conflict between a parent and the school, it is prudent to work with the parent separately, at least initially. However, the parent and teacher often have the same kind wishes for the child and the child can benefit from hearing these first hand. It has been our experience that when using scaling questions in systemic practice, very often the figures arrived at by individuals separately are the same or very close.

Recording stories of success and support

> 'Clients are given the opportunity to comment on the process of helping (critiquing, appreciating or coaching) and to share their expertise with others, thereby elevating their status from passive

needy recipients to active expert contributors.'

(O'Hanlon 1998)

Although I keep my own brief notes of the process in which the participants are invited to share, the unfolding story of the child's success belongs to him/her. Once, I commended the Golden Book to someone from another agency who worked with the same father and son as I did. At this point the father could not see any success in his son's life and undermined the Golden Book. Thus, we could not use such a method of recording the child's considerable success. Instead, I used an audio tape to record my voice, the head teacher's voice, the teacher's and the social worker's voices, telling stories of the child's successes. Eventually the child's voice was taped as he recorded, for the benefit of other boys I might be working with, how it was that he was so successful in school now that he was challenging 'angry'. This spoken document is a powerful reminder of earlier successes and the possibility of future success, confirming what is going well now and what can go well again. It is a part of the child's story. It has become part of his/her history.

It is also part of the school's story. I have heard a head teacher whose first words to me were 'I do not want this child in my school,' say at a multi-agency meeting 'If this child gets accommodated by the Local Authority, you must ensure that he gets transport to this school. it is the best place for him.'

In this account of how I work, I have indicated some aspects of successful solution-focused interactions in a Scottish primary school setting. It is necessary to say that when working with young children, the well-being of the child is paramount and should I feel uneasy about a child's safety, I confer with my colleagues in social work. Ideally, our work will be 'joined-up'. This is more likely now that, in the spirit of the Children Scotland Act 1995, all Local Authority workers have a responsibility for the child. There are still some tensions between education and social work, but I am privileged to have been part of some splendid multi-agency work.

Considerations

I have talked briefly of gender issues in relation to the girls' group. I cannot divorce this from issues of poverty, race or culture. They come under the heading, 'power'. We are part of the culture of power in which we live and work. We are privileged that people interact with us in the ways that they do. We are part of the process. We are also changed when we collaborate rather than advise, co-author rather than interpret. As educators we belong to one of the most apparently privileged groups in any society. We decide what knowledge will be sought after.

In encouraging the child's voice am I doing just that, or am I encouraging the voice that the school wants to hear? Perhaps the child needs to know that he/she has a voice. This may also be true of the teacher. Using a solution-focused approach can encourage all parts of a system to think.

> 'As public and informed intellectuals, teachers have an opportunity to make organic connections with the historical traditions that provide them with a voice, history, and sense of belonging .'
>
> (Giraux 1997)

Working in education, with people who are experiencing or have experienced pain, is a thoughtful process. We must question our role as part of an educational system in a first world society.

> 'I certainly think that the process of self-formation, which includes cognition and emotion, which includes knowing and understanding and being, is crucial. The formative process through interaction, which is what we mean by education, is not only the means, but it is the result hoped for.'
>
> (Wexler 1994)

Some voices

'When a client feels that important information is being withheld, he or she is compelled to guess the therapist's thoughts. This guessing, which we have called counter-diagnosis (Furman & Ahola, 1987), is an activity where the client tries to find out what the therapist actually believes is the true cause of the client's problematic behaviour.'

Solution-focused narrative work can only be done in an open way. I am careful to explain what my notes are about and frequently read aloud what I have written. No one will believe that he/she has the solution if I am saying one thing and writing or thinking another.

I am at pains to respect the anonymity of those with whom I work. I have never worked with a boy called Thomas and I have changed all manner of other examples so as to make them unidentifiable. Because of my concerns as a member of a small population, and given the sometimes extreme nature of the behaviours of the children I work with, I will not illustrate my practice by a case study but will illuminate aspects of solution-focused approaches in relation to outcomes which are real, albeit out of context.

In recognition of the systemic nature of this work, a solution-focused term is the 'ripple_effect'. This describes changes in any part of the system as a result of working in another. The following will illuminate this.

A small boy's disruptive behaviour was discussed by a head teacher and confirmed by the class teacher, who told us it was necessary for someone to supervise her class while she went out to the yard to prise this child away from his grandmother. In the child's dream or miracle he described how he would not be 'fingin' pencils and books around the class. I asked him 'How will you manage that?' He said that when people made him mad he would put his head on the desk and count to ten. At my next visit, when I asked 'So what's been going well then?' he said 'I didn't fling anything about.' While I commended him on this, I made a mental note to check his perception with the class teacher's. Her story corroborated what he had said and she also commented that she had not had to go out to the yard to bring the child in separately for the whole week. (This had been the class teacher's dream.)

So, although the yard issue had not been directly addressed, changes had occurred. This is what is meant by the 'ripple effect'.

Bereavement

A father died in most tragic circumstances leaving two young children, one only months old. The elder daughter was referred to our team because of aggressive and disruptive behaviour in and out of class, resulting in her being sent home on a regular basis. The school was in a rural setting which meant that Mum and her baby had to come a considerable distance to collect the elder child. The school felt bad because of the bereavement and the distance but had to consider issues of safety for other children. Mum had been seeing a psychiatric nurse but had terminated the intervention because she felt labelled by this. The first meeting with Mum happened by chance when I was in school for another reason. We arranged to meet on a weekly basis at a time which did not mean another journey for Mum. Sometimes she brought her baby, sometimes she had a sitter. I would describe her face as wanting to cry and this is what she often did initially. She talked about her husband's death, but also collaborated with the future-orientated, hopeful dialogue. Her dream was that her daughter would be in school all day, that there would be no phone calls and that her daughter would return home independently with her classmates. In this case, I had no doubt that Mum was the client and although I worked with her daughter in class, I put changes down to the 'ripple effect'.

This was not 'brief' therapy: the process took almost a year, during which time the mother and daughter began to smile and took part in a parent-and-child group where Mum supported other families and where her daughter answered questions such as 'So, tell us what you do instead of getting mad?' and 'How do you manage that?'

However, when she was asked 'What did you think was most useful to you about our work together?' Mrs. K answered, 'The fact that you were always there for my daughter.' So be it! The reason for the success must be what Mrs. K thought.

In another school, staff were distressed by the very severe illness of a young mother and the disturbed behaviour of her very young daughter, who was unable to focus on a task, wandered about the class and became very easily upset. The school was torn between keeping the parents informed and further distressing them.

My work was with the parents, who thought that they were 'doing something wrong' with their daughter and had been tearful at school. I set up a Silver Book in which both parents, the teacher and grandmother wrote about the little child's success.

'Angela got dressed without being asked this morning.'

'Angela helped her sister to do a jigsaw.'

Life became calmer through focusing on what was going well and future orientating everyone's thoughts by asking a miracle or scaling question.

Where physical and emotional pain have such an unrelenting presence in people's lives, it is easy to lose sight of hope. This way of working will not take away the pain but shows that it can co-exist with a hopeful future.

> 'One does not become a solution-focused therapist simply by learning to ask an exception question or taking a break before giving an intervention. Rather, becoming Solution Focused is a process of cultivating a world view and a consciousness from which respectful, effective behaviours can flow and that invite and invoke the context in which clients can discover and recover who they are.'
>
> (Simon, Dvorah 1996)

Significant adults

This final example of a piece of work will show that by using a solution-focused/narrative approach it is possible to work through the adults without directly engaging the child. Several agencies were already involved with a family prior to a child's arrival at a new school where difficulties soon became obvious. I spoke with the head teacher and the class teacher, the Special Educational Needs (SEN) auxiliary and the social worker. It was agreed that while child psychiatry was being applied for, I would do solution-focused work with the mother and school. I set up a Golden Book and met Mum on a regular basis. There were also regular interviews with the head teacher and class teacher. We looked at exceptions, miracle questions and scaling. The book went home every night. The very beautiful handwriting of both the mother and the class teacher made the Golden Book a work of art. This child has settled in class and has regulars playtimes in the yard with other children.

On two occasions I have interviewed the child with Mum and the SEN auxiliary. I asked how it was that things had changed and was told that it was good that Mum could read about the hard work done in school. This case turned around relatively quickly. Although the child is the person referred to our service, the work done can be directed through others. This is also a way of engaging significant adults in thinking about the process.

Reflection

The stories I have told, in order to illuminate my practice, are taken from my work in schools. In each case, the child had been or would be excluded from school. The process of reflecting with colleagues from other agencies has been a hopeful way of developing inter-agency trust. This must be of interest to all of us who are involved in social inclusion which calls for multi-agency approaches.

Reflection is an integral part of becoming solution-focused because the interactive solution-focused process is a thoughtful one. In sharing time, space and words with the child, the teacher and the parent, a process in which voices are often strengthened, the voice of the worker is also changed.

This worker has learned a great deal from the families and teachers who have been her co-workers and her solution-focused ways of working are different today from they were yesterday and from they will be tomorrow.

CHAPTER ELEVEN

CONSULTATION:
A SOLUTION-FOCUSED APPROACH

BY PATSY WAGNER AND ELIZABETH GILLIES

Introduction

This chapter offers a description of a consultation model of work as practised by the authors who are educational psychologists (EPs) based in two local education authorities (LEAs) in England, one in Surrey and one in Kensington and Chelsea. We start by describing the context for the work of the EP and then explain what we mean by consultation, school consultation, what it offers and the outcomes of working this way. Following this, we explore the role of a solution-focused approach within the consultation model, before moving on to an illustration of solution-focused consultation through a piece of individual casework. Included in the Appendices is an example of an initial consultation form (Appendix 1) and preparation questions for the teacher prior to an initial consultation and then for a follow up consultation. (Appendix 2)

We have found solution-focused thinking a highly respectful approach that values the things that people bring with them into the consultation, e.g. their strengths, resources, previous successes. It is also a flexible model that can be used at individual, group and organisational levels. We have many examples of successes with individual cases, with classroom groups and in planning and implementing projects, e.g. a mediation service. We are both of the view that teachers working in schools could use this approach and see it as a development in our work. Consequently, although the chapter is written from an EP perspective, we expect that it will have relevance and interest for all adults working in schools who are interested in solution-focused ideas and practice.

The context of the educational psychologist's work

The government directs the state education system mainly through the Department for Education and Employment (DfEE). Schools in the state sector are obliged to achieve outcomes that are prescribed by the government and its agencies. Schools are inspected to ensure that they achieve the outcomes, which are particular targets for pupil achievement. LEAs, which were set up originally to be supportive to local schools, are increasingly expected to ensure that all the schools in their area are compliant with government targets. Schools and LEAs which do not meet the targets are 'named and shamed' and may be closed down or taken over. The pressure on teachers and schools, currently, from both the local and the national context is, therefore, considerable, increasing and unrelenting.

In this very pressured and compliance-oriented climate, the child or young person who has learning or behavioural difficulties which might affect the school's performance may be seen as an unwanted burden. Consequently, teachers' visions and principles of teaching and learning which spring from a desire to help all children and young people achieve are placed under considerable pressure and strain. In such a climate and context, the EP may be seen as a possible solution to the problem, i.e. the EP may be encouraged to assess and diagnose difficulties which confirm that the child is beyond the expertise and/or the resources of the school.

The EP is located in a complex local context, a web of inter-relating systems and sub-systems, role relationships, expectations and attributions.

The expectations of EPs are, typically, for clinical styles of assessment. This results in the EP's role becoming one that focuses primarily on assessment, diagnosis and prescription. However, this way of working is not valued by teachers and schools since it does not help in making a real difference to teachers' concerns. That is, about how to help a pupil make progress with some aspect of his/her learning or social behaviour in school. Hence, there has been long-term dissatisfaction with the traditional role of the EP (Gillham 1978). Teachers, schools and EPs (Lewis 1997) share this dissatisfaction. Thus, the challenge for EPs has been to find a way of developing collaborative relationships with teachers and parents, which enhance the solution-building capacities of school, teacher, pupil and parent. An approach based on a consultation model has provided a creative solution to this problem.

powerful techniques, such as externalising the problem, which help people to distance themselves from troubling aspects of their behaviour. NT has been shown to be extremely useful in working with children and in helping them to work effectively on a range of problems both in schools and in the family in constructive and creative ways (Winslade and Monk 1999; Morgan 1999).

Social constructionism

SC challenges us to examine the way that we perceive the world. It proposes that the way we perceive and understand the world depends on where and when in the world we live rather than any objective reality. It considers that our understanding of the world is a product of social processes and interactions and that language is highly significant and powerful in the social construction of our understanding and of the way that we think and see things (Burr 1995). The relevance and use of such an approach is enormous. For example, SC provides us with a framework of ideas for thinking about and developing a critique of models of psychology and practice and their relevance (or otherwise) to the current historical and cultural context; the deficit discourse of Special Educational Needs (SEN) – the way that much of SEN has been constructed and amplified; how it is maintained by perceptions about problems as located within the person; the associated styles of language and practices, etc. From such critiques we are more able to be exploratory and imaginative about aspects which seem intractable.

What does consultation offer?

Consultation offers to work with the person most concerned about their cause for concern, and to do this with a major focus on the context in which the concern arises (the school and classroom). The aim is to work together to bring about change. In school, consultations take place mainly with teachers. Children or young people and their parents are involved in contributing perspectives and insights to the search for solutions when the concern is over an individual. With pre-schoolers, consultation is carried out primarily with parents in the home setting, with links to the school setting when this is appropriate.

Consultation offers many advantages:

- to help the person most concerned to find solutions to their concerns;
- to work collaboratively with the person most concerned;
- to use frameworks for working together that are clear and supportive to the collaborative work;
- to work in an open-handed way with frameworks and ideas;
- actively to engage with the ideas and views of teachers, parents and chil-

dren and their involvement in developing strategies and solutions;
- to use appropriate psychological models and related strategies and techniques in a manner that is constructive and which makes an effective contribution towards change;
- to work at different levels – of the individual, the group and the organisational – as appropriate to the expressed needs of the school.

What is the evidence that consultation works?

School consultation developed in the 1970s in the United States of America. A range of benefits have been found in that context from using a consultation approach to solving problems in schools, rather than a referral system. Representative findings were:

- student referral rates dropped;
- client gains generalised to other children in the same class as a result of increased teacher effectiveness;
- underachieving children whose teachers and parents received consultation achieved significantly better later;
- teachers found problems to be less serious;
- teachers' problem-solving skills were enhanced by exposing them to either live or modelled consultation interactions;
- teachers reported increased professional skills;
- teachers' attributions for the causes of problems changed from internal-to-the-child to interactional in nature, recognising the importance of ecological factors such as instructional methods and other students;
- using psychologists in consultative roles has provided enhanced learning, psychological wellness, and skills (From Gutkin and Curtis 1990)

A number of EPSs in a range of LEA contexts in England, Scotland and Wales have already undertaken whole-service training and continuing development strategies in the area of consultation. Consultation has been reviewed and evaluated and shows clearly positive and enduring effects. These effects were presented at two National Consultation conferences which took place at the London Institute of Education in the autumn of 1998 and included:

- improvements in outcomes for children in terms of behaviour, learning, achievement and social-emotional development;
- improvements in parental confidence and competence in helping children with their behaviour, learning, achievement and social-emotional development;
- fewer referrals for statutory assessment by schools;
- reduced statementing rates in LEAs;

- increased parental satisfaction with the work carried out by the EP with the school in relation to children who cause concern in school;
- increased parental and teacher satisfaction with the work carried out by the EP jointly with school and parents;
- improved home-school relations over children who cause concern;
- increased teacher confidence, competence and skill in working with children, especially with children who show SENs;
- improvements in levels of achievement in schools as shown, for example, in SAT results.

Other EP services which have adopted the model report similar trends.

What does solution-focused thinking offer to school consultation?

Consultation offers a framework for conversations between EPs and teachers, parents, pupils and other professionals using social psychology to help in making sense of what is happening and in exploring solutions. Given that the core of consultation is a conversation, then the question that follows is: What will the conversation be about? Typically, in school consultation, the teacher comes with a concern. Often it is about a child or young person who is causing concern because of his/her learning or social behaviour. The concern is, for the teacher, something she wishes she did not have. As EPs we then have choices about how we will talk about it and what we will talk about together. Employing the assumptions of solution-focused thinking leads us into conversations about resources, goals and exceptions. The idea that change can occur is promoted through imagining, pretending and experimenting.

The following are some ways in which solution-focused principles have been effectively used in consultation. Clearly, this in not an exhaustive list, nor is the way the examples are presented intended to create the impression that this is a simple task. And, most importantly, solution-focused consultation is about believing that others do have the resources and skills to create change. The questions do not stand by themselves. This way of thinking and the questioning skills are both needed to create change.

Making the most of time prior to the consultation

A solution-focused approach makes use of the possibility for change before the first session. Questions about looking for changes and differences are therefore used. Similarly, EPs using a consultation model can provide questions, as prompts, for a teacher's thinking prior to the consultation. The questions begin the process of consultation by starting to focus the teacher's thoughts on goals and exceptions, and by reminding her of her own strengths and resources in finding strategies and solutions. Typical questions are:

'What do you hope to get from the consultation?'
'If this consultation is helpful what will be different?'
'What strategies have you tried that have been effective?'
'What effects have you noted?'
'When does the behaviour you want happen?'
'What is different about these times?'

Beginning the consultation: clarifying concerns and promoting a solution-focused approach

It is often difficult to resist discussing the problem in great detail. However, connecting with the person over possible solutions is important at an early stage of the consultation. This will create a context of competence and be the start of the 'yes and ...'. Yes there are difficulties and there are also successes.

'What concerns you?'
'Tell me something that is working.'

It is then important to encourage positive and optimistic goals. Referring to the stated aim of the consultation, 'What do you hope to get from the consultation?' and then to ask 'and what else?' is useful to uncover all their goals.

'How do you want things to change?'
'What will he/she be doing differently when things have changed?'
'What will others be doing differently?'
'What else?'
'How could this consultation be useful?'
'How will you know this consultation has been useful?'

Sometimes a teacher may respond to the above by saying that they would like to see the pupil not doing what causes concern. In this situation the miracle question is extremely useful.

'Suppose, you go home, and you go to sleep tonight, and while asleep a miracle happens. The issues you brought here are solved. But you don't know that the miracle has happened. When you wake up tomorrow morning, how will you discover the miracle has occurred?'

(de Shazer 1988)

This question provides a way of exploring in some detail how things might be different through the device of the supposed miracle and can introduce some humour into what might feel to the teacher to be an oppressive concern. It also allows the teacher to think differently, without the teacher feeling that the degree of their concern is not acknowledged or understood.

Exploring perceptions and the possibilities for change

At this stage in the consultation, exploration of perceptions and issues are helpful and important. Asking about life without the problem, establishing areas of competence and exploring effective strategies help develop solution-focused thinking. Staying alert to ideas and details which could suggest a solution and which could be built upon further is also important (Durrant 1993).

> 'When faced with this sort of issue before, what did you do that worked?'
> 'How did you do that?'
> 'How could you do that again?'
> 'How do you cope now?'
> 'What have you done that has been successful?'
> 'What effects have you noted?'
> 'What is different about those times?'
> 'How do you explain the difference?'
> 'What helped you to do that?'
> 'What will you be doing when there is no longer a problem?'
> 'Who will be the first person to notice?'
> 'What will that person notice?'

In our work with concerns at the individual, group and organisational level we have found that asking teachers to use a rating scale of 0-10 seems to help objectify the concern. It appears to create a sense of distance from extremely emotive circumstances, for example, where a pupil or whole class behaviour is causing disruption. It seems to help the teacher stand back and think about when things have been better. It helps the teacher reflect upon the features of the situation that may be relevant in terms of a solution and think about the contribution that he/she has made to improve previous similar situations that caused concern.

Scaling questions can be used in many ways. In particular, we have found them helpful in exploring steps toward achieving goals.

> 'What would life be like at X + 1?'
> 'What is the highest point you have reached?'
> 'When was that?'
> 'What was different about that time?'

'What else was different?'
'How did that effect the situation?'
'How did you do that?'
'On a scale of 0-10 how close are you to the miracle?

Scaling can also be one way of noticing change between consultations. We have found some useful questions to capture the important points in the consultation and then to focus on what will happen next. Encouraging our partner in the consultation to do this piece of work continues the theme of viewing them as competent individuals who can make sense of their situation.

'What ideas have you developed during the consultation?'
'What else?'
'How might these affect what you do next?'
'How close are we to making some plans?'
'What else do we need to consider?'
'What would it take to put these ideas into action in your classroom?'
'What might you try out and what might be a first step?'
'What could you do differently tomorrow?'
'If you were to do this as an experiment, how would that be different?'

Ending the consultation

We think of consultations as punctuations in the work of the teacher, when the teacher can stand back and spend some time thinking about overcoming the concern in a different sort of way. The time following consultation is the time when teachers might experiment. We encourage noticing exceptions and engaging in experimentation as an outcome of consultation.

An effect of consultation is that the teacher has a new way of conceptualising the concern and solution to the concern opening possibilities for further exploration and change. We work with an interactionist and systemic model of psychology and aim, therefore, through the range of questions that we ask, to explore the interactions between the person and the situation and the interrelating systems that impinge on the person. We notice that through the process of consultation, the teacher feels more confident in being able to manage his/her concerns. This is a good measure of how the consultation is progressing. Scaling questions are useful in checking confidence levels and can also be a useful way of ending the consultation.

'How do you make sense of (the concern) now?'
'What other explanations do you have?'

'Which, do you think, make the most sense now?'
'What strategies does that suggest?'
'What might you do?'
'What might you ask others to do?'
'On a scale of 0-10 how confident are you about trying out
these ideas?'

In our work as EP s we see schools and teachers on the receiving end of relentless demands for change. We see little that is appreciative of the efforts that teachers make. Consequently, the idea of compliments is one that we feel is essential. In the consultation model our conversations make this possible. We aim to encourage teachers to celebrate their successes and acknowledge their contribution to finding solutions to difficulties in school through providing constructive feedback.

Follow-up consultations

Continuing the focus on solutions is an effective theme for any further consultations. A useful mnemonic to remember to do this is EARS.

Elicit what has worked and the exceptions. 'What has gone well?'
Amplify the changes. 'How did you manage to achieve that?'
Reinforce the success 'Who else noticed the change?'
Start again ... only if you need to.

An example of school based solution-focused consultation

A nine-year-old girl, Elaine, was discussed during a visit to a primary school. She had recently become reluctant to leave her mother in the morning when they arrived in school. She experienced tantrums and her mother had great difficulty in leaving her in school in floods of tears. Sometimes, Elaine would run out of school after her mother. These times were very difficult for the teacher in trying to restrain Elaine while also managing the rest of the class.

Overall, the piece of work involved three consultations and, of course, all the work in-between the consultations. The initial consultation was with the teacher and Special Educational Needs co-ordinator .The further two consultations took place with the school and both of Elaine's parents.

What helped us move toward solutions?

Identifying goals

The participants were able to state what they wanted to see happen. The miracle question helped them visualize what would be happening when the problem was overcome, e.g. Elaine coming to school with a smile on her face; staff being able to manage the transitions better for themselves and Elaine. The parents also were able to express what they wanted – to be more in control of the situation. On a scale of 0-10 they were at 4 when asked about how close they were to their goal.

Exploring change and possibilities

The school staff were able to explore some of the exceptions e.g. 'sometimes she would run out.' Why did she sometimes stay in class? They were able to think about the times when Elaine already smiled and then how they could encourage more of this to happen. How were they coping with the difficulties in the morning? The 'coping' question is a useful one to use when people need to remind themselves of the skills they are using in difficult situations. What were the effective strategies they were using? What was the best way to support Elaine's parents, especially her mother? How could they do more of this?

The parents were able to report what they were doing that put them at 4 in the scale of control of the situation. At this point on the scale the parents were more or less in agreement of how they would manage Elaine. What had been the highest point? What did they do to achieve this? The scaling question was used during the second school-and-family consultation as a means to monitor progress. In the second session the parents reported that they were now at 8 on the 'control' scale. The parents felt that they were working more as a team; they were clearer about what they expected Elaine to do, they were more able to relax and not expect tantrums from Elaine. They talked in detail about a family outing which had, surprisingly, gone very well for them,. This had been an important time for the family and a huge success. This discussion of a highly successful occasion was encouraged.

Elaine felt able to come into school without tears. She had made some new friends. She had even willingly participated in activities out-of-school on her own. The school staff and parents felt they now had many more opportunities to praise Elaine. How could all involved continue to be aware of and encourage these changes?

Constructive feedback

At the end of each consultation everyone was given time to reflect on what had been discussed. Positive comments focused on skills and resources. This seemed to be vital for all involved in raising confidence in their ability to make a difference. At the end of the third consultation it was felt that there was no real need to meet again. The job had been done. The success of the consultations and the work that went on between consultations was acknowledged.

Following this final meeting a letter was sent to Elaine's parents, acknowledging their work in discovering their solutions and in being able to work through difficult times. Best wishes were offered for their future. There was no further contact.

Reflection

The above case study illustrates the importance of working in collaboration with the key people and those most interested in resolving the issues. In this particular case, all the adults involved were 'customers' who were keen to try to do something different. (See de Shazer 1988 for further reading on describing people's readiness for change.) Collaborative work of this nature and its effectiveness is facilitated by a clear understanding of how the EP can work with the school. This case study also highlights the importance of encouraging clear goal setting. By clarifying in advance the aim and possible destination of the work, it is hoped that everyone will be able to recognize such a place when it is reached. In this particular case, it was clear to everyone when there was no need for further work with the EP.

Exceptions existed in the original information presented and this provided clues to solutions already in place. A critical shift was when the content moved from 'what Elaine does that is a problem' to 'what are we all doing that is working?' One of the main successes of this work was that the school and the parents viewed the changes as being closely linked to their skills and their ability to focus on solutions. This is a major aim of consultation and highlights the contribution of the solution-focused approach to this model of work, as well as to the efficacy of the work at the individual pupil, class and organisational levels in school. That is to say, as a result of working through consultation, a teacher may feel more capable of coping with similar concerns over individuals in the future and the skills and understandings developed may generalize to their classroom practice and learning is enhanced in their schools.

How would we rate this piece of work on a scale of 0-10 and what would it take to be higher up the scale?

In light of the above reflection we think it would be at 8. Ongoing SFBT training with staff in the school would be a positive step forward to promote greater collaboration and solution-focused thinking in our work.

Appendix 1

Consultation Request

To be completed when a consultation with the educational psychologist is required.
To be retained by the school for the EP's regular school visit

To: .... Educational Psychologist

For a consultation over an individual - please begin by filling in each item in this section

Name: .... Birth date:..................... Age:.........

Sex: M/F

Parent(s)/Guardians:................................... School:.................................

.... Address: ....

Address(es): ....

....

....

Tel. no(s):..

Position in family:...................................... Class Teacher:.............................

.... or Form Tutor: ....

.... Year Group:.............................

Year team co-ordinator (if appropriate): ....

Language(s) of the home: ....

Ethnic Group:...

What concerns you about this/these pupil/s, or, what is the issue that concerns you?
....

....
Please write clearly or preferably type, in as detailed and precise a fashion as possible

What strategies and approaches have already been tried regarding your concern?
....

....

What effects have you noted? (including what has worked, when and in what circumstances)
....

....

How would you like things to change? (and what signs have you seen of any changes /differ-
ences)...

....

What do you hope to get from this consultation? ....

....

Other factors: are there any other factors or facts which seem relevant and/or important? ....

....

....

Code of practice action and /or action plus: has the school taken action under the Code of Practice, if so, what, how and when? ....

....

....

Pupil's views: what are the pupil's views of concern that has been raised and of what would help ....

....

....

Parental involvement: what is the history of parental involvement? How have they been involved? Who and when? ....

....

....

Parental views: what are the parental views of the concern that has been raised by the school? ....

....

....

Agency involvement: please check school files and record any involvement of Health Service, incl. Hospital, Clinic, Child Guidance; Social Service; Pupil Support Service; Educational Welfare Service; etc. Please note the Agency - Key Worker - Contact address - Date and period of involvement:

1. ....

....

2. ....

....

Any other comments or concerns: ....

....

....

Completed by: ....
(Name of teacher completing this consultation form)

Designation: .... Date: ....

Please make a duplicate of this Consultation Request for the Consultation Meeting with the EP

Please note that the information on this consultation will be discussed with parents and will be placed in an open filing system at the Education Psychology Service

Appendix 2

Teacher/EP consultation request

It would be helpful to consider the questions below before the arranged consultation. The time for our joint meeting will be about 30-40 minutes. Many thanks.

What do you hope to get from this consultation?
What are the child's positive abilities, interests and attitudes?
What concerns you about this pupil?
What strategies have you already tried?
What effects have you noted?
When does the behaviour you want happen?
What is different about these times?
What other relevant information would you like to share?

Teacher/EP follow-up consultation

It would be helpful to consider the questions below before the arranged consultation. The time for our joint meeting will be about 30-40 minutes. Many thanks.

What has gone well?
How did you manage to get things to work?
What do you need to do to get those things to continue to happen?
On a scaling question where 0 means most concerned and 10 means no concern, where are you now with regards to your concern?
Why are you at this point?
Are there any further concerns?
What needs to happen next?

CHAPTER TWELVE

DEVELOPING SECONDARY SOLUTIONS
EDUCATIONAL PSYCHOLOGISTS
AND SCHOOLS WORKING TOGETHER

BY HUGO STEARN & SEAN MOORE

Introduction

This chapter describes the work of two educational psychologists (EPs) who have been developing, separately and together, solution-focused ways of working within secondary schools. As a result of current social inclusion agendas at both National and LEA levels, EPs in partnership with schools have increasingly been directing their attention towards pupils who are socially isolated, labelled as 'disaffected' or who may be on the verge of exclusion. This has meant working directly with the pupils (and their families), but also with school pastoral support systems and pastoral staff to help teachers find better ways of promoting inclusion.

A traditional model of service delivery for EPs is one in which they are viewed by clients (schools, parents, LEAs) as experts able to carry out assessments and impart knowledge and advice. As a result, much EP time is spent assessing pupils and the educational context in which they find themselves, and in offering management strategies to teachers. This can sometimes have the effect of EPs becoming seen as problem owners. Our experience is that many heads of year and pastoral deputies, in particular, typically find themselves having to deal with a daily basket of 'passed-on' referrals for pupil mis-behaviours of one kind or another, and thus become problem owners them-selves. Additionally, many school pastoral systems, and staff in pastoral support roles, find themselves operating in ways which are highly problem-focused and sanction-orientated. Those schools employing named staff with responsibility for positive behaviour management and pastoral support have, perhaps, greater opportunities, both in terms of time and resources, to develop solu-tion-focused approaches, but for that to happen training and experience are often needed.

Neither 'expert' approaches nor problem ownership necessarily recognise client strengths and resources, nor generate solutions. Having received train-ing in Solution-Focused Brief Therapy (SFBT) ourselves, and being keen to move away from an 'expert' model of service delivery to a more consultative one, we began working with two targeted secondary schools in order to promote solution-focused ways of working. The resulting project was multi-layered, in that it began at an individual case-work level but developed to include training and support for key pastoral and curriculum support staff. In the pages that follow, we describe both case-work and training aspects of the project, present some information about outcomes and probable future direc-tions, and reflect on the whole process.

In applying our own knowledge and experience of solution-focused ideas we made use of the initial four-day training we received at the Brief Therapy Practice in London, and further workshops from their team arranged for our Service as a whole. We also accessed the literature for models of school-focused work, and found the books by Durrant (1995) and Rhodes and Ajmal (1995) invaluable. More recently we have also begun to explore some appli-cations of Ben Furman's work to an educational context. Ben (a Finnish psy-chiatrist) has been developing solution-focused ideas in the context of team development and organisational change.

Project development

This section describes the development of the project, up to this point in time, in two Wiltshire secondary schools (referred to as School A and School B). Both schools are large comprehensives (1000 plus pupils) within market towns, attracting a mixed population of pupils including a relatively high per-centage from the Services. In each school there is a strong curriculum support department and in one, an EBD co-ordinator with an interest in brief therapy whose resourcefulness and enthusiasm we were able to tap into.

In many ways, the development of the project and our thinking about it matches the process described by Redpath and Harker (1999), particularly in its move away from the context of the therapeutic interview to work at different levels – consultation, training, group work etc. Here, we try to build on their analysis by describing some specific outcomes as well as exploring the ideas.

In both schools the interest in the approaches, and wider application of them, was generated by individual casework by the EPs. This is, if you like, a 'bottom-up' approach! In School A, for example, two or three solution-focused pupil interviews were given per monthly EP visit over a period of about a year. The pupils were typically those seen to have significant behaviour problems and/or to be on the verge of exclusion. Because of the relatively successful nature of this work, key staff became interested in learning about how to use some of the techniques themselves. The case-work study presented at the end of the chapter provides a flavour of the context and kind of themes that emerged.

In School B, interest in training and project work was developed via a somewhat different route. Here, the EP for the school began to introduce a solution-focused teacher consultation model with case work. Curriculum support and pastoral staff became used to what are fairly typical solution-focused question frameworks about session goals and preferred futures, as well as a focus on strengths (within the child and within the system) and an exploration of the times when the problem was not happening. Initially, staff viewed the approach as a (hopefully positive) trait of the EP, perhaps as no rationale for the approach had at that point been given. After two terms of working in this way, the EP 'owned up' and subsequently offered a staff development session. As a result, an introductory workshop for curriculum support staff (teachers and learning-support assistants) took place, collectively exploring the approach, its key assumptions and some of the techniques. From that point on scaling became part of the language of the school!

An overview of the input given for the project is given in table 1. The aim of the training sessions was threefold: first, to introduce the principles and assumptions of the approach to key members of staff; second, to give them the opportunity to try out some of the techniques with each other; and third, to encourage them to think about 'how', 'where' and 'when' solution-focused tools could be applied by them in their particular roles. It should be noted that, in the training sessions, the language used was chosen to be as familiar as possible to those in teaching roles, and words such as 'therapy' were avoided where possible and replaced with terms such as 'approaches' or 'tools'. Thus we talked about 'solution-focused approaches to school problems' rather than brief therapy in schools!

	Secondary School A	Secondary School B
Initial Work ⇩	Individual pupil case-work arranged via EBD co-ordinator	Introduction of a solution-focused consultation model by EP
Developments ⇩	Half-day training for EBD co-ordinator by EP	Half-day introductory training session for curriculum support staff
Training	Half-day training session for all Heads of Year, curriculum support staff and others	Half-day training session for Senior Management Team, Heads of Year & curriculum support staff

Table A: Project development in two Wiltshire secondary schools

Initial evaluations

This section reports on how our work was evaluated. We were particularly interested in evaluating the results of the training given, both in terms of teachers' perceptions of and attitudes towards solution-focused approaches, and in terms of any resulting behavioural change by pastoral and curriculum support staff. To this end we devised both solution-focused questionnaires and structured interview formats for use a) immediately following a training session, and b) after an interval of around a month. As the school EPs, we were also able to monitor and help promote any new developments generated as a result of staff interest. Durrant (1995) and others have flagged up a key SFBT principle of how small changes in behaviour can lead to new possibilities and to further, far-reaching changes, which have positive effects on many aspects of future behaviour and functioning. We were hopeful for evidence of this to emerge! A later section of the chapter deals with such developments.

In both schools we were able to evaluate the training given in terms of three dimensions relating to staff perceptions: 'interest', 'usefulness' and 'confidence' in using the techniques. We used scaling to do this. Staff gave positive evaluations, more especially in respect of 'interest' and 'usefulness'. Lower 'confidence' levels were not surprising and, again, solution-focused frameworks were used to explore what would need to happen (in 'baby' steps) for staff to feel more confident in beginning (or continuing) to apply SFBT.

Informal follow up and staff comments suggest that the approach and methods were being seen primarily by them as tools for working with pupils with challenging behaviour, although our focus (as trainers) was on tackling 'school problems' – contextually far broader.

Mostly because of practical difficulties (the need for an EP to visit the school and carry out structured interviews at the end of term), it was only possible for one of the schools to be targeted for a 'formal' follow-up evaluation. In school B, a series of 15-20 minute interviews with 'sample' members of staff were held, covering issues ranging from 'Which solution-focused techniques have you tried so far, and with what result?' to 'What would need to happen now for you to feel that your confidence in using them was greater?' The format was, however, not rigidly adhered to, and staff were given the opportunity to explore possibilities as they arose.

Of the three specific 'named' techniques introduced to staff, and practised by them in their training (problem-free talk, the miracle question and scaling), scaling was found to be the most frequently used. Problem-free talk followed. Some staff had used more than one technique, in sequence, and a number of anecdotal examples of positive outcomes were given. No one had completed a full solution-focused interview with a student. In School B this has now happened.

Although staff in School A were not canvassed in the same way (by follow up questionnaire), the development of in-house solution-focused case-work by the EBD co-ordinator, prior to the training session for pastoral staff, had already shown that positive change within the system had taken place. A cogent example of pre-session change! A further example was provided in the form of the Personal Coping Record, developed and implemented by the same co-ordinator, and shared at the training session. The Personal Coping Record is described below, as one example of a further development.

Further developments

To illustrate how things have moved on, and how new possibilities have arisen and been explored, we highlight two developments out of many.

The personal coping record

This is a pro forma that utilises solution-focused ideas. It was developed so that pupils could record their own behavioural goals ('things to try to do') and monitor their progress toward them ('how things have changed' and 'what still needs to change'). Scaling techniques are used as one way of generating responses. The process is a collaborative one between the teacher most concerned and the pupil.

The Personal Coping Record is designed with a brief intervention of no more than four sessions in mind. Session one could take up to forty-five minutes, whilst the subsequent sessions (if required) no more than fifteen minutes. Although based on the traditional 'report card' idea, it is very different in that pupils are given greater ownership, with a focus on what they have done a) to cope and b) to make the situation better in some way.

The formats are illustrated below. Section A is completed jointly by teacher and pupil. In the record booklet this part is repeated four times. Section B ('How I Coped') is completed by the pupil. Again, this is repeated.

Date.........................Time...........................Meeting with:..

Scaling Scores

Issues.. ....

....

....

Aims...

....

....

Things to try to do...

....

.... By (date).........................

Personal Coping Record – Section A

Week...........................

How things have changed .... What still needs to change ....

....

....

....

How can I tell .... Personal aims................................

....

....

Personal Coping Record – Section B

The mentoring scheme

As a result of a multi-agency initiative at School B, a pilot mentoring scheme has been developed and is currently operating with a group of Year 9 pupils. Adult members of the local community have volunteered (through the school networking system), received training, and are now meeting for up to an hour with these students (also volunteers) on a weekly or fortnightly basis over a two-term period. Within the context of the scheme the mentoring relationship is seen as 'a supportive one in which the mentor helps the mentee identify and work towards goals' (scheme handbook).

The mentors have received two half-day training sessions based around solution-focused ideas in particular: problem-free talk, problems to goals, preferred futures and exceptions. A handbook has also been written for the mentors which gives many examples of solution-focused question frameworks to chose from and adapt as required.

The project has yet to be evaluated, but the mentors responded very positively to the training. A support network has been developed for them, and again SFBT ideas are being used as a way of highlighting what is working well, the strengths and resources of the mentors, and so on.

The 'anger management group'

Also in School B, curriculum support staff are now running a group for Year 8 pupils based around solution-focused approaches to anger management. The materials were selected by staff in preference to other resources available within the school, because of their focus on individual and group solutions, rather than on imposed, 'adult' models.

Reflections on the Project

Work at both secondary schools is ongoing, and in this sense the project, as we have chosen to call it, is not yet at an end. So many positives have come from the experience that it is difficult to reflect upon them all. Crucially, solution-focused work now has a life of its own in both schools, without any 'direction' from us. Interested and key members of staff are taking the ideas forward. In both schools there is a common language. Many pastoral and curriculum staff are using elements of SFBT with pupils rather than referring to outside agencies for 'advice'. Some of the further developments we have highlighted also show that the techniques are being used beyond the level of individual therapeutic intervention.

The training, we felt, was important. We ran this in such a way that the staff had practical, real-life, experiences of the value of the techniques, working on their own solutions to problems shared with others. These activities, in particular, seemed very popular and our time management was compromised as a result!

There was, with the training, some negative comment from staff about perceived opportunities to act in a solution-focused way when intervening with problem behaviours. It emerged in School B that some Heads of Year saw their role as primarily a disciplinary one, and this generated some potential role conflict for them. Additionally, with severe time restrictions imposed upon them in respect of their pastoral duties, some felt that opportunities to use the techniques were limited. As trainers, we attempted to promote the idea of small steps towards change, and working with the techniques in creative ways within a consultation framework, with tutors, for example. The evaluations suggested, however, that even those who were sceptical became more open to the possibilities of the approach.

What also emerged was that on-going support in using the approach was likely to be of value. Many staff lacked the confidence to explore SFBT and its applications without an external resource to offer guidance, support and positive feedback.

The next section of the chapter outlines a case study which demonstrates SFBT at an individual pupil level.

Case Study – A Fisherman's Tale

Terry had a long history of language, learning and behaviour difficulties at his junior school. He was on Stage 3 of the Code of Practice and the psychologist had intermittent involvement. Terry is from a difficult and unsettled home background and he and his siblings are often teased or ostracised by other children, both in and out of school.

Terry transferred to the comprehensive school. Reports in Year 7 comment on his good application and behaviour. In Year 8, several serious incidents occurred where he became very aggressive and violent toward other children, abusive to teaching staff and refused to work in class. He was, consequently, on the verge of exclusion. The school had already undertaken some measures such as putting Terry on report and offering advice. The school asked the EP to become involved.

Terry and the EP met on several occasions. A solution-focused approach was adopted. Initially, Terry wished to relate the history of these incidents, and this was felt to be appropriate. He said that he had frequently been called names because of his body odour, his unkempt appearance and his family circumstances. He had previously come to terms with this over the years, but recently felt that he was having to react when such things were said to him. His mother had run away 'loads of times' and he had been told that 'she won't be coming back' (Social Services had a long involvement with the family).

'Problem-free talk' elicited the fact that Terry was a very keen and competent mechanic and helped his father on a regular basis to strip and repair cars. He was also an accomplished fisherman, often going river and sea fishing with his father and brother, and he was keen to stay at school and improve his behaviour. When asked the 'miracle' question, he said, 'It would be for my mother to come back, and for there to be no name calling and no incidents with other pupils and generally being able to control my anger.' He would also like to be able to write better, especially in copying homework down at the end of lessons.

When asked to scale his behaviour, Terry said that it was 10 out of 10 last year, and 1 out of 10 when the incidents had occurred several weeks previously. During the first interview, he rated his behaviour as 5 out of 10. When asked how he had managed to move up from 1 to 5 on the scale, he said that he was not fighting as much and that when angry he was counting to 10 or walking away. If he felt tense, he would often count to 10 or punch a door or a wall. When asked who else had helped him, he said that his Form Tutor and Head of Year had been friendly and given good advice and they had also been reinforcing the school's 'no bullying' policy with respect to children who were calling him names. He said his father had given him advice on temper control as well.

Terry's goal was to get back to 10 out of 10 in terms of his behaviour. He said he was 9 out of 10 confident that he would be able to get there. He said that he found the EP interview useful and he asked for a further session.

After the EP saw Terry at the second session, she discussed him firstly with his father and later with school staff. Father and staff specifically asked for anger management input for him. His father confirmed that the teasing had been quite painful in the past, for instance, when children were saying to him 'I didn't make my mum run away.' When asked, Terry said his behaviour was still 5 out of 10 and he was complimented for being able to maintain previous levels and not slide down the scale. It was suggested that he do 'more of the same' and also to notice how he coped when he was teased but did not over-react. Because certain aspects of written language appeared in Terry's miracle description, a brief assessment of his learning difficulties was undertaken, and a cursive handwriting programme was subsequently recommended for him. This was then implemented.

At the third session, when asked, 'what's gone well?' Terry replied, 'Everything, people aren't taking the mick, I'm co-operating with teachers.' He rated himself 9 out of 10 and when asked why, he said he had stopped behaving badly and was co-operating, for example by following teacher instructions and completing work. He also said that the changes had been observed and noted by school staff and by his father. His father had seen records of his improvement on the report card and also phoned the school on a regular basis. 'Problem-free talk' during this session led to Terry saying that he had recently caught a 12lb pike. He explained how he caught the fish in great detail and this enabled the EP to comment on the patience and skill needed in this activity and how a fisherman has frequently to cope with frustration when lines get tangled or when fish slip off the hook, etc.

At the fourth session, Terry said that everything was going well and that the bullying had stopped and people were 'nice to me'. He rated his behaviour at 9 out of 10 and reiterated that he was working hard. He had stopped 'behaving badly' and was no longer refusing to do work. He was now 10 out of 10 confident that he could maintain the improvement. A wider range of anger management strategies were discussed when the EP felt confident in augmenting the tactics which Terry had already evolved himself. He said that he was now willing to tell teachers if he was angry and ask if he could leave the room and sit outside by himself (he found this useful). He was trying not to 'explode', he was biting his lips, counting to 10 and, additionally, he was counting all of his fingers slowly three times. This was a good strategy for him. Terry said that the occasions when he had lost his temper were down significantly: approximately forty times in the first half term, but only five times in the second half term. Terry said that he found the interview with the EP helpful (10 out of 10 on a scale) and he wanted a further session. During this, he mentioned that his mother had in fact recently returned to the home.

At the fifth and final session, Terry said that 'Everything was going well.' he was getting good report cards and he felt that he was controlling himself better. He rated his behaviour 10 out of 10 and was 10 out of 10 confident that he could continue to use these strategies effectively. He said he hadn't lost his temper for several weeks. We agreed that this would be the final session for the time being and the EP specifically asked Terry what he had found helpful about the intervention. Terry said that, in particular, he tried to get the scale higher each time and that this was a good motivating factor for him. Subsequently, Terry moved up to the Upper School site and started Year 9. He has not been mentioned since as having difficulties within school.

Comments

Terry's situation was a complicated one, with a long history and the involvement of several agencies. There was a real danger of exclusion in the initial stages. A solution-focused approach helped give a structure to the intervention, a structure which was particularly clear to Terry and also transparent to the school and to the father.

'Problem-free talk' in this incidence was very useful and indicated that Terry had a lot of strengths in out-of-school situations which could be applied in helping him control anger and temper. Terry said he found the scaling helpful and generally the structure allowed input for him to consider a range of anger-management techniques. The EP was able to discuss with staff techniques and strategies – and this case – with others helped generate an interest which then enabled in-service training to proceed in a more favourable light.

Conclusion

For EPs working with secondary schools, we would suggest that there are many possibilities for solution-focused work, and at many different levels. Staff can be empowered to work with some of the tools and techniques, and to develop their own methodologies for particular purposes. We hope that this chapter has illustrated how some of the possibilities can be realised in practice.

CHAPTER THIRTEEN

'BRIDGES TO BABYLON'

BY ANNIE O'LEARY

Introduction

In 1992, having completed a postgraduate diploma in counselling, I embarked on a family therapy course. During this time, I was seconded to a therapy team using solution-focused Brief Therapy. I became very interested in the work they were doing and started attending conferences and work-shops, many of them at the Brief Therapy Practice in London. I introduced solution-focused interventions into my work, and when an opportunity to work with adolescents arose, I decided to try working in a purely solution-focused way, especially as past experience with adolescents had informed me that, generally, they are not interested in looking in-depth at the past, how long a problem has been around, and how it got there. They are, however, interested in finding solutions to their problems, appreciate being treated as equals and often need an advocate. A solution-focused approach would readily fit these criteria. The results were impressive, and I have never looked back.

Setting up the service

Today, having set up a Counselling Service for Adolescents and Young People in 1994, I am employed by an NHS Trust in the south of England. I work as a solution-focused brief therapist and head the small team that forms the Counselling Service. One of my initial priorities in setting up the service was to detail my aims and objectives. I needed to be clear about what we were offering and to whom. I wanted to provide an accessible, responsive, and flexible confidential service to which adolescents could self-refer without parental consent. With this in mind, the Gillick principle has been salient:

> 'People under 16 who are able fully to understand what is proposed and its implications are competent to consent to medical treatment regardless of age.'
>
> (Gillick v Wisbech and W Norfolk AHA. 1985)

The Health Education Authority (HEA) leaflet: Confidentiality and people under 16 (no date) states that 'The duty of confidentiality owed to a person under 16 years, is as great as that owed to any other person.'

The legal department of the Trust backs the right of adolescents to seek confidential advice and treatment providing that they are judged to be Gillick competent. Their backing has on occasion proved invaluable.

Confidentiality was and is an extremely important issue. I had to be absolutely clear regarding the boundaries of confidentiality that I was prepared to work within, and those that the Trust required me to work within. In those cases where the service works within a school context, I needed to be aware of the school's position regarding the breaking of confidentiality, and make my position plain when talking to staff. Getting an agreement between different agencies is not always easy. Some schools were unhappy with a counselling service seeing students without parental consent, and have chosen to seek that consent before referring students. Some refer students directly to us, confident in the legal backing provided by the Trust, and others prefer to use a cover-all phrase in the school brochure informing parents that counselling is available on-site.

As the Trust policy is that no employee working with young people should have a criminal record, it is explicit that anybody working for the service undergoes a police check. It was also considered vital for counsellors to understand what is and is not a child protection issue, and a protocol was developed providing child protection training and access to the Trust Child Protection Procedures.

Other things that were considered before the service came into being were:

The requirements of counsellors for supervision, and for continuing professional development.

All counsellors have regular supervision. Training in record keeping, in writing reports for court, and in court attendance has been invaluable. Of equal importance has been regular attendance at international presentations and conferences at the Brief Therapy Practice in London.

The type of therapy that we would offer – individual therapy, family therapy, working with a friend/partner, group work.

One of the advantages of Solution-Focused Brief Therapy is that it is effective in all of these contexts, so clients are seen in whichever context they prefer.

How the service would be accessed - who would refer to the service and how, would all sessions be booked sessions, or would there be some 'drop-in' sessions?

We take referrals from a variety of health professionals as well as from teachers, parents and students. Several schools in the area 'buy' counselling time from the Trust, and in those schools we provide a counsellor for an agreed amount of time per week. Whilst the majority of clients are voluntary, we are noticing an increase in the number of involuntary clients, particularly from those schools who purchase the service. Referrals are taken in a variety of different ways including verbally, on being spotted in a corridor, by phone, by completing a referral form or by letter. I have found that booked sessions are generally better used than drop-in sessions.

When will the service be available - between what times?

It became apparent fairly quickly that the majority of adolescents wanted to be seen during school hours and in school, although provision is made for those with different requirements.

The length of the sessions.

What started out as 45-minute sessions has now become more flexible, as the majority of students prefer to be seen within the time frame of one lesson, and lesson times seem to vary from between 30 and 45 minutes. Sessions with children of Primary School age are often only 20 to 30 minutes long to accommodate a shorter attention span.

The location - where would the service be offered?

We have always striven to provide a flexible service, and clients are seen in schools, at health clinics, in GP surgeries, at home, and in my office. The majority however, choose to be seen in school.

Consulting suites with one way mirrors do not feature highly on our agenda! Clinic rooms with weighing scales, and examination couches, sick rooms in schools, and small windowless 'cupboards' are more likely to be part of the experience.

How we would inform people about the service?

I designed a referral form – which has been re-worked on several occasions – to send to potential referrers. Posters put up in schools and clinics have been used successfully to advertise the service. We have yet to design a leaflet describing the service, what is available, and the qualifications and experience of the counsellors.

In the early days before the service took-off, I spent invaluable time visiting and introducing myself and the service to the school nurse teams, to GPs, the health promotion department, GUM clinic staff where sexually transmitted diseases are treated, to family planning clinic staff, health visiting teams, schools across the district and other potential referrers to the service.

Subsequently, I have found it extremely helpful to attend staff meetings at the beginning of the school year to introduce myself, and talk about the way I work, talk to pupils in school assemblies about what I do, and the kind of problems that I may be able to help them with.

How the service would be monitored and improved:

Outcome information and statistical information was considered important from the start. It is invaluable to be able to give feedback to the agencies with which we work. Schools purchasing the service clearly have an interest in knowing the number of clients seen, the number of times they were seen, the age/sex ratio, types of problems dealt with and whether there was a satisfactory outcome.

The questionnaire that I designed to evaluate the service is sent to everybody seen for counselling, one term after their last therapy session. More recently we designed an interim survey for use in school with students who are seen for longer than either six sessions or a term (whichever happens first). This has been extremely useful in helping teaching staff to identify any small changes that the client is making, hence beginning to de-stigmatise those pupils who have acquired a 'bad' reputation. An End of Counselling Survey sent to referring teachers again underlines the changes that the client has made, as well as providing outcome information.

Outlining a counselling session

The service initially provided for adolescents between the ages of 11 and 18. Individual clients are offered an initial assessment session, at the end of which they decide whether they feel it will be useful for them to come again. Today, we see an increasing number of primary school children. They are usually seen with one or both parents or guardians, and/or with a teacher. More recently, experimenting with some of Ben Furman's work, I have started seeing the parents/guardians alone for an initial session before involving the child (Furman 1999).

There is no set frequency of sessions – clients are asked at the end of a session when they would like to see me again and most opt for every two or three weeks. I have found that the flexibility of this model allows me to have a case load of between two and three times the number of spaces available in a week, i.e. I usually have between 15 and 18 hours available each week to see clients. I can, therefore, carry a case-load of between 30-50 clients without having a waiting list. It also allows for clients in crisis to be seen promptly for an initial assessment session. They are not limited to a certain number of sessions, and our evaluations have shown that people are seen for an average of four sessions.

Although clients are usually seen in the context in which they want to be seen, there are times when it may be helpful to include others in the therapy, so on occasion I suggest a joint session with one or both parents, with a teacher, or a social worker. However, unless there is a child protection issue, the choice of including others in their sessions lies ultimately with the client.

As an employee of an NHS Trust, it is vital that I work within the recognised Child Protection Procedures and, consequently, it is important to clarify the limits of confidentiality with each client. When I see somebody for the first time, before they begin to talk about their problem, I discuss the times when I will have to break confidentiality. I have designed a 'confidentiality slip' which re-iterates the limits of my confidentiality, and - in case of litigation - clients sign and date the slip before we start the therapy.

My experience of working with adolescents has underlined the necessity of building rapport quickly. If my clients do not feel respected and understood during the first session, they are unlikely to give me a second chance. George, Iveson and Ratner (1990) consider it salient: '… problem-free talk at the beginning of the session is extremely important ….' They also talk about clients being 'esteem-blind' and that is my observation, too. So, during an initial session I ask three simple questions which I have developed over the years, and which I call the 'Keys for Co-operation'. I have found these questions extremely useful in helping to build rapport quickly. I use them in the following sequence, so that they build on each other:

> 'What do you enjoy?'
> 'What are you good at?'
> 'What does it take to be good at … (some of the things that
> they have mentioned)?'

The Keys provide a vehicle both for competence seeking and for giving clients invaluable constructive feedback using their own language. Client feedback shows that many people value this intervention, and I believe that in using the Keys for Co-operation within the first session and subsequently compliment-ing people on the skills and resources that they already have, I dramatically increase the chances of forming a 'customer' relationship with my client, where the client and I are able to work co-operatively in order to do some-thing about the problem.

An assessment session usually begins with me introducing myself, talking about the way that I work, defining the boundaries of confidentiality, and telling the client about the evaluation of the service – stressing the importance of returning the final questionnaire! I go on to ask for basic details about them and their support structures – I often have no information bar a name. I ask them to tell me a bit about what has brought them to see me and why at this particular time. The answer may be anything from a detailed description of the problem – and at this point we will spend as long as the client wants to looking at the details of the problem – to a somewhat more disconcerting 'I don't know, Mr Bloggs sent me.' Either way, the answer will give me an impres-sion of whether the relationship that I have is either a Customer relationship, a Complainant relationship (where the client is bothered about the problem but does not yet see him or herself as part of the solution, and our work will involve my encouraging continued co-operation) or a Visitor relationship. When a client is sent to see me, they may feel that they have no complaint themselves, so our work will start with building a sufficiently good relationship to interest my client in returning to see me with something to work on (Berg and Miller 1992). Clearly the type of relationship that we have will be impor-tant in deciding how to progress with the work that we will do.

We look at whether they have had counselling before and if so, what was most useful, and what was less helpful. This information can be used to guide me in our work.

I ask about the family (which is often pertinent) and look at what they hope will be different when they no longer need counselling. There may be some discussion about whether what they want is feasible, and if not, what I am able to offer. We are beginning to co-construct goals and agendas which will be expanded on by the use of the miracle question (de Shazer 1988).

'Is there anything else that we haven't talked about yet that you think may be important?' often proves a valuable question – sometimes the envisaged direction of the therapy can be changed as a result of the answer, as when a fourteen-year old was referred with aggressive behaviour and in answering this question mentioned that he had found out two weeks previously that his father was not his real father.

Scales of 1-10 are useful in measuring progress, in exploring future steps, in searching for exceptions and to ascertain confidence of change and motivation to change (Miller, Hubble and Duncan 1996). I use a pictorial representation of a ladder in the initial session to evaluate how bad a client feels their problem is. By comparison with a similar representation in the final survey, this measure can be used in assessing therapy outcome. I also find scaling questions useful in looking for client competence:

> 'What was the lowest that you remember being on this scale,
> and how have you managed moving from there to where you are
> now?'

In the light of my description of the various locations in which I work, and the time limits of the sessions, I have found it impractical to take the traditional solution-focused 'break' during a session. I therefore aim to end each session with positive feedback and at the end of my working day, I spend time going through my notes deciding and noting the constructive feedback that I will give my client at the beginning of the next session. After opening a session with positive feedback, there is an opportunity for clients to comment on what I have said, before I go on to ask what has gone well and what they have been pleased about since we last met. Complimenting clients at the beginning of sessions not only provides essential positive feedback, but also serves to connect sessions. Subsequent sessions may be spent in further construction of goals – for instance, by asking the miracle question if it has not been asked during the first session, by looking at the times when the problem does not happen, or happens less, and what happens instead (exception seeking), looking at what will be happening when the problem is no longer around (preferred future) and asking scaling questions to ascertain motivation and to check progress.

Case study

Sonia was a fourteen-year-old girl, who self-referred after learning about the availability of a counsellor within the school during a school assembly. She was thoughtful and quietly spoken, and appeared more mature than her fourteen years.

Session 1

I opened the session by talking about the way that I work, and gathering basic information. I asked Sonia how she would know that it had been worth her while coming to see me. She replied that it would be helpful having somebody to talk to who was not in her life.

She told me that it was the first anniversary of the death of a close aunt.

There had been several family deaths throughout her childhood, including the suicide of another aunt. She mentioned that she had been bullied at primary school.

We talked about what she would like to be different, at the point in her life when things were the way that she would like them to be, and when she felt that she no longer needed counselling. This intervention was used to create an expectation of change (Synder et al. 1991 in Miller, Duncan, and Hubble 1997) state that psychotherapy studies show how fostering a positive expectation of change may be a pre-requisite for successful treatment.

Sonia felt that she would like to be stronger, and rely less on others. She also wanted to stop feeling angry about the past, and to stop resenting people. We talked about the things in her life that she would like to continue – one of several interventions which I use to begin to establish client competence. Sonia replied, 'Doing well at school, having an excellent relationship with my family, doing a lot of drama, and having a fairly good social life.'

I asked if there was anything else that it may be useful for me to know. She said that her sister was important to her. Using the Scaling Ladder she rated herself at 6. I asked what small changes she had noticed since she made the appointment to see me. Beyebach et al. (1994 in Miller, Hubble & Duncan 1996) state that subjects who reported improvement prior to treatment showed a greater sense of self-efficacy. Sonia answered, 'I've felt more positive, and more helpful, and I've thought about things more.'

We moved on to consider the Keys for Co-operation. Sonia enjoyed a variety of things. History, acting and debating were among the subjects and activities she felt she was good at, and we looked at what it took to be good at those things. She decided it was '...being able to think about the long term, and to follow things through, able to understand and to analyse things, being confident and not caring what others think, being able to forget yourself, having a thick skin, able to listen, and to think and act quickly, being open-minded and able to admit when you are wrong.'

I ended our first session, by re-iterating these strengths and resources, so underlining some of the skills which she would be able to bring to bear in solving her problem.

Session 2

The second session began with focusing on and complimenting Sonia again on the strengths and resources that we had uncovered in the previous session: 'The more the client is told of what is noticed, the more they are likely to continue with the new behaviour.' (Source unknown.)

Sonia commented that she is not always good at all of those things. This gave us an opportunity to talk about the possibility of transferring skills from one area of one's life to another. We looked at the good things that had happened since we had last met, and I went on to ask Sonia the miracle question.

She described the day after the miracle in detail, creating a positive image of life when the problem was solved. For me, however, the miracle question is more than this. It can give a clear idea of the practical steps that clients can begin to take in creating their own miracle, e.g. when Sonia described having bagels and cream cheese for breakfast, making daisy chains with friends, or going for a walk with her sister. I also use the miracle question as a vehicle for asking what difference it will make if all the things described in the miracle were to come true – in Sonia's case she would feel calm, at peace and understood. I use this difference to rate how close to their 'miracle' my client is, and to discover what they have already done to get them to that point on the scale (looking again for client competency).

I asked Sonia what for her, was the opposite of feeling calm, at peace and understood. Her answer was 'feeling angry and resentful.'

We rated feeling angry and resentful versus feeling calm, at peace and understood. At this point Sonia felt at about the half-way point on this scale (a 5). Her 'good enough' point was 9. I asked what her lowest point had been on the scale, and what had been going on at that time. She replied that she had been at 1 during the previous year at her uncle's funeral. I acknowledged her feelings and complimented her on having moved so far up the scale after such a difficult event, and we explored how she had moved herself from 1 on the scale to 5 where she was now. She answered as follows:

'I talked to a few people about how I felt, I threw myself into school, into drama, and into a variety of other activities, I met an aunt of mine for the first time, and I thought things through and talked myself out of it.'

I asked who would be the least surprised that things would ultimately work out for her (introducing an 'other person perspective' and so providing a view of the client that she may not always acknowledge). Sonia thought her father would be the least surprised: 'He knows I'm capable of fighting through, and of providing for myself.'

The session ended with my repeating those words to her and allowing space for a reflective silence before agreeing the details of our next session. In my work, I often use feedback in this way as I have found that leaving clients with positive statements to reflect on between sessions can provide effective levers in helping them to move forward in therapy.

Session 3

During our third session we used the 'miracle scale' – scaling Sonia's problem at its worst at 1 on the scale and the day after the miracle at 10. She felt at 7. We spent the rest of the session exploring the differences that people would notice in her after the miracle, when she was calm, at peace and felt understood. Once again I introduced other people's perspectives.

Session 4

In session 4 we talked about other difficult times in Sonia's life, and how she had overcome these difficulties (looking again at client resources).

I asked an adaptation of one of the questions that Yvonne Dolan uses in *Resolving Sexual Abuse* (1991):

> Imagine that you have grown to be a healthy, wise old woman,
> and that healthy, wise, older you can talk to you now.
> What advice would she give you to help you through?
> What would she tell you to remember?
> What could she say to comfort you when things are not going
> so well?

The original question was used by Dolan in her work with people who have been abused. I have found it one of the most subtle and useful solution-focused questions to ask of any of my clients, and I never cease to be amazed at the insightful way that people answer it.

Sonia's answer was as follows:

> 'You've got through things before and you can do it again. It's
> human nature to fight things and to feel grief – it's part of life.
> What doesn't kill you makes you stronger. People surprise you,
> and the most strange people can be the most help. You'll be sur-
> prised at how strong you can be – if you want to, you can cope
> with anything because that's how people survive. There are a lot
> of good things in the world – you have to look for the good in
> everything. Look for the beautiful things and lose yourself in
> them.
>
> 'Remember there's always light at the end of the tunnel.
> There's always something to learn. Remember the good things
> you've done, and when things have gone well and how you got to
> that. Treat things as a challenge. There are a lot of people who
> love you and who care what happens.'

Throughout therapy I randomly check by asking the client:

> Are you still getting what you want?
> What have you found the most useful thing that we have done
> today?
> How else can I be helpful to you?

On this occasion, Sonia said that she was getting what she wanted, although it wasn't what she had expected. I did not pursue this.

When I asked how else I could be helpful, she said that there were still things she wanted to talk about, and that she would like to work at ways of relaxing. I demonstrated two different relaxation techniques and suggested she try them both to see which one she found most useful.

Session 5

We met for our fifth session after the Easter break. Sonia reported that she had found both of the relaxation techniques helpful in different ways. When I asked what she had been pleased about since we last met she replied, 'I feel I've come through things, gone a step further.'

I asked what she felt she'd learned about herself since she first started coming for counselling and she answered, 'I can cope on my own for a time. I can move on from the past. I can respect myself for who I am.'

I said that I thought that sounded pretty good. We reviewed the work that we had done to date, looking at the things that she had wanted from counselling in the initial session. Sonia felt that she was stronger and relying less on others, that she no longer felt let-down and alone. She was feeling less angry and resentful, and said that she thought that it would completely resolve over time.

As things begin to improve, I introduce more future-focused questions, looking to the time when the client is no longer in need of therapy. I asked where Sonia saw the counselling sessions going. She replied that she needed to teach herself to try to live for the day, and talked about insecurity and a lack of control. We scaled insecurity versus security and she put herself at 6/7 on the scale. She felt that 8/9 would be good enough. The first sign that things were beginning to move up the scale would be that she would not worry in lessons if she had to sit by herself.

George, Iveson and Ratner (1999) say that clients often see exceptions as something that emphasises the problem. However, once the therapist starts describing them as successes, the client may begin to see his world differently. We discussed the times when Sonia did feel secure:

'At the family holiday house.'

'In the company of my cousins.'

'When I go out with my sister.'

I asked about any times when she felt secure but was not either in familiar places or with familiar people (looking for resources within the client herself rather than in other people). She replied that she liked the anonymity of London and big cities, and that she felt secure in herself, adding that her insecurities were usually about other people. I did not pursue that at the time.

Toward the end of the session I asked Sonia what she had found the most helpful thing that we had done that day, and she said that she had found it helpful to reason things through, and to realise that she was getting on pretty well and that she did not have to be perfect.

Session 6

I saw Sonia again one month later. She said that things were stable, and that she was feeling positive and secure.

I checked how she felt on the angry/resentful versus calm/at peace/understood scale, and she put herself at about 8 on the scale, adding that it was OK and saying that she thought she would stay at around this point on the scale. I asked whether she was still getting what she wanted and Sonia said yes, she was no longer worried about being lonely.

We discussed the relaxation techniques that she had been practising, and talked about sleep routines. Sonia added that she had decided that today's session would be her last. I congratulated her on achieving her goals, and said that I had been impressed by how hard she had worked. I checked how she would be able to keep things on track. She said that she needed to keep things in perspective – to take time to sit down and think, and to keep talking to people about how she feels.

Sonia felt that there was nothing more that she needed to talk about, and after reminding her of the different ways in which she could contact me in the future, we ended our final session.

Reflections

One of the things that drew me to Solution-Focused Brief Therapy in the first instance was the de-mystification of the role of the therapist, and the lack of jargon. When the client is the expert, and the therapy is client-led, the result is a respectful model which is helpful in working with people from different cultures and races. My experience is that it enables the most difficult ideas to be explored in a supportive and non-judgmental way, allowing young people the possibility of examining their thoughts and feelings on a range of subjects from panic attacks to sexuality and gender issues. The ability of the therapist to join with clients and build rapport, is vital in facilitating such exploration.

Solution-Focused Brief Therapy has been criticised for not paying attention to client feelings, I do not believe this to be the case. Many of today's most well known Solution-Focused Brief Therapists stress the importance of listening to the client. Steve de Shazer (in George, Iveson, and Ratner 1999) says

'Instead they listened to the client, found out what she wanted and worked with her toward getting it.'

Neither, as somebody who will shortly be seeing one of my clients for the seventy-eighth session (over a period of four years), can I go along with the criticism that solution-focused therapy is a quick and superficial fix. In this case I initially saw the client as the result of bullying at school. Since then we have worked with her bulimia, and more recently with a history of sexual abuse which she is only just beginning to recognise, let alone be able to talk about.

It has been argued that solution-focused therapy is only suitable for moti-vated clients with clear goals but this has not been my experience either. Over the years, I have seen many clients, some of whom arrive apparently not knowing why they have been sent to see me. I have found that if, during an initial session, I listen carefully and remain respectful, the majority will find something they would like to work on. Part of our work will then concern clar-ifying the goals – what does the referrer want to achieve and what does the client want to achieve? – and breaking them down into small, manageable steps. I am also convinced that being able to build rapport rapidly plays an important part in their decision to come again – hence my development of the Keys for Co-operation. Of those who do not find anything that they would like to work on at that time, several have returned for therapy at a later date. Sometimes it is enough to sow the comforting thought that therapy is available when required.

How does solution-focused therapy differ from other models?

Solution-focused therapy is an ideal way of working with young people who, in my experience, are often not concerned with examining the history of a problem in any depth – although I hasten to add that it does provide the scope for that if it is what the client wants to do. How many other therapies examine the times when the problem is not there (looking for exceptions), focusing on what the client is doing instead of 'doing the problem'? What a brilliant way of keying into client resources, as well as underlining the fact that there are times when something other than the problem is happening!

In looking to the future, to a time when the problem is no longer there, a positive focus is maintained, which is not found in many other helping models. Complimenting clients also differentiates this model from others where feedback may be given more in the form of advice. The emphasis on client competency helps rapidly to identify client resources, and to use them in solving the presenting difficulty. This model also provides methods of meas-uring change as it happens. Working with a solution-focused approach can provide a coherent structure which is helpful in keeping both client and therapist focused, and is readily adaptable by a variety of professionals to suit a diversity of situations. As it is constantly evolving, it remains a very 'alive' model, and as a therapist I find it a satisfying way of working. Our client evaluations indicate a high level of client satisfaction and effective outcomes – the latest evaluation showing that 83% of clients rated the counsellors work as either excellent or good, 84% said that they were either very happy or happy that the counsellor cared about them and their problems, and 76% said that they would recommend the counselling service. I have a fairly eclectic therapy background – Person-Centred/Transactional Analysis/Gestalt/Personal Construct – and have chosen to base the work that I do on a solution-focused model because it works – and as de Shazer (1985) said: 'If it works don't fix it.'

Full Permission has been given to Annie O'Leary by the client concerned, to use excerpts from work done during counselling sessions to illustrate the Case Study. All names used in the case study have been changed in order to protect client identity, as recommended in BAC guidelines.

CHAPTER FOURTEEN

DISCOVERING THE EXPERT

BY MAGGIE STEPHENSON
AND HARDEESH JOHAL-SMITH

Introduction

This chapter describes some of our experiences in learning to do things differently, in a solution-focused way. It has been a process of exploration, experimentation, discovery, and at times, fascinating rediscovery. On our journey we have challenged some of the beliefs which we held to be at the centre of educational psychology, particularly that of the psychologist as the expert problem-analyst and solution-provider. This is not to say that psychologists cannot and should not be these things, it is just that we have begun to change our view of where we feel our expertise can best support the process of helping others find useful solutions to their own problems.

The development of our solution-focused thinking stems from the work of de Shazer (1985, 1988, 1991, and 1994). We have also avidly read the works of other leading writers in this field such as O'Hanlon and Weiner-Davis (1989), Durrant (1994), Murphy and Duncan (1997), Miller, Duncan and Hubble (1997) and White and Epston (1990). On a more local front, the work of Rhodes and Ajmal (1995) continues to be a most useful and regularly used reference. We are also grateful to the Brief Therapy Practice for their ongoing support and encouragement and would recommend their publications (George, Iveson and Ratner, 1990 and Letham, 1994).

In addition, our thinking and practice has also been influenced by friends and colleagues and the many people we work with in schools and elsewhere in the wider sphere of a psychologist's work in an LEA. Our thanks to them all for their generosity and support in helping to develop and shape our ideas.

Why do something different?

Over the last decade, we have seen a steady growth in the volume, range and complexity of work demands placed upon LEA psychologists. More recently, factors such as limited resources and statutory requirements have significantly added to overall demands and workload pressures. Operating effectively within these constraints is never an easy task, even with strong time management and good working practices. Working harder, smarter and quicker often just didn't seem enough to get the job done effectively and at the same time achieve a sense of real satisfaction.

We wanted to try to redress the balance; to do something that would be as effective in meeting the demands made upon us and at the same time create an environment for growth, development and enjoyment for ourselves and the people we work with.

Small beginnings

We had been interested in solution-focused brief therapy as an approach with individuals and families for some time and had started in small ways to incorporate some of the ideas into our practice in schools. In so doing, we found ourselves spending more time with staff discussing ways forward and less time observing and assessing individual youngsters. It is important to understand that our start was very much 'in small ways' because working with a solution-focused approach was quite different from our then-practice as educational psychologists (EPs). In essence, we began to move away from the isolated sole-practitioner model, toward a more collaborative approach.

Some of these 'small ways' were in fact very small. For example, we tried out questions such as 'what else?', 'how did you do that?', and 'how will you know when ...?' When feeling braver, we also tried the miracle question, scaling and exception-finding questions.

After some experimentation, we began to notice that it felt good working in this different way – for ourselves and for those we were working with. For example, in one school, staff remarked how useful and hopeful these conversations were. It was also noted that 'the problem' wasn't being discussed so much, yet the conversation was still very constructive. Parents, teachers and children all noted at various times that they were unaware they had already being doing so much to help themselves. There was positive change in the outcomes in that seemingly stuck situations were beginning to be resolved successfully. Our enthusiasm and confidence, therefore, steadily increased and we started to share and discuss cases with each other. These discussions led to the establishment of a local interest group that created regular opportunities to discuss cases and share ideas on further applications of the approach, e.g. work with staff groups, peer consultation and supervision activities, facilitating meetings and enabling discussion groups.

Early learning

From our shared interest in the use of solution-focused approaches, it was natural to reflect on our changing practice. As a result of our discussions, a number of common ideas began to emerge and crystallise:

– **It is OK not to be the expert on the problem content.** We realised that being the 'expert' on the content material was not necessarily crucial in helping others find useful solutions to their own problems. This shift in our 'thinking and doing' as psychologists was a significant step. In so doing, we gave ourselves permission that it was acceptable to become facilitator of the process of change rather than presenter of expert advice on the problem. Whilst at times we sought the permission of those we worked with to try something different, our increasing sense was that the respectfulness and trusting relationships that developed from these conversations were key to it being accepted as an approach.

– **Knowing what you know.** Moving away from being 'content rich' about the problem in our conversations, to talking about goals and ways to achieve them gave us opportunity to become more interested in listening for the direction of the conversation. In so doing, we began to focus and reflect on the skills and qualities important for useful conversations and consultations. In fact, many of the skills we know (and sometimes forget) are important in helping conversational relationships to develop and flourish, namely those of genuine and respectful listening and understanding, warmth, empathy and trust. For example, when talking to a teacher about a behavioural issue surrounding a youngster, it was not important to focus on the exact detail of what was or was not happening; more what he would like to be happening. Questions such as, 'Suppose John was behaving in a way you would like. What would be happening? What would you be doing? What would his classmates be doing?' all proved helpful in eliciting ways forward without focusing on the actual behaviours occurring.

– **Guide the flow.** Early on we realised the importance of 'going with the flow' of the client whilst at the same time providing some guidance this along a useful path. This meant trying hard to work with the client's agenda (their goals rather than our own). This does not mean becoming involved with the client's problems, rather eliciting in a solution-focused way what their goals for change are. Once this is achieved, the task becomes one of working together to find useful ways to obtain the desired results utilising the strengths and resources available to them. One useful way we found of doing this was to ask them what they would like to achieve from coming to the session, i.e. 'What would make coming here today a useful and helpful thing for you to have done?'

Reassuring research

Although the development of our practice produced some very encouraging results, we often pondered on the question, 'So what is it that works?' This tough question was answered, at least to some extent, by the research work of Lambert (1992, well described in Murphy and Duncan 1997) who investigated the factors involved in outcome success. Data collected from thousands of clients across a variety of settings and problems identified four key factors as significant contributors to outcome success (see fig. 1).

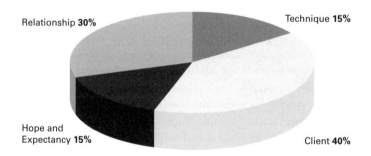

fig. 1

These findings indicate that:

- 40% of effective change is due to factors people have within their power to utilise. These are their personal strengths, resources, qualities and skills.
- 30% of effective change is due to factors related to the development of a good working relationship between the worker and the client. These factors are things such as empathy, warmth, acceptance, encouragement and support in risk taking. Taken together, these factors help build a collaborative relationship which can support clients in identifying, appreciat-

ing and harnessing their own strengths and resources in finding solutions to their problems.

- 15% of effective change is due to factors related to 'expert interventions'. There are innumerable models of working and practice techniques and clearly they have all been credited with success at sometime or another. A solution-focused approach is a model of working and a set of expert techniques. The key is that any expert intervention or technique used, if it is to be of any benefit, needs to be acceptable to the people we are working with. This way of working seems to be an excellent way of enabling the personal relationship factors to flourish.
- Lastly, 15% of effective change is attributed to factors known as placebo factors. These factors are centrally those of hopefulness and expectation that things will get better. In other words, the simple fact of expecting and hoping things will improve can go a long way to making it so.

This research study gave us reassurance and encouragement by validating our feelings of what was important in our developing practice.

Next steps

In addition to the ongoing solution-focused work with individual cases in schools, we also began to explore the use of this approach in our work with school staff. This often involved talking with them about how they coped and managed in tough situations, both class-based and school-wide. Regular work in one school provided us with valuable feedback from the headteacher on reports received from staff of a sense of increased confidence and competence in handling certain situations as a result of our involvement. Staff suggested that this was not due to any specific advice we had given but rather a confirmation of their skills and competencies. For example, in supporting a youngster with very challenging behaviour, a teacher was asked just how she was managing such a difficult situation so well and how she knew this was the right thing to do.

We wanted to increase our effectiveness in facilitating change at this level. We also needed a way to do this within existing resource constraints, i.e. limits on the number of school visits available and pressures to find time for other activities such as report writing. These thoughts led us to the possibility of using letter writing to supplement our dialogue with schools.

Letter-writing as a means of providing constructive feedback *to* children and adults

We explored the use of constructive feedback letters as a way of capturing the essence of our conversations for our clients to refer to again and share if they wished. In these letters we hoped to offer concrete evidence to support clients in recognizing and utilising their competencies and resources, in order to achieve useful change for themselves. The letters also provided an alternative to detailed reports as record of our involvement, thus freeing up valuable time.

Case study

The following case study is an example of our use of letters as constructive feedback. We chose to use this case as there were many lessons learned along the way and we wanted to share how sometimes making changes can take time and requires nurturing.

The girl who became 'cleverer'

Laura was fourteen-years old when she first came to our attention. She was a Year 9 Grammar School student about to move up into Year 10. She was reported to have stopped performing in all subject areas and told an alarmed staff that she could no longer read! She was sent for various medical tests to rule out any physiological cause. Nothing was found to be wrong. The school then referred Laura for psychometric assessment that indicated her to be experiencing general learning difficulties. At this point a letter was received from a concerned speech and language therapist also noting Laura's language skills at this level. Laura's teachers were very worried by these findings, as they had no experience of working with learning difficulties of this type.

In talking with Laura about her interests many strengths were noted, such as her excellent sporting and general outdoor skills and her love of animals. She was a very pleasant youngster and good company, with a well-developed sense of humour and many friends. In talking about what had brought her to the session, she spoke about her learning difficulties. Her goals were discussed for some time, before it was realised that the psychologist was really getting Laura to discuss her school's goals! A change of questioning found that her goals were about outdoor life and getting a job that would allow her physical activity. This was much more productive. The miracle question was used along with scaling activities to identify where she was in terms of her goals. With this change of questioning, Laura became noticeably more engaged and interested in working out small steps of change for herself. These were mostly about moving on in her out-of-school activities and helping her mother feel less anxious about her situation. One outcome of this was that the 'problem' was not discussed anymore, and it was quickly established that she had many abilities.

At this time, a clinical psychologist also became involved with the family. He continued using a broadly solution-focused approach with Laura and her mother and began noticing significant changes in the home. This was apparent to both Laura and her mother and their anxiety about school lessened greatly. Their identified 'good enough' point on their scale was almost being reached and they were finding this work very helpful.

In sharp contrast, staff anxiety in school was increasing, as Laura was still not producing coursework. As a group of highly committed teachers, they found it difficult to accept that Laura was failing and so supported her more. Laura happily accepted this situation and still produced little work. The two psychologists, therefore, arranged to meet with all Laura's teachers to discuss the way forward.

At the meeting there was an explosion of emotion from many of the staff who felt they could do no more to support Laura. It became evident early on that the staff were a very angry, frustrated, caring, committed and problem-focused group. Staff were asked how they would like things to be different, in terms of a preferred outcome for themselves as a group and for Laura. This met with limited success, as did attempts to find small exceptions to the expressed concerns.

We therefore quickly recognised the need to be flexible in our approach in an attempt to achieve the following:

- **To acknowledge and validate their concerns.** We started by asking each teacher to talk about what he/she would like to achieve with Laura. This solution-focused question was interpreted as an opportunity to express deep concerns and problem talk. Clearly, it was important for staff to have sufficient time to express and talk about those concerns. We took care to note that it was indeed a difficult situation and that we could see their concerns were very real.
- **To find exceptions.** During the meeting we asked several times about when the problem was less of a problem. For example, we asked, 'In your lesson, when Laura works a little better, what is happening?' Interestingly, whilst we felt that our attempts at eliciting exceptions had met with no success, at the end of the meeting several staff approached the psychologists to share recent examples of how, when Laura had been supported in different ways, she had indeed performed better.
- **To offer constructive feedback.** Given that time constraints and the

strength of feeling of the group made it difficult to give much constructive feedback, it was felt more appropriate to put our thoughts in writing.
In this letter (fig. 2) we attempted to identify all the extra support and
hard work the staff had been doing and to acknowledge what a difficult
situation it was for everyone (psychologists included). We also wanted to
highlight the small 'signs of change' that were being noticed at school
and the larger 'signs of change' at home.

Dear All

Thank you for making the time to meet with us on Tuesday, it was
very much appreciated. Following our visit we would like to
convey our impressions to you.

   We became very aware of just how deeply concerned you are
for Laura's welfare, and were very impressed by the great efforts
you have made to help her overcome her difficulties.

   We, too, have been endeavouring to support Laura for the past
year, and have taken a strong interest in seeing her through her
difficulties. This is why Laura was seen for individual sessions with
.... and then referred on for brief therapy at TMS.

   We were encouraged to hear of the improvements Laura has
been making in certain subjects. This has occurred despite the
fact that the direct, tangible support for her has been reduced. We
have all been included in a vicious cycle; the more we have tried
to help Laura, and the greater the sense of urgency, the more she
has 'switched off'. However, by not giving up on her you have
given Laura the opportunity now to come out of her self-imposed
state, if she is ready to. It may be the case that she is ready to
accomplish this in the near future, as her mother tells us she has
seen very marked changes at home.

   Laura will most likely need some support to catch up, just like
any pupil who has missed school. The most important step to take
at this point is to reduce the sense of urgency that has been conveyed to Laura. This will enable her to take responsibility for her
own progress, which is necessary for her to improve. In our view,
this is best done by treating her like any other pupil in every way.

   A meeting has been scheduled in school to discuss Laura's
immediate educational needs. Laura herself will be there and will
need to take an active role in the discussion and any decisions
made. Hopefully, this meeting will spur her on to make further
progress. We are looking forward to meeting you again in

September, and wish you a relaxing break and a nice summer holiday.

Sincerely yours

....

Educational Psychologist   Clinical Psychologist

fig. 2

At the next staff meeting several weeks later, the atmosphere seemed much lighter. To our surprise every teacher had a copy of the letter. When asked what changes they had noticed since the last meeting, many positive things were remarked about Laura. Staff reported how, now they had a unified approach toward Laura, she was responding very well to it. This enthusiasm by staff to elaborate on what was now working was further reinforced by questions and comments such as: 'That's really interesting, how did you achieve that?' and 'What were you doing that was different?' Talking about things going well and how they had managed to achieve this with Laura gave a sense of hopefulness that things would continue to progress.

The EP saw Laura periodically at her request after this point and generally noted in-between session changes and returned to the scales created in previous sessions. Scales in these earlier sessions had been about being able to complete tasks in lessons and getting qualifications in her outdoor activities. As the scales were returned to, Laura was able to remember each time what they were measuring and her previous scores on them. She continued to work well throughout the rest of the year. She was also seen briefly to arrange special exam arrangements towards the end of the Spring term. Several letters were sent to her throughout this period, as well.

Laura left school with 8 GCSEs!

Letters... more letters and sometimes notes

Letter writing as constructive feedback has increasingly become a regular feature of our work with individual youngsters, parents, teachers, staff groups, and head teachers – in fact, pretty much anyone we have meetings with! Sometimes these letters are as lengthy as in figure 2 and others are considerably shorter and even in note form (fig 3).

Dear

Just thought I'd write you both a quick note after the brilliant school meeting on Friday. I was really impressed by the small number of youngsters discussed at the meeting and also the general feeling around the school. For those kids we did discuss, we were able to talk in more detail and generally make more suggestions as we had more time.

I wanted to write because I think you and the rest of the staff are really making a great difference to the school; despite all the ongoing hardships of the usual parental, social, economic difficulties, not to mention transitory nature of your school population, you are making this fabulous progress. All those social skills, playground activities, circle time, learning and behaviour support and staff meetings (and more) are obviously doing the trick!

I think the addition of 'Sure Start' will just help you continue on this track.

This is not formal, hence the terrible grammar and fax (!). I just thought I wanted to say what a great job you're doing, without (hopefully) sounding patronising.

See you soon

fig. 3

At the time of sending these letters the feedback was that people really appreciated the summary and support. Reflecting now, our thinking has moved on again and we would pay even more attention to the suggestions that people at the meetings had made and would place less emphasis on our own suggestions.

With youngsters, we sometimes suggest they could use their letters as 'rainy day letters' when they think that they need reminding of their goals, or when they just want to read nice things about themselves (fig. 4).

Dear

As agreed at our meeting, I am just writing you a quick note. I want to say again how impressed I was by your willingness to chat today. I was struck during the meeting by how well you understand your own difficulties and how well you know what to do about them. You came up with all the ideas in the 'miracle'. That also brings me to the point of how well you understand your parents and how considerately you thought about them. You certainly seem to know about how you can make them feel happier!!

The things that you wanted me to remind you of were your 'miracle'. So, here they are:

Getting to school on time.
Happier form tutor.
Class quiet for 5 minutes.
You have everything you need in your bag.
Decent handwriting.
Being out of your room more.
Playing music quieter.
Eat a bit more.
Go out with friends and invite them round more.
Smaller phone bills.
Pay more attention in class.
Handing things in on time.
Doing more with friends.

Meanwhile, to help you in class you were going to pick several teachers and approach them about copying off the board. We also talked about a 'sign' on your door at home to help you remember things for school. We mentioned having a 'sign' inside your workbooks to help remind yourself to hand work in. You are going to practise reading and spelling and possibly play games that help your memory such as; pairs games; snap; Cluedo and covering pictures and trying to remember what was on them.

I think, as I told you today, that you have a lot of strength to help you and that is why I know (with help) you will change the bits that you want to change. I hope the laptop is helpful.

See you in three weeks time.

....
Educational Psychologist

PS – This letter is addressed to you. If you want, share it with your parents or ...., **but only if you want.**

fig. 4

So how useful are letters? Feedback *from* people

The way we have evaluated the usefulness of our letters has been very simple – we asked the people who receive them! Listed below is a selection of comments made in response to our request asking people of what they thought of the letters:

- 'Feeling listened to.'
- 'Being "in it" together.'
- 'Things aren't as bad as I thought they were.'
- 'I didn't realise he could do so many things.'
- 'This letter makes me feel "cleverer". It's pointed out the things I can do.'
- 'I liked getting my own letter.'
- 'It brought tears to my eyes! I'm going to frame it!'
- 'It helped me believe that I will get there.'
- 'Makes me feel proud of my achievements.'

In addition to us asking directly for feedback, very occasionally we receive surprise feedback letters that tell us clearly what the recipients thought of their letters and the approach itself (fig 5):

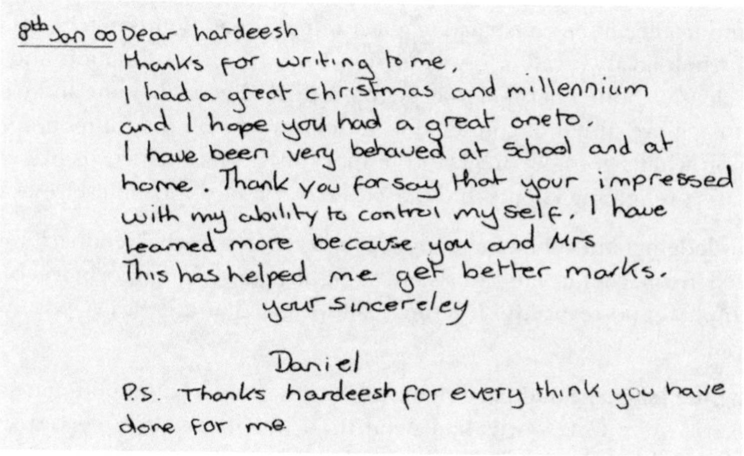

8th Jan 00 Dear hardeesh
Thanks for writing to me,
I had a great christmas and millennium
and I hope you had a great oneto.
I have been very behaved at School and at
home. Thank you for say that your impressed
with my ability to control myself. I have
learned more because you and Mrs
This has helped me get better marks.
your sincereley

Daniel
P.S. Thanks hardeesh for every think you have
done for me

fig. 5

Top tips

From the various comments we've had over time, we've pulled together some 'top tips' for letter writing (fig. 6). These contain many of the core elements of solution-focused constructive feedback:

Validate	the client and their feelings, attitudes etc.
Access Strengths	remind them of their own abilities.
Look Forward	reiterate the 'preferred future'.
Interest	let the client know that you are interested in them.
Deliberate	possible solutions defined on paper for client to ponder.
Admire	client strengths.
Teamwork	from co-operation to collaboration.
Encourage	client to review own 'expertise' to handle own difficulties.
Success	hopeful for the future

fig. 6

What have we learned?

The importance of co-constructing goals and agendas. Solution-focused thinking has helped us by allowing us to step back from the situation and think more clearly about what it is that people involved actually want and what we want to achieve. It has encouraged us to focus more on the future and not so much what's going wrong. More importantly it has helped us place more emphasis on helping clients find a useful way forward for themselves.

The importance of co-constructing goals and agendas. Solution-focused thinking has helped us by allowing us to step back from the situation and think more clearly about what it is that people involved actually want and what we want to achieve. It has encouraged us to focus more on the future and not so much on what's going wrong. More importantly it has helped us place more emphasis on helping clients find a useful way forward for themselves.

Acknowledging and validating people's experiences. Verbal feedback we have received from clients has consistently highlighted the importance of non-judgemental and respectful listening. They note that this is very positive and validating.

Getting the language and pace right. In the case study, Laura said that she did not like it when long words had been used with her and preferred smaller ones she could understand! This highlights the need to cue into the language being used. By talking with clients on a level they can relate to, they seem to respond positively. The first staff meeting also taught us the importance of keeping with the pace of clients. The pace must be at a comfortable level for people and we learnt that it isn't imperative to work through all the elements of a solution-focused meeting in one session.

There are always exceptions. A solution-focused approach has helped us to listen out for times when the problem is absent or less and to underline the importance of these. Discussing these times raises the importance of people's own strengths and resources in managing and coping with difficult situations. Hearing about small changes seems to help people believe that further change is possible.

For us, letter writing has proved a very effective way of encapsulating the above in black and white, for people to read at their leisure. They act as a permanent record for people to keep and share if they wish. They can act as a reminder of goals and resources and seem to help perpetuate changes already happening in a person's life. Feedback from Laura noted that the letters made her feel, 'cleverer' because they pointed out all the things she could do well!

A difference that makes a difference?

Reflecting on our reasons for trying something different, our evaluations indicate that this approach is at least as effective as other ways we could work. The added bonus has been that it is also an extremely enjoyable and satisfying way of working. It has enhanced our working relationships with schools and has also given us a sense of real growth and development in our practice.

CHAPTER FIFTEEN

SOLUTION WORLD

BY IOAN G. REES

Introduction

This chapter is dedicated to viewing solution-focused work from a child and adolescent perspective, rather than from the adult-worker perspective. Recently, exciting information has emerged about what children find useful in solution-focused intervention. Whatever the role from which you apply Solution-Focused Brief Therapy (SFBT) skills, whether as a class or subject teacher, a special educational needs co-ordinator, a counsellor, an education welfare officer or educational psychologist, this information can inform practice.

In the beginning …

I recall being in the same room as a solution-focused worker for the very first time and it seemed like 'deja-vu'. I felt as though I'd been in that room so many times before – but hadn't realised it. Changing my own pattern of work had remained elusive until that moment. Then, SFBT became a liberating alternative. It made instant sense; I had re-discovered the effective yet respectful approach to working with children that had always been within me, but hadn't yet sprouted wings.

SFBT contributed immediately to the re-structuring of my work philosophy, that children, families and schools, not only hold the secrets to the unravelling of their own difficulties, but also the resources by which to do so.

Inevitably, however, buried secrets and resources are nearly always invisible to those troubled deeply. I consider that adopting a careful and patient solution-focused approach serves to embrace the great human struggle to unearth these vital virtues, freeing them to become functional assets in shaping better futures. This in essence encapsulates the SFBT paradigm for me.

Traditionally, practitioners of most therapeutic models reflected upon 'process and outcome' from their own, adult perspective. However, by considering the perspective of the child or adolescent, a new insight and exciting knowledge about what they regard as being useful in overcoming their difficulties is revealed. It serves also to remind us of the collaborative nature of each encounter!

In my case, practice led to research, and I was drawn to investigating children's experiences of SFBT. A series of interviews with both solution-focused educational psychologists (EPs) and children elicited comparative narratives about their shared therapeutic encounters. A variety of questionnaires provided additional information about their perceptions in relation to the process and outcome of their joint work. The entire data has provided a fascinating account of child and adolescent experiences of SFBT.

Our brave new world

My research indicates that children appreciate joyous ways of solving serious problems. The simplicity of their messages during feedback about sessions is both enlightening and inspiring. They form the basis for this chapter.

Working simply and keeping our approach simple is difficult, it takes practice. The Buddhist exercise of 'cultivating a beginner's mind' at every opportunity is worthwhile. For children and their families, therapeutic experiences become demystified when one is 'simple'.

Results of this research suggest that it is the simple things that children most appreciate within SFBT. However, they also report enjoying some 'technical' aspects too: the miracle question, yes; scales, yes. They even notice talking about 'exceptions'. But these are not the factors which they feel influence change most. For them, the novelty of the experience itself, the special relationship based upon common understanding, being liked unconditionally, being heard and being able to talk hopefully of dreams and aspirations, constitute the essential ingredients for the possible re-authoring of their lives. Given the choice, they also consider biscuits, tea or squash, comfortable chairs and an unhurried conversation to be additional contributors(although not essential) toward positive outcomes!

Bill O'Hanlon (a possibility therapist) speaks of 'Possibility Land'. Like Bill, I have also come to see that children can be transported within a 'land', taking them to places where otherwise they would not have been, potentially becoming someone other than who they were. SFBT can help achieve this.

'Utilization' was the central tenet of the great Milton Erickson's thera-peutic work, and by utilizing the genius of Disney® it is possible for us to view SFBT from the child's perspective, not our own. All Disneylands® are attrac-tive and appealing to the young (and not so young), our 'world' needs to be, too.

In this chapter we can share in children's accounts of SFBT translated into a new form: a day at our Disneyland®; welcome to what I call, 'Solution World'!

A Solution World

SFBT is a Solution World. Visiting there, even for a brief encounter, is poten-tially healing and therapeutic. There is so much to do and see, so much to learn about oneself and others, but most of all it is a place where joy lives, laughter is heard and dreams talked about. No matter whether a first time visitor or a veteran of the park, the opportunity for personal progress always exists in Solution World.

Following a day in Solution World, how then do children recall the expe-rience, and what will have changed them from when they first entered? What can we learn from their stories of Solution World?

The turnstile at Solution World

There is only one first time. Michael Hoyt (single therapy session researcher and worker) refers to this as the 'first hello' or primacy factor. Here, we need to be novel and immediately accepting of the child; to join in a memorable way. Either talk about what seems right at the time or consider what they don't expect – and do it!

'Two's company, three is' ... not necessarily a crowd. Check to find out from the child whom they may wish to accompany them in Solution World. For example, they may call upon a friend, a key adult or parent to be there. Indeed, Michael White (a narrative therapist) assists us in enveloping such additional supporters, viewing them as 'external witnesses' or 'audiences' to Solution World activity.

A map and the 'rules of engagement'

There are maps and maps, and in this case a map refers to the flexible, theo-retical framework of SFBT. However, a map of Solution World only provides an overview of possible routes and an appreciation of the diverse directional choices open to us. It is not designed to be a schema and should never limit possibilities.

The Solution World map does not tell you where to go first, so start where you and the child feel comfortable; play a game (for example, Winnicott's 'squiggle-wiggle' game), have a chat, go for a short stroll. There are no barricaded or well-trodden paths; you are free to roam the park together (although in the case of a Risk Assessment or Disclosure scenario, the correct, professional steps as advised by your Authority will also need to be considered.)

Negotiating 'rules of engagement' around the park can be useful and discussed early on, or alternatively just kept in silent awareness until later. Some 'rules' which may emerge from collaborative discussions are, for example;

– Taking care of each other – staying together at all times, not getting lost.

'Moving' together and staying close are crucial, both perceived and actual. If you go too fast, or too slow, in what you do and say you'll run the risk of becoming separated or dislocated from the reality of the experience from the child's perspective. Scott Miller (Institute for the Study of Therapeutic Change) calls it 'checking your pulse'. He refers to the fact that two significant factors that can lead to the relapse of symptoms are, first, not listening sufficiently, and second, going too fast. Some lines you may wish to consider:

'How are we doing? Tell me if you feel I'm going at a snail's pace with my questions? I can change gear!'

'Does this feel comfortable to you, this much talking about things?'

Also, mind your body language. Take regular breathers. Keep reviewing how far you've come together and reflect on shared understandings. If misinterpretation is creeping in, or you feel that you're constantly re-phrasing what you or the child says, then you've probably missed the point or gone too fast! Don't be afraid to stop and ask to go back for a re-telling of the story. A line to consider:

'That story you just told me about the other children in your Year group sounded really interesting. It seemed to have some clues in it about how you're getting on so well. Do you mind telling it to me again?'

– Honesty is the best policy.

Show humility in asking for guidance around the park. Matthew Selekman (1995) refers to this as 'the Columbo approach'). Also, share with them what their story stirs in you. Possible lines:

'I'm really curious about what you've just said. Help me understand how that makes you feel …'

    'Get me off the hook here – tell me a bit more about …'

    Orienteer collaboratively – 'How about I hold the compass and you hold the map?'

How are you going to stay together in Solution World if you are intent on going separate ways? Share the map and compass, orienteer collaboratively. A line:

    'I was thinking (dangerous thing) maybe we could talk a bit about X or Y next, what do you think? Does it seem like a good time to do that?'

Don't forget, children accommodate us greatly, they remind us when we go off track and they let us know when we stand in their way. Trust their ordnance skills.

Now that you've read some 'rules' and you have a map, you're on your way! Go ahead, in no particular order, and visit some, or all of the park areas which children report as enjoyable and helpful.

Liberty Square at Solution World

Liberty speaks of the rights, privileges and freedom of every individual we meet. Solution World's Liberty Square is a place where the granting of authority and the honouring of identity occur explicitly.

When children tell us of how important it is for them to feel accepted and comfortable in our company, they are acknowledging that we have communicated respect for their rights. Ensuring both their physical and emotional comfort in the new and unfamiliar relationship they face is a priority.

At Liberty Square they value the soothing opportunity to tell their side of the story, having the hurt acknowledged and the suffering validated. Their stories are privileged information shared, treasured testimonies of true-life experiences opened and trusted to us. Let them know this. In turn, this creates the space into which they step, finding new opportunities for moving forward.

Reflecting upon Liberty Square at Solution World from the child's perspective reminds me of a line of W.B. Yeats:

    'I lay my dreams beneath your feet, tread carefully, for you tread on my dreams.'

Adventureland at Solution World

In Adventureland at Solution World a relationship is established, joy is introduced to experiences of surviving and healing, heroic stories are recited and suppressed dreams are awakened.

Children commonly refer to how different SFBT is to any other 'intervention' or 'treatment' they have previously encountered. For some, this difference makes all the difference. 'Doing something different' relieves the child from engaging in a 'tyranny of escalating sameness.' Indeed, nearly without exception, SFBT is seen as being novel. It would appear that the joyful engagement in respectful conversation is quite often a new experience for many children, and also for their families as a whole. Such novelty adds weight to the momentum of change, however small, which may already be taking place (from pre-session changes) and should be treasured as a jewel in our crown as solution-focused practitioners. There is a powerful, combined effect for children of breaking free from old stories about themselves and experiencing a 'beneficial uncertainty' that Lyn Johnson (1995) refers to as the 'healthy curiosity one holds about what is about to happen next.' That is what Adventureland at Solution World seeks to create.

So what makes SFBT novel to children? What is unexpected and the surprising for them?

Could it be the ...

- unexpected adventure
- respectful relationship
- being able to laugh
- feeling comfortable
- freedom to tell their story
- being heard
- gaining hope
- realising their healing knowledge
- realising their survival knowledge
- invitation to speak of their dreams and aspirations
- unearthing and exposing of proudest attributes
- becoming other than who they were
- discovery of new possibilities
- miracles?

Children, especially 'veterans of therapy' (as discussed by Scott Miller), even at a very young age usually display the 'articles' of their lives which they believe adults want to see or hear. Beneath these stories are invisible tales of silent courage in addressing the difficulties in their lives. However, by shining a light on such 'invisible presences' (Michael White), or 'extra-therapeutic factors' (Scott Miller), we choose to be curious about past and present events which help shape an alternative sense of future, social authenticity.

We must refrain from professing to understand what is 'surviving' or 'healing' for one child compared to another, but can feel confident in knowing about inviting 'rich' descriptions (a term from narrative therapy) of personal healing and survival knowledge, and in so doing communicating our 'struggle' to understand their experiences.

Frontierland at Solution World

Frontierland at Solution World provides a greater 'technical' challenge. Certain questions and theoretical tools come more into play, although they seem not to hold any inherent value in the absence of a partnership with Adventureland at Solution World. However, they do not pass unnoticed by children.

Activities in Frontierland at Solution World are reported to provide a reference point for both us and the child, against which future progress and/or events can be plotted. It provides a statement of position on our map of change. Michael White would describe this feature as the 'landscape of change'. Here are some of the most common examples of applications used and noticed;

Scaling

Scaling is recalled by most children as an activity that provides hope by perspective. However, some that encounter a scaling question on immediate entry into Solution World find it a solution-forced and unhelpful experience. Therefore, timing issues can apply to the efficacy of this technique.

Good days

Descriptions by the child of 'good days' experienced can also be a Frontierland at Solution World activity, enabling rich narration of their knowledge and skills at exceptional and preferred historical junctures.

Exceptions

Children don't live by the 'exceptions' of their complaint but, for us, exceptions constitute points of entry, ways 'in' to help re-author alternative perspectives and story lines. Exceptions, however, (also known as 'unique outcomes') are not so until the child confirms their validity and true existence. When this occurs and a unique outcome can be embraced and celebrated, new paths reveal themselves and new conversations are made possible about the past, present and future.

Frontierland at Solution World continues our journey around Solution World, breaking into new ground by use of 'referencing' techniques. Children notice these but, it can be easy for us, particularly when the going gets tough or, when we are weary, to depend upon them as main attractions, forsaking other important Solution World areas. A warning is sounded.

Tomorrowland at Solution World

Tomorrowland at Solution World is, as it says, future-orientated. And, although the whole of Solution World can be visualized as a futuristic park, with change being the focus, it is within Tomorrowland at Solution World that the concentration of experiences, which inspire hope and expectancy, abound.

Here, children speak of possible selves. Conversations are held about possibilities for becoming somebody different from when they first entered the park. Space is created for them to step into reviewed social identities, based upon previously invisible, positive truths about themselves, recovered or discovered within the park. These positive truths support one or more alternative, preferred social identities which embrace their true-life purpose, intentions, hopes, dreams, plans, aspirations, visions, values and commitments. In other words, they see and start becoming who they really want to be. Bill O'Hanlon would describe this, once again, as becoming the 360° person you were at birth, referring to the notion of an integrated self.

The miracle question, and any of its many hybrid forms, is a good example of a vehicle in which children can be transported to projected, desired outcomes where they can establish their chosen social identity. I am of the belief, however, that for some, this question can be as limiting as it is liberating. A miracle, for some, locates desired change beyond the point they believe can be reached. I find that sensitivity, in each case, toward the usefulness of the question requires its amendment to include the possibility of there not just being one big miracle, but many little ones. There should be cautious avoidance of the 'either/or' life choice it can offer a child. Listen and watch the child carefully to ensure that his/her description of a miracle scenario does not serve to cast a shadow across the value of a current position in life. As Gestalt therapy has it: 'You have to be where you are to get to where you're going.' For me, therefore, valuing and validating the present, whilst also being able to hold up the possibility of change, is the true and intended purpose of this question.

Lastly, be sure to have a conversation about life immediately beyond the exit, particularly in terms of the child's intentions and possible actions. Following extensive research, de Shazer and others (e.g. Prochaska) seem to have got it right with regard to pitching the levels of post-conversation 'homework'. Their descriptions on the subject constitute a useful rule of thumb, while bearing in mind that there is no substitute for the tailored, go slow, salient, fun approach which children seem to prefer.

Café at the turnstile of Solution World

Traditionally, this is the 'break' taken from the SFBT session to review progress and plan for the future. It can provide valuable time for reflection on the shared experience so far, and on any thoughts you may hold about life beyond the turnstile. Similarly, for the child, it can be a time for useful thinking or simply relaxing. Either way, children tend to report a value in being afforded time for reflection.

On return, we can be honest about what we've learned. We need to acknowledge and validate the suffering that the complaint has caused. We need to pay respect to the fact that, although we may have been in Solution World before, for the child it may have been the first time. Compliment with sincerity, always adducing the facts on which you have based your positive statements.

Check over your joint plan. You will also need to commit yourself to work on the new project ahead ... so think about it.

The merchandise shop at Solution World

SFBT merchandise can be trendy and cool. It is not unusual for children to share, show and display merchandise as testimony to their experience or as trophies of the day. Some refer to merchandise as a 'piece of the therapist' but this could be seen as locating us as 'expert' within the whole encounter. I like to consider merchandise as something tangible, something which gives an account of the day at Solution World and of any new intentions arising from it, for example, a sort of personal scrapbook.

Merchandise can take on many forms. Michael White speaks of therapy 'documents' which children refer to whenever they feel the need to remember, be reminded of or gain strength from words. 'What if ...' relapse-prevention and contingency plans are very useful, based on unearthed healing and survival knowledge revealed at Solution World.

Also letters, cards, postcards, contracts and child-friendly reports are all easily manufactured. Less common merchandise, yet still very effective, are audio-recordings of 'summary conversations' between the child and us (and/or whoever), outlining the day, possible selves and possible futures.

Next, walk out through the turnstile together.

Finally, say your own 'farewell', remembering the potency of the 'recentcy' factor – that is, the last memory they will have of you.

Disney always parts sweetly, by reminding us that 'If you can dream it, you can do it.'

Final note

What if we became lost and the day was a disappointment? Ask yourself honestly the questions on the checklist. Did I, for example:

> decide where I was going before entering the park;
> run;
> fall and never recover;
> not like what I saw or heard and rushed to leave the park;
> take plenty of breathers;
> make laughter impossible;
> show too much interest in other people in the park;
> become distracted by one particular activity and miss out on others;
> think too much about where it was all heading and not on where it was;
> repeat failed activities and techniques too many times;
> stay too long at café;
> forget to open the Merchandise shop?

Future research

For those interested in conducting a research project or study in the field of SFBT, particularly in its application to educational contexts, there is plenty to be done. The data which enabled the writing of this chapter was collected as part of a doctoral study, funded by the Economic and Social Research Council (ESRC). This new and exciting field of practice will require ongoing inquiry by practitioners, of both of a qualitative and quantitative nature, in order that application of the model becomes increasingly widespread and efficacious.

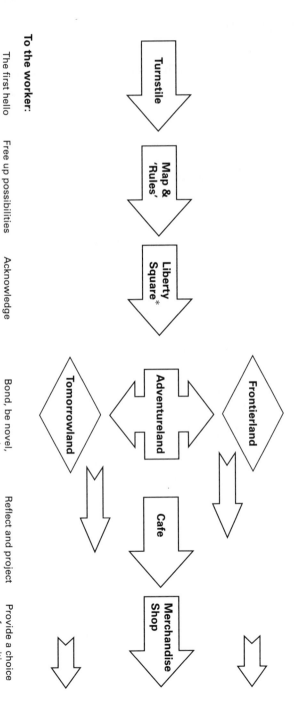

To the worker:

Turnstile	Map & 'Rules'	Liberty Square*	Adventureland	Cafe	Merchandise Shop
The first hello	Free up possibilities and negotiate context	Acknowledge and validate	Bond, be novel, agree on goals	Reflect and project	Provide a choice of securities

To the child:

Look – a new opportunity!	Trust and negotiate	Share and feel healing	Build a future and see possibilities	Check and Plan	Take a reminder

*At Solution-World

Figure: Visual depiction of Solution World and the process perceptions of worker and child

EPILOGUE

At the heart of education is the desire for students to learn and grow and to become independent adults. Solution Focused Brief Therapy shares the essence of this. Ultimately we are only visiting people and a measure of our effectiveness is the degree to which people move on independently in their work and make ideas their own. We are guessing that you had good reasons for picking up this book and would like to thank you for getting this far. Suppose you were to take away one idea that is useful:

- How will you know? What would you and others notice different that will tell you?
- What will be the smallest sign that it is useful?
- Imagine that tomorrow you are taking the first step towards this, what will you be doing and how will you be doing it that will tell you that you are on your way?

And finally. We see this book and the Education conferences as the start of a dialogue. We would like to keep this conversation going; to develop one community with a common goal of generating new and unique applications of solution-focused thinking in the context of education. To this end all the authors have included a point of contact at the back of the book develop and we hope this is just a beginning ...

Contact Details

Yasmin Ajmal Tel 020 8968 0070
Brief Therapy Practice, 4d Shirland Mews , London W9 3DY
yasminajmal@brieftherapy.org.uk

Jean Day Tel: 020 8290 6784
Teacher/Counsellor, Behaviour Support Team
Pupil & Student Services, Bromley BR1 2SQ

Elizabeth Gillies Tel: 01483 744050
Senior Educational Psychologist
Surrey County Council, Educational Psychology Service, Local Education
Office (NW), Alexander House, 55a-61a Commercial Way, Woking GU21 1HN

Michael E Harker Tel: 01475 715430
Senior Educational Psychologist
Inverclyde Council Psychological Service, Highholm Centre, Highholm
Avenue, Port Glasgow PA14 5JN

Vavi Hillel Tel: 020 7428 0966
Co-ordinator of ABC Peer Counselling Anti-Bullying Campaign
Acland Burghley School, Burghley Road, London NW5 1UJ

Bryony Howe Tel: 020 7275 0066
Senior Educational Psychologist
chowe@eidosnet.co.uk

Hardeesh Johal-Smith Tel: 01227 772992
Educational Psychologist
Kent Psychological Service , Clover House, John Wilson Business Park, Thanet
Way, Whitstable Kent CT5 3QZ

Margaret Kay Tel: 01236 702136
McGlone & Kay Consultancy, Atrium Business Centre, North Caldeen Road,
Coatbridge, Scotland ML5 4EF

Suzanne Loggie Tel: 020 8290 6784
Counsellor/Teacher
Behaviour Support Team, Pupil & Student Services, Bromley BR1 2SQ
susanne_loggie@yahoo.co.uk

Madan Mall Tel: 07803 082300
Senior Social Worker

Catherine McGlone
Behaviour Support Teacher
catherinemcglone@yahoo.co.uk

Sean Moore Tel: 01453 833940
Chartered Educational Psychologist

Annie O'Leary Tel: 01797 222484
Solution Focused Brief Therapist/Counsellor

Ioan G Rees Tel: 01758 770653
Sycol Foundation, PO Box 5035, Cardiff, Wales CF5 6WQ
ioangrees@sycol.co.uk

Maggie Stephenson Tel: 01227 772992
Senior Educational Psychologist
Kent Psychological Service , Clover House, John Wilson Business Park, Thanet
Way, Whitstable, Kent CT5 3QZ

Hugo Stearn
Educational Psychologist
hugo@stearn.fsnet.co.uk

Gillian Strachan Tel: 01241 435035
School & Family Support Worker
ednsfss@angus.gov.uk

Bernadette Stringer Tel: 07879 497 590
Area Senior Social Worker

Patsy Wagner Tel: 020 7598 4848
Educational Psychologist
Educational Psychology Consultation Service, 108A Lancaster Road, London
W11 1QS

Sue Young
The Little House, 22 Humber Road, North Ferriby, East Yorkshire HU14 3DW

WHERE TO GO NEXT...

If you work in the field of education and are interested in further reading on the subject of applying Solution Focused Brief Therapy within this exciting context, then you are in luck. There are many excellent sources of information and inspiration available and we include but a few in this 'brief' list which will serve hopefully as an uncomplicated guide to possible, next steps.

Principles, practises and techniques

de Shazer, S. (1985), Keys to solutions in brief therapy. New York: Norton.

de Shazer, S. (1988), Clues: Investigating solutions in brief therapy. New York: Norton.

de Shazer, S. (1991), Putting difference to work. New York: Norton.

de Shazer, S. (1994), Words were originally magic. New York: Norton.

George, E., Iveson, C. and Ratner, H. (1999), Problem to Solution: Brief Therapy with Individuals and Families. London: BT Press.

Children

Furman, B. (1997), It's Never Too Late To Have a Happy Childhood: From adversity to resilience. London: BT Press.

Selekman, M. D. (1997), Solution Focused Therapy with Children: Harnessing family strengths for systemic change. New York: Guilford.

Adolescents

Selekman, M. D. (1993), Pathways to change: Brief therapy solutions with difficult adolescents. New York: Guilford.

Parents

Metcalf, L. (1996), Parenting Toward Solutions: How parents can use skills they already have to raise responsible, loving kids. New York: Prentice Hall.

'The Solution-Oriented Parenting Group', Chapter 7 (pp160-170) in Selekman, M. D. (1993), Pathways to change: Brief therapy solutions with difficult adolescents. New York: Guilford.

School

Davis, T. E. and Osborn, C. J. (2000), The Solution Focused School Counselor: Shaping Professional Practice. Philadelphia PA: Accelerated Development.

Durrant, M. (1995), Creative Strategies for School Problems: Solutions for psychologists and Teachers. New York: Norton.

Kral, R. (1995), Strategies that work: Techniques for solution in schools. Milwaukee WI: Brief Family Therapy Center Press.

Murphy, J. J. and Duncan, B. L. (1997), Brief Intervention for School Problems: Collaborating for School Problems. New York: Guilford Press.

Murphy, J. J. (1997), Solution-Focused Counseling in Middle and High Schools. Alexandria VA: American Counseling Association.

Rhodes, J & Ajmal, Y. (1995), Solution Focused Thinking in Schools. London: BT Press.

Research to support practice

Hubble, M. A., Miller, B. L. and Miller, S. D. (1999), Heart and Soul of Change: What works in Brief Therapy. Washington DC: American Psychological Association.

Internet solutions

If you have access to the internet then you will be able to visit several UK and international sites devoted to solution-focused work.

www.brieftherapy.org.uk

Yasmin works at the Brief Therapy Practice. This is their home site. Find out about courses, services, conferences and international presentations for personal and professional development. It's all here.

www.sycol.co.uk

The Sycol Foundation was founded by Ioan. See what this growing Cardiff-based team can offer in terms of professional workshop training, conferences and supervision.

www.brief-therapy.org

The Brief Family Therapy Centre, Milwaukee. Web-site for Steve de Shazer and Insoo Kim Berg. Check out their 'hot-tips'.

www.talkingcure.com

Scott Miller and members of the Institute for the Study of Therapeutic Change have a regularly updated site relating to many topics, including up-to-date outcome research on efficacy.

www.brieftherapy.com

Enter Bill O'Hanlon's Possibility Land. Bill's books, tapes and services are all here.

www.reteaming.com

Ben Furman, from the Brief Therapy Institute of Helsinki introduces Reteaming to the web.

www.brieftherapysydney.com.au

Michael Durrant and the Brief Therapy Institute, Sydney.

www.fkc.se

The Mellansjö Institute & School in Sweden provide inspiration on applying the solution focused thinking in education.

Solution-focused lists

Why not become a member of the solution-focused, global community? Two solution-focused lists provide great opportunity to listen and contribute toward contemporary debates which span continents. You'll find that 'solution-talk' is fast becoming an international language! To join, visit:

http://www.enabling.org/ia/sft

Harry Korman, Swedish solution focused consultant and therapist posts extensive links in the field. You can also subscribe to Harry's solution-focused list, hosted by a Canadian University at this site.

www.topica.com/lists/brieftherapy

You can subscribe to Bruce Neben's solution focused list, hosted by Topica.com via this web-site or by sending an e-mail to: brieftherapy-subscribe@topica.com

Finally, as our 'community' is forever growing, it is important we set aside opportunity to meet face-to-face with others from all over Europe and further afield, in order to share ideas and stories. For this purpose, the European Brief Therapy Association (EBTA) hosts a wonderful annual conference (usually during the spring or summer months) open to all who are interested in learning more or maybe make their own, unique contribution. For more information on EBTA, contact Ioan or Yasmin.

References

Foreword

Cade, B. W. (1995), Discipline: Insolence, Offensiveness and Violence. Education Australia, Issue 29 pp 6-9.

de Shazer, S. (1999), 'Radical Acceptance', paper published on the Brief Family Therapy Centre web site. (see html://www.brief-therapy.org).

Korman, H. (1998), Contribution to the Solution-Focused Therapy Internet Discussion List (see http://maelstrom.stjohns.edu/archives/sft-l.html).

Rosenthal, R. & Jacobsen, L. (1968), Pygmalion in the classroom. New York: Holt, Rinehart & Winston.

1. Introducing Solution-Focused Thinking

Murphy, J. J. (2000), Solution-Focused Counselling in Middle and High Schools. American Counselling Association.

de Shazer, S. (2000), Brief Therapy Practice Conference.

White, M. (1997), Narratives of Therapists Lives. Dulwich Centre Publications.

2. How to Build Solutions at Meetings

De Jong, P. and Berg, I. (1998), Interviewing For Solutions. Brooks/Cole Publishing Company.

Durrant, M. (1993), Creative Strategies for School Problems. Eastwood Family Therapy Centre, Australia; Bell Graphics, Alexandria, NSW.

McMahon, M. O. (1990), The general method of social work practice: A problem-solving approach (2nd ed.). Prentice Hall: Englewood Cliffs, NJ.

Redpath, R. and Harker, M. E. (1999), Becoming Solution-Focused in Practice: Educational Psychology in Practice, 15(2), pp.116-121.

Rhodes, J. (1993), The use of solution-focused brief therapy in schools. Educational Psychology in Practice, 9(1), pp.27-34.

Rhodes, J. and Ajmal, Y. (1995), Solution-focused Thinking in Schools. London: BT Press.

3. From the Impossible to the Solution

de Shazer, S. (1985), Keys To Solution In Brief Therapy. New York: Norton.

George, E., Iveson, C. & Ratner, H. (1990 & 1999), Problem To Solution. London: BT Press.

Rhodes, J. & Ajmal, Y. (1995), Solution Focused Thinking In Schools: London: BT Press.

Furman, B. & Ahola, T. (1992), Solution Talk

de Shazer, S. (1994), Words Were Originally Magic

4. Brief Therapy in an Education Support Service

George, E., Iveson, C. & Ratner, H. (1990 & 1999), Problem To Solution. London: BT Press

Acock, A.C. & Hurlbert, J.S. (1990), Social Network Analysis: A Structural Perspective for Family Studies. Journal of Social and Personal Relationships, Vol. 7 pp.245-264.

Beck, A.T. & Emery, G. (1985), Anxiety Disorders and Phobias: A Cognitive Perspective. New York: Basic Books.

Dryden, W. & Feltham, C. (1992), Brief Counselling. Buckingham: Open University Press.

Mall, M. (1993), Culture of the Excluded Child: Unpublished MA Research Dissertation, University of Central England, Birmingham.

Nelson-Jones, R. (1991), Life Skills. Trowbridge: Dotesios Ltd.

Rogers, C. (1951), Client Centred Therapy: London: Constable.

Rutter, M. (1999), Resilience concepts and findings: implications for family therapy. Journal of Family Therapy 21, pp.119-144.

Sapir, E. (1929), The study of linguistics as a science. Language, 5, pp.207-214.

Stringer & Mall (1999), A Solution Focused Approach to Anger Management with Children, a group work manual for practitioners. Birmingham Questions: Publication.

Vygotsky, L.S. (1962), Thought and Language. Cambridge M.A., MIT Press.

Wharf, B.L. (1956), Language, Thought and Reality. Cambridge.

6. Solution Focused Anti-bullying

De Shazer, S. (1985), Keys to Solution in Brief Therapy. New York: Norton.

Maines, B. and Robinson, G. (1992), The No-Blame Approach. Bristol: Lame Duck Publishing (now Lucky Duck).

Molnar, A. and Lindquist, B. (1989), Changing Problem Behaviour in Schools. San Francisco: Jossey-Bass.

Rhodes, J. and Ajmal, Y. (1995), Solution Focussed Thinking in Schools. London: BT Press.

Young, S. (1998), 'The support group approach to bullying'. Educational Psychology in Practice, 14 (1) pp.32-39.

8. Solutions to Emotional & Behavioural Difficulties

Andersen, T. (1987), The Reflective Team: Dialogue and Meta-Dialogue in Clinical Work. Family Process 26, pp.415-428.

Boscolo, L., Cecchin, G., Hoffman, L. and Penn P.(1987), Milan Systemic Family Therapy. New York: Basic Books.

DfEE, (1994), Code of Practice on the Identification and Assessment of Special Educational Needs. UK: HMSO.

de Shazer, S. (1982), Patterns of Brief Family Therapy: an ecosystemic approach. New York: Guilford.

de Shazer, S. (1985), Keys to Solution in Brief Therapy. New York: Norton.

de Shazer, S. (1988), Clues: Investigating Solutions in Brief Therapy. New York: Norton.

O'Hanlon, W.H. and Beale, S. (1994), A Field Guide to Possibility Land. London: B.T. Press.

O'Hanlon, W.H. and Hexum, A.L. (1990), An Uncommon Casebook. The complete clinical work of Milton H. Erikson, M. D. New York: Norton.

Palmarini, M. P. (1994), Inevitable illusions: How mistakes of reason rule our minds. New York: Wiley.

Selekman, M. D. (1997), Solution-focused therapy with children. New York/London: The Guilford Press.

Senge, P.M., Kleiner, A., Roberts, C., Ross, R.B. and Smith, B. J. (1994), The fifth discipline fieldbook: Strategies and tools for building a learning organization. New York: Currency and Doubleday.

9. Wrapping New Narratives in Golden Paper

Anderson, H. & Goolishian, H. in Gergen & McNamee (1992) Therapy as Social Construction. Sage.

Dahlberg G., Moss P. & Pence A., Beyond quality in Early Education and Care Postmodern Perspectives. London: Falmer Press.

Durrant, M. (1995), Creative Strategies for School Problems. New York: Norton.

DES (1978) Special Educational Needs: report of the Committee of Enquiry into the Education of handicapped Children and Young People (the Warnock Report). London: HMSO.

Efran, J. S., Clarfield, E. in Gergen and McNamee (1992), Therapy as Social Construction: Sage

Gitlin A. et al (1992) Teachers' Voice for School Change. London: Routledge.

Grey P., Miller A. & Noakes, J. (1994), Challenging Behaviours in Schools. London: Routledge.

Harre, R. (1985), Situational rhetoric and self-presentation; Language and Social situations. Social Psychology series pp.175-180.

Hill, M. (1999), Signposts in Fostering. BAAF.

Miler, R. Duncan, Hubble (1997), Escape from Babel. New York: Norton.

Watters, F. (1988), Innovating Practice: Professional Development Initiatives: Scottish Education Department Regional Psychological Services, pp.239-261.

White, M., (1995), Re-Authoring Lives: Interviews and Essays. Dulwich Centre Publications.

White, M., (1995), School & Education: Exploring new possibilities: Dulwich Centre Newsletter, Nos. 2 & 3 pp.51-66.

10. 'A Thoughtful Process'

Berg, I. K. (1994), Family Based Services. New York: Norton.

Berg, I. K. (1996) cited in Simon, Dvorah Handbook of Brief Therapy.

de Shazer, S. (1991), Putting Differences to Work. New York: Norton.

Freire, P. (1996), Pedagogy of Hope. New York, Continuum, cited in Grey, M. (2000) The Outrageous Pursuit of Hope. Darton, Longman & Todd.

Furman, B. & Ahola, T. (1992), Pickpockets in a Nudist Camp – The Systemic Revolution in Psychotherapy. Dulwich Centre Publications.

Giraux, Henry A. (1997), Pedagogy and the Politics of Hope. West View Press.

Kral, R., & Kowalski (1989) After the Miracle: The Second Stage in Solution Focused Brief Therapy. Journal of Strategic & Systemic Therapies 8, pp.73-76.

O'Hanlon, B. (1998), New Possibilities in Brief Therapy: Collaboration, Inclusion, Validation and Change. London: BT Press.

Simon, D. (1996), Handbook of Solution Focused Brief Therapy.

Wexler, P. (1994) Dulwich Centre Newsletters I & II.

White, M. (1997), Narratives of Therapists Lives. Dulwich Centre Publications.

11. Consultation

Χ Burnham, J. (1986), Family Therapy: first steps towards a systemic approach. London: Routledge.

Burr, V. (1995), An Introduction to Social Constructionism. London: Routledge

Χ Conoley, J.C. and Conoley, C.W. (1992) School Consultation: practice and training. Boston: Allyn & Bacon.

Consultation Development Network (1998), Developing Consultation: LEA presentation notes at workshops 18/9/98 and 6/11/98. London: University of London Institute of Education [www.mailbase.ac.uk/lists/epnet/files/consult.rtf].

Χ de Shazer, S. (1985), Keys to Solution in Brief Therapy. London: Norton.

de Shazer, S. (1988), Clues: Investigating Solutions in Brief Therapy. New York: Norton.

Dowling, E. & Osborne, E. (1994), 2nd. Edition, The Family and the School: a joint systems approach to problems with children. London: Routledge.

Gillham, B. (Ed) (1978), Reconstructing Educational Psychology. London: Croom Helm.

Gutkin, T.B. & Curtis, M.J. (1990), 'School-based consultation: theory, techniques and research' in Gutkin, T.B. and Reynolds, C.R. (Ed.), The Handbook of School Psychology, New York: Wiley. Second Edition.

Hargreaves, D.H. (1972), Interpersonal Relations and Education. London: Routledge Kegan Paul.

Hoffman, L. (1981), Foundations of Family Therapy: a conceptual framework for systems change. New York: Basic Books.

Lewis, L. (1997), An exploration of Special Educational Needs Co-ordinators' perceptions of the role of educational psychologists. Research Report, MSc Educational Psychology, University of London, Institute of Education.

Morgan, A. (Ed.) (1999), Once Upon A Time...Narrative Therapy with Children and their Families.

Ravenette, A.T. (1968), Dimensions of Reading Difficulties. Pergamon.

Wagner, P. (1995), School Consultation: frameworks for the practicing educational psychologist - a handbook, Kensington and Chelsea Education Psychology Service, 108A Lancaster Rd. London W11 1QS.

White, M. and Epston, D. (1990), Narrative Means to Therapeutic Ends. New York: Norton.

Watkins, C. et al. (2000), Educational Psychology in Practice. 16(1), 5-58.

Watzlawick, P. and Weakland, J.H. (1977) Studies at the Mental Research Institute Palo Alto 1965-1974, The Interactional View. New York: Norton.

Winslade, J. and Monk, G. (1999), Narrative Counselling in Schools, Powerful and Brief. Corwin Press: California.

White , M. and Epston, D. (1990), Narrative Means to Therapeutic Ends. New York: Norton.

13. 'Bridges to Babylon'

Berg & Miller (1992), Working with the Problem Drinker. New York: Norton.

de Shazer, S. (1985), Keys to Solution in Brief Therapy. New York: Norton.

de Shazer, S. (1988), Clues Investigating Solutions in Brief Therapy. New York: Norton.

Dolan, Y. (1991), Resolving Sexual Abuse. New York: Norton.

Furman, B. (Nov. 1999), Kidskills, London: Conference at the Brief Therapy Practice.

George, Iveson & Ratner (1990), Problem to Solution. London: B.T. Press.

HEA leaflet. (Date unknown), Confidentiality and people under 16. Available from the Health Education Authority – copyright of text belongs to the BMA.

Miller, Hubble & Duncan. (1996), Handbook of Solution-focused Brief Therapy. San Francisco: Jossey Bass.

15. Solution World

de Shazer, S. (1982), Patterns of Brief Family Therapy: An Ecosystemic Approach. New York: Guildford Press.

de Shazer, S. (1985), Keys to Solutions in Brief Therapy. New York: Norton.

de Shazer, S. (1988), Clues: Investigating Solutions in Brief Therapy. New York: Norton.

de Shazer, S. (1991), Putting Difference to Work. New York: Norton.

de Shazer, S. (1994), Words were Originally Magic. New York: Norton.

Miller, S., Duncan, B. & Hubble, M. (1997), Escape from Babel. toward a unifying language for psychotherapy practice. New York: Norton.

O'Hanlon, B. & Beadle, S. (1996), A Field Guide to Possibility Land: Possibility Therapy Methods. London: Brief Therapy Press.

Prochaska, J. O., Di Clemente, C. C. & Norcross, J. C. (1992), 'In search of how people change.' American Counsellor, 47, pp.1102-1114.

Selekman, M. D. (1993), Pathways to change: Brief Therapy Solutions with Difficult Adolescents. New York: Guildford.

White, M. & Epston, D. (1990), Narrative Means to Therapeutic Ends. New York: Norton.